40

Insight

Getting to "Retired!"

Joseph M. Maas

CFA®, CFP®, CLU®, ChFC®, MSFS,

CCIM, CVA, CM&AA, ABAR

and

John A. Flavin

ChFC®, CFP®, CCIM, AIF®, CLU®

Merrell Publishing Company, LLC

Seattle, WA

Merrell

Published by Merrell Publishing Company, LLC
701 Fifth Avenue, Suite 3520
Seattle WA   98104

info@merrellpublishing.com

First Edition.

ISBN 978-1512213478

Printed in the United States of America.

Disclaimer

This book is presented solely for educational purposes and is not intended to represent or be used as an exhaustive financial resource. The information contained in this book is made available for illustrative purposes, explaining only the basics of 401(k) planning.

The author and Merrill Publishing Company, LLC, emphasize this material is not offered as financial, legal, accounting, or other professional services' advice. It is highly recommended you seek the services of a competent professional before making any decisions regarding your business or personal finances.

Best efforts have underscored the writing of this book, but the author and publisher make no representations or warranties of any kind and assume no liabilities of any kind with respect to the accuracy or completeness of the contents, and specifically disclaim any implied warranties of use for any particular purpose.

Neither the author nor Merrill Publishing Company, LLC, shall be held liable or responsible to any person or entity with respect to any loss or incidental or consequential damages caused, or alleged to have been caused, directly or indirectly, by the information contained in this book, or disruption caused by errors or omissions, whether such errors or omissions result from negligence, accident, or any other cause.

The case studies with their characters and references are fictional, and any likeness to actual persons, either living or dead, is completely coincidental. The 401(k) case studies represented in this book were created to show only the highlights of how a plan sponsor can implement a 401(k) plan, and how a plan participant can benefit from a 401(k) plan.

The reader is advised to consult with a professional financial advisor who has experience establishing new company 401(k) plans, and experience advising plan participants with making choices relevant to their individual financial situation.

Dedication

Joseph M. Maas

This book is dedicated to my loving wife Molly, my precious little princess Madison, my amazing new son Andrew, my Church, my mother, Anne Maas, and in loving memory of my father, Henry Maas.

John A. Flavin

I wish to dedicate this book to Shannon, my devoted wife, my three wonderful children, Rhys, Charlotte and Simon, and my mom and dad, Charlotte and Dan Flavin.

We also dedicate this book to all the professionals with whom we have worked throughout the years who have guided and instructed us so we may continually improve the services we provide our loyal and deserving clients.

About the Authors

Joseph M. Maas
CFA®, CVA, ABAR, CM&AA,
CFP®, ChFC®, CLU®, MSFS, CCIM

Joe Maas is an unusual financial advisor because he is certified in so many areas of expertise. Mr. Maas has earned certificates from nine prestigious organizations, and with over two decades of financial industry experience, he offers refined professional advisory skills to business owners, private wealth clients, and trusts.

Mr. Maas holds a variety of world renowned professional designations; he is a CFA (Chartered Financial Analyst) charterholder, which is the world's most respected investment professional's achievement. In addition to the CFA, Mr. Maas is a certified valuation analyst (CVA) and is accredited in business appraisal review (ABAR). Mr. Maas's professional capability also includes being a certified merger and acquisition advisor (CM&AA) trained and experienced in buying and selling middle-market companies with revenues from $5 million to $500 million.

Mr. Maas earned his reputation as a CERTIFIED FINANCIAL PLANNER™ (CFP®), having fulfilled the requirements of the Certified Financial Planner Board of Standards, and is also a chartered financial consultant (ChFC) qualified to provide comprehensive advanced financial planning.

Adding to Mr. Maas's many skills are his specialties in life insurance and estate planning as a chartered life underwriter (CLU®), in addition to being a certified commercial investment member (CCIM) with expertise in commercial and investment real estate. In 2000, Mr. Maas earned his Master of Science in Financial Services (MSFS) from The American College.

Mr. Maas established his company, Synergetic Finance, as a 360-degree financial services boutique, providing a variety of solutions under one roof. With a team of capable and broadly experienced financial advisors, Mr. Maas provides a complete mix of integrated financial services.

An expert in his field, Mr. Maas is a member of numerous professional organizations; he has participated as a guest lecturer for the Washington State Bar Association, and taught corporate finance as an adjunct professor at Seattle Pacific University. Mr. Maas also studied finance in Japan, Hong Kong, China and Thailand.

In his personal time, Mr. Maas enjoys traveling with his wife and daughter, and serving local charities.

Joe Maas makes an excellent choice as the quarterback of your financial team...it's rare to find a financial professional with such a variety of expertise who will proficiently advise and guide your financial interests to new levels of security and income.

Certified Financial Planner Board of Standards, Inc. owns the certification marks CFP®, CERTIFIED FINANCIAL PLANNER™, and federally registered CFP (with flame design), in the U.S., which it awards to individuals who successfully complete CFP Board's initial and ongoing certification requirements.

John A. Flavin
ChFC®, CFP®, CCIM, AIF®, CLU®

John Flavin is a senior managing principal with Synergy Financial Management . In this role, John coordinates the efforts of Synergy's other team members in executing the financial planning and investment process. Because of his excellent attention to detail, every client's financial plan is assured of successful implementation.

Mr. Flavin graduated with a Bachelor of Science degree from Boston College where he earned both academic and athletic scholarships. After completing a postgraduate program in Baltimore, Maryland, John moved to Seattle and began his career in the financial services arena. Mr. Flavin holds the CFP, AIF, CLU, ChFC, and CCIM designations, as he is always looking to grow professionally to better serve his clients.

In addition, Mr. Flavin is very active locally and internationally. He has served as the past Finance Council Chairman for a local parish, volunteers with various high school programs, and coaches at a local gym. Internationally, he and his family have established schools, health care centers, and built homes for the poor in Nicaragua since 1989. He is an accomplished classical violinist, and has played since the 3rd grade.

Mr. Flavin has three younger children with his wife, Shannon, and you can often find them running from one activity to another as they enjoy their family time together.

This Book is for You

...if you are a business owner who wants to
start a new 401(k) plan for your company,
or an employee in a company that has,
or should have, a 401(k) plan.

Business Owners:

This book is extremely valuable because it provides the essential
information you need to know for creating a new 401(k) plan...a plan
that could reduce your company's taxes, increase your company's
valuation, provide a retirement savings program that will attract,
reward and retain your employees, and benefit you personally
by expanding your own retirement funding. This book is a must-
read because it tells the whole story about navigating the steps of
evaluating, selecting and hiring an investment advisor, a third party
administrator (TPA), a record keeper, and the nitty-gritty about
custodians. Your responsibilities as a fiduciary are reviewed in detail
to protect you, and by the end of this book, you'll know precisely how
to proceed with adding this rewarding retirement savings program to
your company, guiding you and your employees toward the rewards of
"Getting to Retired!"

Employees:

You'll love this book because it will teach you how to use your
company's 401(k) plan to enjoy a safe and comfortable retirement.
This information shows you how to take control of your financial
future, and provides you with an in-depth look at how investment
experts think about money, revealing many of the tools they use
to build sizeable fortunes for their clients. Now you have access to
knowledge that can change your life...for the better!

The Insight Series from Merrell Publishing Company

Available Now:

- Exit Insight: Getting to "Sold!"

- 401(k) Insight: Getting to "Retired!"

New Books Coming Soon!

- Investment Insight: Getting to "Diversified!"

- Start-up Insight: Getting to "Funded!"

Acknowledgments

We wish to personally thank the following people for their help with creating this book:

Our editor, Dr. Daniel Levine; your expertise, enthusiasm, and dedication were invaluable to the success of this book.

Connie Peterson, Katie Vercio, and Mark Girouard for your continually insightful advice and helpful commentary.

Chris Scott for the expert technical skills and steadfast diligence.

Lindsay Lush for innovative cover design.

Synergetic Finance's valued clients, Seattle Pacific University, the CFA Institute, the Certified Financial Planner Board of Standards, the American College of Financial Services.

Synergetic Finance

Synergetic Finance is an integrated financial services firm — a financial ecosystem — specializing in Financial Management, Business Valuation and Consulting, and Mergers and Acquisitions including commercial real estate investments.

Serving as a trusted partner, we provide objective guidance and proven expert solutions based on a thorough understanding of your specific situation and goals. As our client, you will benefit from a collaborative relationship that addresses — and anticipates — your needs. We follow a disciplined process that provides a structured approach while allowing customization to your circumstances.

Whether you are seeking to value and grow your company, to optimize your investments, or ensure the orderly succession of the ownership of your business, our approach is comprehensive, and designed to meet your near and long term financial goals.

Additionally, to help serve you, please sign up for news about our publication release dates. Go to http://synergeticfinance.com/contact/index.html

Figure 1: Synergetic Finance.

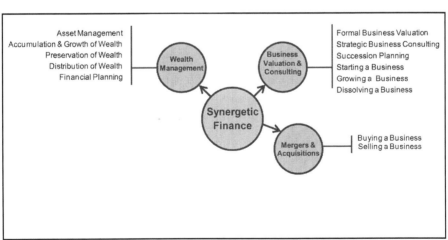

Contents

Section 1:
Overview of the 401(k) Plan

When you have finished reading this chapter, you will:

- Know the advantages of having a 401(k) plan for your business

- Understand the difference between open and closed architecture, and the difference between a bundled and unbundled 401(k) plan

- Possess introductory knowledge about the five key 401(k) professionals your plan will need

- Know the three different types of 401(k) financial advisors and recognize which one would serve your company best

- Be able to explain your role as the plan sponsor

- Identify the two sources of 401(k) plan contributions

- Be familiar with the basic components of a 401(k) plan

You've decided to look into the idea of establishing a 401(k) plan for your employees. Of course, with every new project there are a lot of assumptions and unknowns, so let's begin by reassuring you that the path ahead is not that complicated, mostly because you are now holding this book in your hands.

"401(k) Insight: Getting to "Retired!" was written especially for you and others like you who want a clear and comprehensible guide that provides the insight needed to establish a 401(k) plan for the benefit of yourself and your employees. It's really not that hard to do when you follow the expert advice in this book and use the services of a professional financial advisor.

One of the great features of a 401(k) plan, and maybe one of your main reasons for wanting a 401(k) plan, is that your business may more readily attract employees, and retain them. Retirement benefits are a significant factor in employee loyalty, and a 401(k) is a strong inducement.

You don't have to own or manage a big corporation to have a 401(k) plan...because small business owners, such as sole proprietorships, are also eligible. Did you know that a 401(k) allows a business owner and employees to set aside more funds annually than an IRA? In 2014, IRAs had a limit of $5,500 ($6,500 if you're 50 or older), while a 401(k) allowed as much as $17,500 per year ($23,000 for those who are 50 or older).

In addition, a small business can also receive a tax credit of up to $500 a year during each of the first three years to compensate for some of the costs of establishing and administering the plan.

Yet another good feature is that your plan's financial advisor will provide several important services such as setting up the 401(k) plan, educating your employees about how they can receive the most benefit from the plan, and offering you and your employees critical investment advice periodically throughout the years.

There is a lot of interesting and valuable information for you to know, and this book will help you understand all the important details you need to establish and successfully maintain a great tax-saving retirement-building program for the benefit of your employees...and yourself.

401(k) Plan Types

There are three basic kinds of 401(k) plan designs. One is "open architecture" or unbundled plans, one is "closed architecture" or bundled plans, and the third is a combination of the two, sometimes referred to as alliance plans. Here's what they are:

Open architecture: An open architecture 401(k) plan means the plan may select and invest in any assortment of mutual fund families, and stocks and bonds (ETFs: Exchange Traded Funds). This type of 401(k) plan allows the plan sponsor (you) and your investment advisors to customize your plan's service providers and investment funds so the plan and investments target your financial goals and those of your employees. This type of plan also requires that all fees incurred through the buying and selling of these investments are clearly itemized on your statements; there are no hidden fees.

Closed architecture: With closed architecture 401(k)s, investment choices are limited to the investments offered by the 401(k) provider. Also, since the fees are bundled, they may be more difficult to identify. Currently, most plans offered through mutual fund families or insurance companies are closed architecture plans. With closed architecture plans, one single vendor provides all the plan services, including investment, recordkeeping, administration, and education services. These plans provide little flexibility or customization and prevent the ability to use any mutual funds not managed by the service provider. Closed architecture plans are a one-size fits all, "one-stop-shopping" option, which may not be the best choice if you prefer having a wider range of available investments.

Combination plans: Combination plans mix elements from both the unbundled and bundled models. Usually, the plan's vendor serves the sponsor with recordkeeping, administration, and employee education, and establishes business relationships, or alliances, with other service providers to offer a wide variety of investment choices and specialized services. The expenses for recordkeeping and administration are often borne by the partners in the alliance through 12(b)1 fees or other types of revenue sharing, making the combination/alliance plan competitive with the two other plan types.

Summary: The following table provides the generalized advantages and disadvantages of all three 401(k) investment types.

Figure 2:   Bundled, Unbundled, Alliance Plan Types.

	Bundled	Unbundled	Alliance
Able to have the best service options	No	Yes	Yes with investment options; possibly not with other services
Investment option diversity through multiple mutual fund families	Possibly, but only if plan is big enough.	Yes	Yes
Changing investment options is easy within the plan	Yes, usually only within the limited options.	Yes	Yes
Costs	Low to Medium	Medium	Low to Medium
Plan sponsor's administration is easy.	High	Medium	High
Point of contact is one person.	Yes	No	Yes
ERISA attorney assistance needs.	Medium	High	Medium
Employee education services	Standardized, usually with limited customization available	Customizable to plan sponsor's needs	Standardized, usually with limited customization available
Technological integration	High	Medium	High
Complexity	Low	High	Medium

The Players

There are five key professionals involved in your company's 401(k) plan, and another five professionals who are important, but on a mostly secondary level.

Here is the list of the five key professionals: your financial advisor; third party administrators (TPAs); record keepers; custodians; and you, the plan sponsor. The secondary list is composed of the trustee, auditor, attorney, accountants, and education firms. Let's take a quick look at each of these professionals.

Figure 3: 401(k) Participants.

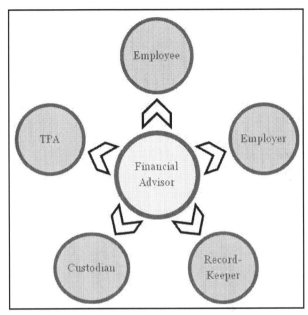

The financial advisor: The financial advisor is the most important professional on your 401(k) team, because this person is educated, trained, and has the experience to help you with a number of critical 401(k) activities. Your financial advisor can help you determine the financial goals for your plan, create and implement the plan, monitor the plan, report the results, and make recommendations for changes that help your plan provide the most financial return possible.

Three Types of Financial Advisors: The first type of financial advisor fits into the consultant category. The consultant acts like an investment advisor because he or she will advise on all three types of plans, and will help you set up your plan, but consultants do not manage the funds in your plan. A consultant may meet with you periodically, either every quarter or only once per year, to review the performance of the investments in your plan. Consultants usually charge a flat fee while some receive an hourly rate, and they have no financial interest beyond this simple relationship.

The second type of financial advisor is the broker/salesman. Brokers represent the mutual funds on their approved list, so their interest is focused solely on your selecting investments offered by their company. They usually sell combination plans. A significant feature of their service is that the broker/salesman is paid on commissions, not fees; also, a broker/salesman is usually not a fiduciary. On the positive side, you will have the familiarity of working with just one company; however, on the other hand, the list of funds available through this single fund family may not contain the best funds that are available in the different investment sectors. For example, the broker's mutual fund family may have a high-performing mid-cap fund but only average performing large-cap and small-cap funds. In addition, the variety of sector-specific choices may be limited, which typically provide diversification (safety and growth) as the different economic cycles ebb and flow. Choosing only from a broker's selection, you may not have the best choice of funds available. The broker is paid by commission for his or her work.

Also in the closed architecture category are 401(k) plans offered by insurance companies. Insurance companies offer an altogether different type of investment. Instead of direct investment in funds, insurance companies use mirrored funds, crediting and debiting your account depending on the performance of the fund being mirrored. You'll find that costs are higher with an insurance company's 401(k) plan because the insurance company has factored in mortality expenses along with the normal expenses for asset management. Given the choices that are available, there is no reason to pay more than needed.

The third type of financial advisor is a registered investment advisor (RIA). An RIA is a professional who is registered with the Securities and Exchange Commission, or, in some cases, with a state's securities agency, and is licensed to give advice about investing in stocks, bonds, mutual funds, and exchange traded funds. When you work with an RIA, you can select from the full universe of investments and customize your 401(k) plan to specifically meet your financial objectives because an RIA typically uses unbundled plans. An RIA is independent, often serves as a fiduciary, and is paid either with a fixed fee, an hourly fee, or a percentage of the asset value they are managing for their clients. Since an RIA is independent and can offer you the opportunity of selecting any investment you wish, an RIA may be the best choice for working with your company's 401(k) plan.

Key:

You don't have to create and manage the 401(k) all by yourself! Your company can hire trained professionals, and they are paid from the plan.

Third party administrators (TPAs): Though the employer is the plan sponsor, administrative support is provided by the TPA. The TPA provides the "third party" services the employer requests. A TPA is an important member of your 401(k) plan because this professional is responsible for administering the plan's services, and also assuring your plan's compliance with laws and IRS regulations so your plan legally receives the appropriate deductions. The TPA also provides plan design consulting and plan document preparations. Yes, you could save some money if you completed these tasks by yourself, but unless you're an accountant and have the time to generate extra reports, it might be best to hire a TPA to do the work for you. The TPA sets up your retirement account and makes sure it meets IRS regulations, calculates and allocates the employer's contributions, prepares your plan for compliance testing, files the annual 5500 forms, maintains and archives all documents, and tracks employee eligibility. If you do not have a TPA on your 401(k) team, you'll have to do all these things yourself.

When you choose a TPA, you want to select someone with whom you can work well. Your financial advisor probably has a database of TPAs he or she has worked with over the years, and can recommend a TPA that best suits your personality, and who best understands your company's particular investment philosophy. When you work with a TPA, you only have to fill out a few forms and the TPA will do the rest. Your TPA will also keep you informed of changes in IRS legislation affecting your plan. During the year, you'll receive reports on your account's performance; at year end, you'll receive a form for your tax returns.

A TPA may receive compensation either with an annual fee or commissions on your earnings, but usually the fee is a percentage of the total funds in your account. A competent TPA will save you time and trouble in many ways, removing a degree of your control in exchange for peace of mind.

Record keepers: The record keeper has the very important task of keeping scrupulous records showing the variety of contributions in and out of the 401(k) investments, and also crediting or debiting the investment earnings for each of the participants' accounts. In most cases, the 401(k) recordkeeping must be coordinated with the company's payroll. Recordkeeping must note each participant's account activity and individually record all employer matching contributions. An additional level of complexity occurs when the plan participants direct their own investments, rather than when the investments are pooled. The record keeper must periodically provide participants with account statements, process distribution checks, and value the investments as they increase or decline.

Unless a company is quite large, it is usually advised that 401(k) recordkeeping become the responsibility of third-party firms that specialize in this service. Of course, if your plan is a closed architecture plan and you are participating in a mutual fund's or insurance company's 401(k) plans, your plan's activities will be monitored by the record keepers employed by those companies. In some cases, a bank may be your third-party administrator, and the bank will assign a record keeper to keep track of your plan's activities. There are also payroll companies that will do the recordkeeping for you as part of the payroll services they provide. You may also find there are third party administrators (TPAs) that will also perform the record-keeping tasks for you. Again, should you choose to work with a registered investment advisor (RIA), your advisor will have a database of record keepers that he or she has worked with over the years and would be a good fit for your company's plan. You should negotiate the record company fees when you first establish the 401(k). These costs can be covered by your company, or you may choose to have the plan participants bear the recordkeeping costs through deductions from each participant's account.

Custodians: The custodian is another key team member for your 401(k) plan because it's the custodian that acts as a watchdog for the hundreds of thousands or millions of dollars in your 401(k) retirement accounts. As you might imagine, there are quite a few laws and regulations that must be followed to ensure that these retirement funds are handled properly and in a legally compliant manner.

The custodian is a named trustee, holding all the plan's assets in a trust. The custodian is typically responsible for managing the funds, though there are occasions when another fiduciary, or named managers, can direct the custodian. The custodian is also usually required to process investment contributions and transactions, prepare financial statements, disburse funds when requested by plan participants, and pay the trust's fees and expenses. Often a custodian will assign their responsibilities to service providers, permissible under ERISA regulations.

Types of Custodians: The first type is a broker-dealer. A broker-dealer is a brokerage firm that purchases and sells securities through its own account and then resells the securities to its clients, such as you, earning a margin on the reselling. There are discount broker-dealers like Schwab and TD Ameritrade which provide the securities for a small margin. There are also wire house brokers, which are brokers who are not independent because they work for a wire house firm such as Bank of America's Merrill Lynch, or a company like Morgan Stanley. Wire house brokers tend to have a higher margin since these are broker-sold plans and commissions must be included. A second type of custodian is mutual fund companies. You or your financial advisor can arrange to purchase your 401(k) plan's investments through mutual fund companies which then act as the custodian of your plan's funds. The third type of custodian is insurance companies because they also offer 401(k) plan investments, and serve as the custodian of those funds. Of course, we've already mentioned that your fees will be somewhat higher because the insurance companies incorporate mortality rates in their fees.

The custodian must be approved by the IRS for these guardian responsibilities, must report all transactions to the IRS for tax compliance, and assure that these retirement funds are not mixed improperly with any other funds. The custodian is the safeguard that guarantees both the safety and legality of retirement funds, and protects them from embezzlement and other mishandling. Be sure that your custodian is approved by the IRS because this provides the greatest protection for you and your funds. Of course, custodians receive a fee for their services.

Plan sponsor: Well, this is you. Your company is sponsoring the 401(k) plan, so you're the plan sponsor. As the plan sponsor, you have a number of important responsibilities. Some of these we've already covered above, but this is a good place to review. The most important detail is that you are the number one fiduciary; this means that you are the primary party responsible for, and with authority over, the plan's assets. This is why it's so important to use the services of an experienced financial advisor who can also quarterback a highly skilled professional team that serves your legal and financial obligations.

Here is a general list of your responsibilities, to give you an idea of what is required through your authority as the plan sponsor:

1. Your plan document must be written so it complies with all requirements of the IRS code.

2. Your 401(k) plan must be administered properly according to the terms you've set up.

3. You must review your plan annually to confirm the plan is operating according to its terms and all laws and regulations.

4. Monitor the law for changes and update your plan as needed.

5. Communicate as required with the plan's participants.

6. File all required forms and paperwork with the IRS and with the Department of Labor.

7. If your plan requires testing, conduct it in a timely manner.

8. Maintain accurate records for all participant accounts.

9. Invest the funds as mandated and determine all associated fees.

10. Be aware of all your fiduciary responsibilities and take action to fulfill them.

As you can see, as the plan sponsor, all the responsibility lies with you, so it would be very wise if you chose to use the services of an experienced financial advisor who could be your 401(k) team's quarterback, guiding the activities and monitoring the performances of the third party administrators, record keeper, and custodians as needed.

Frankly, the circumstances that would serve you best is when you hire the services of a financial advisor (RIA) who enthusiastically takes a professional interest in your plan's participants, in the growth of your plan's investments, and the financial and legal well-being of your company. The best of all worlds is when you find a professional money manager who becomes an advocate for your plan and provides you with the best advice, price and service. A truly excellent financial advisor will make it a point to meet with you annually to review your plan, host educational seminars for your employees, conduct plan research, provide steady support, and work with you to customize and achieve the financial goals of your plan's participants. A professional financial advisor of this stature is rare because the service you'll receive will be exceptional and likely to be quite profitable, funding your retirement with comfort and security.

The next group of five professionals is also important to the success of your 401(k) plan. They are not as predominantly conspicuous as the preceding group, but they are necessary components to the smooth operation of your plan!

Trustee: The trustee is the company or organization that receives the investment funds, holds them in your company's name, invests the funds, and pays out the assets when required to do so. The trustee has no authority to act except under your direction.

Auditor: An auditor is unnecessary if you have a plan with less than 100 participants; otherwise, your plan's funds will be audited to ensure that all legal requirements are being met, and that the funds display the proper documentation of monies flowing in and out of the plan.

Attorney: The attorney is available as a resource for various legal questions that may arise, such as when your company first establishes an employee benefit plan that raises legal issues regarding employee contracts, or your company is involved in a merger or acquisition that affects benefit plans, or when your 401(k) plan needs resolution with a fiduciary decision.

Accountant/Payroll Administrator: Your company's accountant or payroll administrator is the individual responsible for payroll, and because your company's 401(k) plan will be deducting funds from each participant's paycheck and transferring those sums into the 401(k) plan's investment funds, this person will be steadily engaged with making these deductions and assuring the funds are transferred properly and on schedule.

Important:
Educating your employees about their 401(k) plan
is as important as providing this powerful pretax
investment opportunity. When your employees
understand the value of this savings and investment
tool, their retirement years could be significantly better.

Education Firms: As the plan sponsor, you are responsible for
educating the plan participants about your company's 401(k) plan.
It's obvious you may not be the best source of information for your
employees, so you might consider hiring a company that specializes
in educating plan participants about your company's 401(k) plan. In
most cases, your employees will probably be eager for information on
saving money for retirement and investing it for growth so they can
enjoy a comfortable retirement. Most people do not know a lot about
investing, so inviting a professional education firm to hold workshops
and employee information sessions could be welcome. Of course, if
you've been able to locate and retain a financial advisor to coordinate
the aspects of your plan, this individual could also provide educational
services to your employees as well as also overseeing the operations
and effectiveness of the other team members. A professional financial
advisor may be the solution to the variety of obligations you would
otherwise have to arrange yourself.

Laws and Regulations

In this section, we're going to briefly review the 401(k) laws and
regulations, giving you a good understanding of the legal obligations
and parameters of this exceptional employee benefit program.

Fiduciary: A fiduciary of a 401(k) plan is a person who is legally
responsible for the plan's assets, and acts on behalf of other people's
financial interests. As the plan sponsor, you are the fiduciary, but
you are also permitted to hire a professional who can share fiduciary

responsibilities with you and alleviate your many tasks. If you choose, your 401(k) plan's investment advisor can be appointed as a fiduciary to manage your plan's investments on behalf of you and your employees.

 ## Definition:

Fiduciary: A fiduciary of a 401(k) plan is a person who is legally responsible for the plan's assets, and acts on behalf of other people's financial interests.

Section 3(38): Congress passed a federal law in 1974 called the Employee Retirement Income Security Act, or ERISA. This law set the minimum standards for private industry pension plans. In Section 3(38) of ERISA, the definition of a fiduciary is very clearly stated as being a bank, an insurance company, or a registered investment advisor (RIA). In the vernacular, a 401(k) plan fiduciary is referred to as a 3(38) fiduciary. Once you have named your 3(38) fiduciary, you, as the plan sponsor, give control to your fiduciary to make investment decisions on behalf of your plan's participants. As the plan sponsor, it is critically important that you choose an experienced, capable, and effective 3(38), and having selected this person, it is your responsibility as the plan sponsor to monitor his or her performance. Even though you have appointed a fiduciary to invest your plan's retirement funds, you are still responsible for ensuring that this fiduciary performs appropriately.

Section 3(21): A 3(21) fiduciary is a co-fiduciary serving as an advisor and receiving a fee for his or her investment advice. A 3(21) fiduciary shares fiduciary responsibilities and liabilities with other plan co-fiduciaries, such as investment committee members, or board members who are also plan fiduciaries.

Non-Fiduciaries: ERISA regulations do allow non-fiduciaries to offer investment services as consultants, but they do not have discretionary authority to make decisions. These non-fiduciaries have no legal responsibilities or liabilities for the funds, with the responsibility and liability remaining solely with the named fiduciaries. As the plan sponsor, you need to know where the liability lies, because it lies with you unless you delegate it appropriately.

401(k): The laws and regulations for 401(k) plans are quite extensive and very tightly regulated by the IRS and the Department of Labor. In a nutshell, here are several details to review and understand:

Eligibility: Employees must meet eligibility requirements to participate in the plan. While a plan sponsor can set more flexible eligibility requirements, an employee must be eligible to enter a qualified plan after attaining the age of 21 and completing one year of service, or attaining the age of 21 and completing two years of service if the employee is immediately 100% vested upon entry into the plan. A year of service is usually 1,000 hours. Also, a plan cannot exclude part-time or seasonal employees by job classification, and an exclusion of employees by job classification must not relate to age or length of service.

Contributions: There are two types of contributions, one from the plan sponsor, and the other from the employees. As the plan sponsor, you can choose how much of your employees' annual salary you wish to match with employer contributions, as permitted by the regulations. As for the employees, in 2014, for example, they could contribute a maximum of $17,500 per year. After the age of 50, employees could contribute up to an additional $5,500 per year ("Catch-up Contribution Limit"). The maximum total annual contribution per employee could not exceed $52,000 ("Annual Defined Contribution Limit") and also may never exceed 100% of the employee's annual salary. It is also important to note that employers are not required to continue providing a 401(k) contribution; you can suspend making a contribution with due notice. On the other hand, employers may also decide to renew making contributions at a later date.

The following table illustrates changes to 401(k) plan ceiling limits from 2008 to 2014:

Figure 4: 401(k) Plan Limits by Year.

401k Plan Limits for Year	2014	2013	2012	2011	2010	2009	2008
401k Elective Deferrals	$ 17,500	$ 17,500	$ 17,000	$ 16,500	$ 16,500	$ 16,500	$ 15,500
Annual Defined Contribution Limit	$ 52,000	$ 51,000	$ 50,000	$ 49,000	$ 49,000	$ 49,000	$ 46,000
Annual Compensation Limit	$ 260,000	$ 255,000	$ 250,000	$ 245,000	$ 245,000	$ 245,000	$ 230,000
Catch-Up Contribution Limit	$ 5,500	$ 5,500	$ 5,500	$ 5,500	$ 5,500	$ 5,500	$ 5,000
Highly Compensated Employees	$ 115,000	$ 115,000	$ 115,000	$ 110,000	$ 110,000	$ 110,000	$ 105,000
Non-401k Related Limits							
403(b)/457 Elective Deferrals	$ 17,500	$ 17,500	$ 17,000	$ 16,500	$ 16,500	$ 16,500	$ 15,500
SIMPLE Employee Deferrals	$ 12,000	$ 12,000	$ 11,500	$ 11,500	$ 11,500	$ 11,500	$ 10,500
SIMPLE Catch-Up Deferral	$ 2,500	$ 2,500	$ 2,500	$ 2,500	$ 2,500	$ 2,500	$ 2,500
SEP Minimum Compensation	$ 550	$ 550	$ 550	$ 550	$ 550	$ 550	$ 500
SEP Annual Compensation Limit	$ 260,000	$ 255,000	$ 250,000	$ 245,000	$ 245,000	$ 245,000	$ 230,000
Social Security Wage Base	$ 117,000	$ 113,700	$ 110,100	$ 106,800	$ 106,800	$ 106,800	$ 102,000

Timeliness of Deposit: According to the Department of Labor, which oversees the ERISA program, 401(k) deposits must be made in a timely manner, which typically means at the next payroll. Specifically, the employer must deposit the contributions no later than the 15th business day of the month following payroll distribution. However, this is the extreme range of the permissible window, and deposits should be made as quickly as reasonable.

Taxes: Contributions to a 401(k) fund are made on a pretax basis; all monies earned on these retirement funds grow tax-deferred. However, Roth IRA contributions are made on an after-tax basis, and all monies earned grow tax-free.

Withdrawals: A plan participant is allowed to begin withdrawals from his or her 401(k) account once they reach the age of 59 ½. Any money withdrawn will be taxed as though it were regular income.

Early Withdrawals: If a plan participant withdraws funds before the age of 59 ½, there will be a 10% early distribution penalty and the money will be treated as regular taxable income.

408(b)(2): This section of ERISA defines the regulations regarding fee disclosures. Administrative fees for working with 401(k) plans can significantly reduce the growth of investment funds over time, so ERISA regulations describe the legally permitted compensation for investment services, and require the disclosure of these services and the related compensation to plan participants.

ERISA: The Employee Retirement Income Security Act of 1974 is a federal law. Its purpose was to establish the minimum requirements for employee pension plans in private industry and to protect plan participants by establishing responsible fiduciary conduct, requiring disclosure of important information, and providing legal remedy for concerns brought before the courts.

Plan document: ERISA requires the plan sponsor, or the plan sponsor's administrators, to provide important information to the plan's participants. The participants are legally required to be notified about their company's 401(k)'s rules, their personal financial information, and certain documents about the plan's management. One of these key documents is the summary plan description (SPD) which informs participants about what the plan provides and how the plan is being administered. The SPD contains such details as eligibility, how the benefits are calculated, how the benefits will be paid, and how a claim for benefits can be filed. If changes are made to the plan, all plan participants must be informed with a written description of the changes. In addition to the SPD, participants must receive an annual report summarizing the plan's activities and results.

Summary

The intention of Section 1 is to provide an overview about your role as the plan sponsor. In this section we discussed open and closed architecture, introduced the primary and secondary 401(k) team members, and also reviewed several of ERISA's key legal requirements. This information sets the stage for Section 2 which more completely prepares you to be an effective plan sponsor.

 Section 1 Review Questions:

1. Which of the following is not done by the TPA?

    A. The TPA is responsible for the administration of the plan.

    B. The TPA periodically provides participants with account statements.

    C. The TPA assures your plan's compliance with laws and IRS regulations.

    D. The TPA calculates and allocates the employer's contributions.

2. Which of the following is not done by the record-keeper?

A. The record-keeper keeps scrupulous records showing the variety of contributions in and out of the 401(k) investments.

B. The record-keeper also credits or debits the investment earnings for each of the participants' accounts.

C. The record-keeper guarantees both the safety and legality of retirement funds, and protects them from embezzlement and other mishandling.

D. The record-keeper usually coordinates the 401(k) recordkeeping with the company's payroll.

3. Which of the following is not your responsibility as the plan sponsor?

A. Review your plan annually to confirm the plan is operating according to its terms and all laws and regulations.

B. Monitor the law for changes and update your plan as needed.

C. Communicate as required with the plan's participants.

D. Pay for your employees' financial education outside your company's 401(k) plan.

4. A fiduciary of a 401(k) plan is a person who is legally responsible for the plan's assets, and acts on behalf of other people's financial interests.

A. True

B. False

5. What is the name of the federal law Congress passed in 1974 that set the minimum standards for a private industry pension plan?

    A. ERIKA

    B. ERISA

    C. ELISA

    D. ESILA

6. Eligibility requirements for plan participants can vary from plan to plan.

    A. True

    B. False

Answers

1. Answer: B. The record-keeper provides participants with account statements.

2. Answer: C. The custodian guarantees both the safety and legality of retirement funds, and protects them from embezzlement and other mishandling.

3. Answer: D. You are responsible only for educating your employees about your company's 401(k) plan.

4. Answer: A. As the plan sponsor, you are the fiduciary, but you are also permitted to hire a professional who can share fiduciary responsibilities with you and alleviate your many tasks. If you choose, your 401(k) plan's investment advisor can be appointed as a fiduciary to manage your plan's investments on behalf of you and your employees.

5. Answer: C. ERISA is the acronym for Employee Retirement Income Security Act.

6. Answer: A. The plan sponsor decides the preferred eligibility requirements, within the regulations.

Section 2:
Essential 401(k) Knowledge
for Plan Sponsors

Chapter 1:
Introduction

When you have finished reading this chapter, you will:

- Be able to cite the six services provided by an RIA

- Know the 10 important details you and your advisory team should discuss when contemplating a 401(k) plan

- Understand both the benefits and the disadvantages of establishing a 401(k) plan for both your company and your employees

- Possess an initial awareness about a variety of retirement plan alternatives that might be better for your company than a 401(k)

This section of the book is written for the plan sponsor, to provide pertinent information from the employer's viewpoint. Employees are welcome to read this section as well because this will more completely inform plan participants about the administrative elements of a company's 401(k) plan, educating employees about the intricacies of hiring the key players and setting up a new plan. Also in this section is a case study that provides an example of a fictional plan sponsor's experiences, illustrating typical events that may also occur in your forthcoming experience.

Contemplating a 401(k)

The chances are you're contemplating a 401(k) plan because your company is doing well financially and you realize that by establishing a plan and having your company contribute to it, you can accomplish several important goals. You can reduce your company's taxable income, thus saving money your company would otherwise be paying in taxes and, by establishing a 401(k) plan, you can provide a significant and wholesome benefit for your employees. The financial benefits could potentially increase your own personal finances as well, because you can also become a plan participant and set aside thousands of dollars annually in your own pretax retirement account. A 401(k) plan is very appealing to employees and you may find you'll attract and retain good employees who value this benefit with their loyalty; employees who feel recognized and rewarded usually perform better in their tasks. All these various considerations are likely to have an impact on improving your company's productivity, and thus your bottom line.

Note:

One of the great features of a 401(k) plan, and maybe one of your main reasons for wanting a 401(k) plan, is that your business may more readily attract employees, and retain them. Retirement benefits are a significant factor in employee loyalty, and a 401(k) is a strong inducement.

Because a 401(k) plan can be complicated, your best choice could be to acquire the services of an independent registered investment advisor (RIA) who specializes in providing professional money management to employers and 401(k) participants. This way, both your company and your employees receive the most benefit for their retirement dollars. As mentioned in the introduction, should you choose a broker-dealer or an insurance company, you may either be restricted in the funds your retirement plan can hold, or you may be paying higher than normal fees and thus costing your retirement funds a significant portion of the growth they would otherwise enjoy. Hiring the services of an expert RIA is, in our opinion, the wisest choice available to you.

 Note:

A Registered Investment Advisor (RIA) may be the wisest choice for setting up and managing your company's 401(k) plan.

When seeking the services of an RIA, look for an advisor who will maintain low fees, thereby increasing returns, and who will enroll and educate your employees, closely watch market conditions, measure and explain your fund's results quarterly, and also provide investment guidance through the fluctuating performance of economic cycles. Your RIA will become a trusted partner and fiduciary, designing, monitoring, and managing a 401(k) plan that serves your company's goals.

All companies, even companies with just one employee, are eligible to set up a 401(k) plan. When contemplating a 401(k) plan for your company, here are some details you should be prepared to discuss with your advisory team.

1. Explain your company's type of business entity: sole proprietorship, partnership, corporation, or LLC

2. The number of employees in your company

3. The compensation you receive and the compensation range for your employees

4. Your age, and the age range of your employees

5. The amount of money you and your employees are likely to want to set aside annually

6. The level of employer contributions and deductions desired through the plan

7. Maximizing contributions for you and other executives

8. The stability of your company's profits during the last few years, and your company's anticipated profits over the next five years

9. Whether or not you want your company's plan to be competitive for attracting and retaining employees

10. Later, when you've selected your advisors, a discussion about these details will help your RIA design the best 401(k) plan for your company

The Benefits and Disadvantages of a 401(k)

Employer's benefits: Employers benefit in several ways from offering a 401(k) through their company:

1. Employer contributions, in the form of matches and profit sharing which are offered through the plan, are all deductible and may be on a vesting schedule to promote tenure with the employer

2. An employer's contributions are discretionary since each year you can decide whether or not to continue making contributions, provided you are within the regulations

3. Administrative fees for 401(k) plans are also tax-deductible

4. If this is your company's first 401(k) plan, you can receive a tax credit of up to $500 a year for each of the first three years

5. A 401(k) plan can help your company attract and retain good employees

6. A 401(k) plan demonstrates you care about your employees by helping them fund their retirement

Employer's disadvantages: Though not many, there are a few:

1. Due to the disclosure and reporting requirements of ERISA, you will need professional assistance to help you create and then administer your company plan

2. Unless you are a financial investment expert, you might also require investment advice from an experienced registered investment advisor RIA. The plan cannot discriminate between your highly and non-highly compensated employees by permitting your executives to defer a substantially higher percentage of their compensation

Employees' benefits: Employees receive a number of benefits:

1. 401(k) plans allow participants to select from a variety of investment choices including money market funds, stocks, bonds, mutual funds, ETFs, company stock, and more.

2. Employees benefit when the employer matches a portion of the employee's contribution

3. 401(k) contributions and investment earnings are all tax-deferred

4. Some plans permit loans and withdrawals for specified reasons

5. Employees have the flexibility to participate in the plan, and the flexibility to change the amount of their contribution

6. Employees often find it easier to save for retirement because the deductions are taken out of their payroll before they access their paycheck

7. Employees older than 50 may be entitled to contribute a larger annual amount than younger employees

8. If your plan chooses, employees may roll over assets from other retirement plans into your company's 401(k) plan

9. All the funds in a 401(k) plan are completely protected under federal law in case an employer suffers bankruptcy, or the company goes out of business

Employees' disadvantages: Here are four to consider:

1. Since a 401(k) is a defined contribution plan, there is no guarantee of a specific benefit in retirement; the employee is accepting the risk for investment choices

2. The investment funds are subject to market performance, so while the funds may prosper, they may also diminish, resulting in financial loss

3. Annual contributions are limited to $17,500 for employees under age 50; older employees can contribute an additional $5,500

As with everything, there are benefits and disadvantages to 401(k) plans. However, by scrutinizing the previous lists, it is clear that 401(k) plans provide a substantial opportunity for employers and employees to optimistically consider the valuable effects of establishing a company plan.

 Important:

For most company owners, and most employees, the benefits of a 401(k) plan far outweigh the disadvantages.

Popular 401(k) Features

In a survey of 1,200 plan sponsors conducted by the IRS in 2012, key findings revealed that the most popular 401(k) plan features were as follows:

1. 96% of these plans offered catch-up contributions for older employees

2. 79% permitted rollover distributions from other retirement plans

3. 76% allowed hardship withdrawals

4. 68% authorized matching contributions

5. 65% sanctioned non-elective profit sharing contributions

6. 65% approved of employee loans

7. 64% required participants to be 21 years old or older, while 20% had no age requirement at all

8. 54% obliged participants to have a minimum of one year's employment before joining the company's plan, while 13% had no service requirement

9. 41% allowed participants to adjust their deferrals at any time

10. 22% offered a Roth option, which permits employees to pay taxes on their salary, but then funds deposited in a Roth may grow tax-free until distribution

These findings may influence your discussion and decision when designing your own company's plan.

<u>401(k) Plans with Traditional and Roth IRA Options</u>: Since we're discussing 401(k) plan features, this is a good opportunity to mention that for companies with a traditional and/or a Roth IRA investment option, employer contributions based on the Roth contribution must be made to the traditional portion of the plan, whether or not the plan participant defers 100% of his or her contribution to the Roth category. This is required by IRS regulations. Employer contributions that are matched on Roth deferrals are pre-tax.

401(k) Plan Alternatives

Even though you are considering a 401(k) plan for your company, you should know there are several alternatives which might be a better fit for you and your employees. This book is not designed to review these alternatives in depth, but a simple list with brief explanations may help you further your own research.

 ## Key:

A 401(k) may not be the best solution for your unique circumstances; there are other choices...

Small companies: The alternatives available to your company depend on the level of deductions and/or contributions desired by the owners or other key employees. Different plans offer different solutions, so it's important to select the best plan for your circumstances. Self-employed individuals or small business owners should consider the following alternative retirement plans:

Payroll Deduction IRA Plan: With this plan, employees establish either a traditional or Roth IRA with the financial institution of their choice, and then authorize a specific payroll deduction to fund their account.

Simplified Employee Pension (SEP) Plan: In a SEP plan, employers contribute a set monthly amount to their employees' traditional IRA accounts.

SIMPLE IRA Plan: SIMPLE is an acronym for Savings Incentive Match PLan for Employees. This plan allows both employees and employers to contribute funds to their employees' traditional IRA accounts.

SIMPLE 401(k) Plan: Similar to the SIMPLE IRA plan, the SIMPLE 401(k) plan allows an employee to defer some compensation, however the employer must also make a matching and legally prescribed contribution.

Keogh Plan: A Keogh plan is a qualified tax-deferred pension plan specifically for a self-employed person or a partnership.

Large companies: Larger companies can avail themselves of all of the above plans except for the Keogh plan, and in addition there are nine more alternative choices. Smaller companies have these choices, too, though they may or may not make fiscal sense. Smaller company plans tend to have more profit sharing and defined benefit or cash benefit plans since there are fewer employees participating in profit sharing, and less obstacles for passing discrimination testing.

Profit Sharing Plan: Employers have flexibility with designing the key features, and may choose to contribute to the plan from company profits or other sources. The money in this plan can grow through a variety of investment vehicles, and is generally not taxed until distribution.

Money Purchase Pension Plan: With this type of plan, the company makes annual contributions to the employees' pension accounts that are not related to the company's profits.

Age-weighted Profit-sharing Plan: As it sounds, this plan allows employers to make retirement contributions based on an employee's age as well as their salary.

New Comparability Plan: A new comparability plan creates classes of employees in a company, and permits the employer to maximize contributions for selected employees who are in employee groups or classes.

Thrift/Savings Plan: A TSP is a retirement savings plan for employees and retirees of the federal government, in addition to members uniformed service organizations such as the military, police, firefighters, EMTs and paramedics.

<u>Defined Benefit Plan</u>: Employers can also establish a pension plan, known as a defined benefits plan, in which the employer deposits a specified amount. The employer bears the funding and investment risk.

<u>Target Benefit Plan</u>: With a plan of this type, contributions are based on retirement benefit projections; results are tied to the performance of the investments and are not guaranteed.

<u>Cash Balance Plan</u>: The employer makes annual contributions to each individual's account, and on retirement, the originally defined dollar amount is available to the retiree. The monetary value in the account may increase or diminish over the years, with the risk being borne by the employer. This is a hybrid defined benefit plan where the participants' accrued benefits are expressed more like a defined contributions plan, and paid as a lump sum.

<u>Employee's Stock Ownership Plan (ESOP)</u>: This plan is for companies owned by the employees, in which shares of the company are divided among the workforce, and on retirement, each employee can then sell their company shares.

Nonprofit organizations: There are also retirement plans for tax exempt organizations, AKA nonprofits. Because of their unique nature, a careful review of the options is recommended.

Nonqualified plans: Also worthy of comment are nonqualified compensation plans. Because these plans are not required to abide by strict requirements, they are more flexible, e.g., employer contributions are not capped. However, the term "nonqualified" raises a yellow flag because the plan is not as attractive from a tax perspective, nor are the assets protected should the company go bankrupt or out of business.

With this much variety of choices, an employer should carefully consider which retirement program best suits the company's and employees' needs. A 401(k) plan might be the best choice after all, and in making your decision it is prudent to ask the advice of an experienced professional such as a Certified Financial Planner (CFP) or other professional trained or certified in retirement planning.

The purpose of the case study: The fictional case study in the next chapter is presented to illustrate a scenario which may be similar to your own, providing insight through the medium of a story. Michael Kendall is a fictitious person who was featured in an earlier book, Exit Insight: Getting to "Sold!", written to guide owners with assessing the true value of their business and then increasing the value with specific actions as they position their company for sale at the maximum price. We'll be reintroduced to Michael and his circumstances, and follow his experience with creating a new 401(k) plan for his company. As you read the following chapter, consider your own unique situation and note how this information may provide the solutions you seek. The essential key to your success is consulting with a financial advisor who has years of experience with creating 401(k) plans for a range of companies in size and industry, and this advisor's strong professional network of service providers who will best facilitate your plan and benefit your company.

Summary

This chapter considered the advantages and disadvantages of establishing a 401(k) plan for your company. For many, the advantages are much more compelling than the disadvantages, but, of course, the decision to proceed or decline must be based on your own unique set of circumstances.

For most companies, a new 401(k) plan will be an advantage if it reduces company taxes, retains and attracts employees, and benefits the employees' retirement savings. Perhaps the only significant disadvantage to starting a 401(k) is that it will require the services of outside consultants to establish and administer; but even though you'd have a new company feature to monitor, when you hire a team of experienced professionals, the plan will almost run itself and will not require your constant attention.

It's about the same for the employees; their benefits outweigh the disadvantages...tax-deferred savings, possible employer matching funds, a managed savings and investment program with standard investment features, and a healthy ceiling for annual contributions; so what's not to like?

We also reviewed several alternatives to a 401(k) plan to provide insight to other available options; and now we'd like to share our scenario of Michael Kendall, a fictional business owner who, like you, is interested in exploring the idea of starting a 401(k) plan, and not spending too much money for the privilege.

 ## Chapter 1 Review Questions:

1. Which of the following is a service that is not provided by an RIA?

   A. Preparing your plan for compliance testing

   B. Measuring and explaining your fund's results quarterly

   C. Closely watching market conditions

   D. Enrolling and educating your employees

2. Are all companies, even with just one employee, eligible to set up a 401(k) plan?

   A. True

   B. False

3. Which of the following four choices is a benefit for your employees?

   A. Funds that match a percentage of the employees'
   contributions, in full or in part, are all tax-deductible

   B. Saving for retirement is easier because deductions are taken
   from payroll before paychecks are issued

   C. Administrative fees for 401(k) plans are also tax-deductible

   D. A 401(k) plan can help attract and retain good employees

4. Based on an IRS survey in 2012, a popular plan feature is allowing
catch-up contributions for older employees.

   A. True

   B. False

 Answers

   1. Answer: A. It's the TPA who prepares for compliance testing

   2. Answer: A. Every company can start a 401(k) if they wish.

   3. Answer: B. Employees contribute to their 401(k) account
   before tax is assessed, and before they receive their paycheck;
   automatic deductions are easiest for saving and investing.

   4. Answer: A. 96% of the 1,200 plan sponsors surveyed by the
   IRS in 2012 offered this feature in their company's 401(k) plan.

Chapter 2:
Case Study for Pacific Specialty Lighting Supply, Inc.

When you have finished reading this chapter, you will:

- Recognize the value of consulting with a financial advisor who will also serve as a fiduciary

- Be familiar with 401(k) plan features, such as expenses, eligibility, matching contributions, and more

- Realize the importance of an advisor who will guide you with selecting a TPA, record keeper and fund custodians

- Understand the essentials of assessing and comparing 401(k) plan proposals

- Value the importance of setting 401(k) plan goals

In this section of the book we're going to present the case study of a fictional company, Pacific Specialty Lighting Supply, Inc., and its fictional owner, Michael Kendall. We originally met this gentleman in our earlier book, "Exit Insight: Getting to Sold!", which tells the story of Michael and Mary Kendall, a married couple looking forward to their retirement years. Michael suddenly panics when he realizes he may not have properly estimated the true value of his business, and now, almost too late, may not be able to exit the business with enough money to fund their retirement dreams. "Exit Insight" explains in detail how a Certified Valuation Analyst (CVA) can precisely measure the current value of a business, and then work with the owner to increase the business's valuation and position the company for a maximum value sale.

Now we will rejoin Michael Kendall and consider the 401(k) plan he chose to adopt for his company as an illustration of the thinking and the significant details that compose a typical 401(k) plan, and which now may assist with the further development of your ideas for your own company's plan.

Looking in on the Kendalls

Please meet Michael and Mary Kendall. In their mid and early 50s, they live in Bellevue, Washington, and have three children.

Michael has been in business since graduating with an MBA from Indiana University in 1985. Starting as a mid-level manager for a shipping company, Michael shifted into the telecommunications industry as it began to have explosive growth with the advent of computers, the Internet, and cell phone distribution. In 2003, Michael started his own company, manufacturing specialty light bulbs for electronic devices. Michael's business grew slowly at first, and as he developed his specialty niche and new products were brought to the market, Michael's company grew to $4 million in annual sales.

Michael and Mary have discussed their future and concluded that Michael should begin taking his retirement seriously. Michael had given some thought to this over the last few years, but never took the advice of his CPA to create a financial plan. Michael thinks his personal investments have been doing well, but he doesn't have any accurate way to benchmark their progress because his retirement goals have been so vague. So, while it appears that he and Mary have a healthy retirement fund, he isn't sure; and with property values rising, the eventual sale of the family home, it was assumed this money would create additional retirement income, but how that source of retirement money fits into the overall plan...well, he really hasn't any assurance he's on the right track, and he knows it.

Important:

Planning for the future entails building a retirement fund, knowing the true market value of your business, and preserving your estate. A Certified Financial Planner (CFP®) can assess your financial circumstances and make recommendations that will secure your financial freedom.

Their situation is further complicated by the emotional insecurity Mary is feeling. Mary realizes the extent of her vulnerability should anything happen to Michael. This has been a nagging worry that has lately turned into a gnawing fear, and Mary has clearly told Michael how frightened she really is. Michael enjoys risky sports like skiing, windsurfing and skydiving, and fatal accidents are not unusual. What would she do if Michael died suddenly? Or what if Michael was in a coma, or had a broken spine? Why isn't Michael improving his golf game instead of waxing his skis? Mary needs Michael to tone down his active lifestyle while beefing up whatever planning and insurance she would need to live on if a disaster happened. If Michael was seriously damaged, do they have enough disability insurance? Who would manage the business if Michael couldn't? Would there be enough income until Michael could return...and what if Michael could never return?

And then, Mary is also asking smart questions about how the family is situated from now until Michael can retire...which raises all the hundreds of questions about their retirement. When is Michael retiring? What is their retirement income? Will they keep or sell their home? Can they move to a warm dry retirement village? How will they be cared for if they need long term care? What are their friends doing, or will they be forced apart? What about the kids and grandkids? What is the financial plan from now until Michael finally retires? Retirement planning takes time, and Mary doesn't think Michael has invested any serious thought into planning their finances from now until retirement, and then beyond, through the years of retirement.

Questions like these buzzed around Michael and Mary like angry hornets...

The truth is, like most business owners, Michael never consulted with a financial planner, so the details he and Mary need to know about having a comfortable retired life are unknown. Responding to Mary's sense of urgency, Michael saw the wisdom of consulting with a financial consultant, so he asked a few friends for a recommendation. The consultant a friend recommended was an established local professional who had helped other businessmen and their families develop their retirement plans, so Michael felt comfortable making an appointment.

When Michael met with the financial advisor, he realized his visit was overdue and planning their retirement should have been initiated long ago. He was glad he was now beginning to understand, and soon remedy, the situation he and Mary were in. This financial advisor presented Michael with a single 401(k) option because the advisor represented an investment company with only closed architecture plans. During the following week, Michael studied the information and then made a second appointment with the advisor to discuss creating a new 401(k) plan for his business. The advisor was good at what he did, and about a week later he presented Michael with a draft of the basic costs for a new 401(k) plan, and based on the closed architecture of the investment company he represented. The plan was consistent with Michael's goals, but Michael realized he had nothing with which to compare it. Just like buying a car, it pays to do a comparison analysis by visiting several showrooms and doing your own independent inquiries.

In order to satisfy his interest for acquiring the most cost-effective and best quality plan available, Michael decided to contact an independent RIA, this time through the advice of his CPA, who could offer alternatives to the plan Michael reviewed. However, Michael was now a bit more savvy and wanted an advisor who would serve as a consultant and fiduciary, a professional who valued a team approach, and whose team included a CFA charter holder (chartered financial analyst), a CFP (certified financial planner), and an AIF (accredited investment fiduciary). The advisor recommended by his CPA had created a number of open architecture 401(k) plans for other businesses about the same size as Michael's, so Michael made the appointment to have this second advisor perform an independent analysis to help Michael determine how best to proceed.

The Goals for Michael's 401(k) Plan

After Michael had decided that a 401(k) plan would be a great idea for his company and for his employees, he held a meeting to discuss the idea with his staff. Michael's staff of 14 employees was very excited about the prospect of having a 401(k) plan, and it was agreed that Michael and his employees would start the plan by rolling over their IRAs into the new company plan. The new financial advisor had made some inquiries, and discovered that Michael's plan would be funded by $4 million in assets by the end of its first year through a combination of rollovers, employer matching contributions, and employee tax-deferred payroll contributions. This gave the 401(k) plan a healthy financial start, and provided the figures that appear in Figure 6: 401(k) Plan Comparison.

Michael had four goals for the company plan:

Goal 1: Provide a strong retirement plan for his employees that allow maximum annual contributions.

Michael sincerely cares about his employees, and this kindness and consideration was developed from having worked with this group of exceptional people for over a decade. Michael knew each person quite well, and had attended their weddings, visited them in the hospital when accidents or health had been an issue, knew their children and happily attended birthday parties and athletic events, held company picnics, and visited them during the joys and sorrows of their lives. If it was ever possible to have a family of coworkers, this was that family. Michael felt deeply indebted to all of them because through the years this staff had been loyal and hard-working, and had built the company from a simple three-man shop to a healthy going concern. This staff had provided Michael and Mary with a comfortable life, and now also had the potential for providing the security of a happy retirement. Michael wanted to reward his employees as much as possible, so he wanted the plan to be friendly and flexible, and focused on helping his employees secure their retirement. In fact, Michael had considered a defined benefit plan, much like a pension plan, but in reviewing this option Michael realized his costs would be too high, and this option was unaffordable. The 401(k) plan was the best choice for the company and the employees; the 401(k) plan allowed the maximum level of tax-deductible contributions other than a defined benefit plan. Michael was also an employee of the company and this would be good for him and Mary, too.

Goal 2: Retain and reward employees.

Michael valued his employees and wanted them to know how much. Based on his research, Michael discovered that having a company 401(k) plan was highly regarded by employees across the nation and in every industry, and it was a useful tool for retaining employees and also attracting new talent. Michael decided to enhance his company's 401(k) plan by offering employer matching contributions. Based on the calculations that his accountant made, Michael felt that a 3% match was affordable, would be well received by his employees, would have an effect on incentivizing them to actively participate in the company plan, and would be another token that expressed his personal sense of obligation and gratitude for their support throughout the years. Michael also decided to reserve the right to make additional discretionary profit-sharing contributions to their retirement accounts, should the company's health allow him to do so. Michael wanted to reward his employees with every opportunity.

Goal 3: Provide Michael and Mary with tax-deductible savings and contributions.

As an employee, Michael was also able to make his own tax-deferred contributions to his company's 401(k) plan, in addition to the company's 3% match. Based on the conversations he'd recently had with his new financial advisor, Michael knew that establishing a personal retirement plan would help him and Mary bridge the gap between what they had now, and what they needed to have for the retirement they wanted. Michael had only seven years until retirement, and now that several other important tasks for improving his company's valuation had been achieved, it was time to get moving on establishing a company 401(k) plan which would augment his and Mary's retirement funds. The money going into their 401(k) account would also provide another advantage by reducing his annual income tax; his executive's salary would be comprised of less taxable dollars since funds were being diverted into his tax-deferred 401(k) account.

Goal 4: Reduce company taxes and build value with company loyalty.

Another solid reason for establishing a company 401(k) plan was that his accountant had confirmed the company's taxes could be reduced because of the projected amount of annual employer contributions. By matching his employees' contributions with 3% of the company's money, and paying for some of the fees and expenses of the plan, his company would be able to reduce corporate taxes and use that money to benefit his employees instead. And, because the 401(k) would increase employee loyalty and retention, Michael was also improving the valuation of his company.

Plan Features

Michael's discussion with the financial advisor who had been referred to him by his CPA focused on eight features:

1. Plan's Expenses: Michael decided his company would pay for the plan's fees and expenses, instead of having a pro rata share of these costs billed to his employees' retirement accounts. Companies with smaller plans usually have their employees pay the plan's expenses, but Michael was assured that his company had sufficient cash flow to

handle the expenses, and he was willing to incur these fees because these expenses would reduce his company's taxes and help his employees save even more money for their retirement.

2. Eligibility: Michael wanted as many of his employees as possible to have the option to participate in the 401(k) plan, so he decided that the eligibility requirement would allow all employees with one year of service, or 30 consecutive days of employment, to join. Michael sometimes had part-time employees help out when there was a production crunch, or when an employee was on maternity or health leave. Michael was willing to be generous, but not to a fault. However, if any part-time employee worked for 30 consecutive days, even if they dropped back to part-time afterward, they retained the right to stay in the plan. Michael wanted very low barriers of entry; with this requirement, most full-time people would be eligible within the first 60 calendar days, and this satisfied Michael's interest in having a friendly and flexible plan.

Key:

A 401(k) plan can choose to match employee contributions, or not. When matching, the owner decides the amount to match. A match can be dollar-for-dollar, or $.25 per dollar, or any other designation. Typically, the company matches employee contributions based on an analysis that best serves the company by reducing taxes.

3. Matching Contribution Vesting: Michael wanted to establish a vesting schedule to assure his employees would stay with the company. As you can see from the table below, after five years of service, the employee would be eligible to receive 100% of the company's annual matching contributions of 3%, and any discretionary matches also made by the company.

In the top portion of the following tables, an employee is earning $50,000 a year in net wages. This employee is allocating 8%, or $4,000 a year ($333.00 monthly) to his or her 401(k) account. The company has a 50% match, so every year the company contributes $2,000 to this employee's 401(k) account, for a total annual contribution of $6,000.

In the lower set of tables, you can see that this fictitious company can choose to have either a "three year cliff" vesting policy in which the employees are not vested, or not entitled, to keep any company matching funds until after three years of employment; or the company could choose a "graded" vesting policy, in this case over a period of six years, with the gradual vesting of company funds. Each company's 401(k) plan can select the vesting policy that best suits its particular financial needs and goals.

Figure 5: Matching Contribution Vesting Table.

Assumptions:	
Wages (Net of Payroll Tax)	$50,000
401K Contribution %	8.00%
Company Match	50.00%
With Company Match	
401(k) Annual Savings	$4,000.00
Company Match	$2,000.00
Total Contribution	**$6,000.00**

Vesting Example			
Three Year Cliff		**Six-Year Graded**	
Year	%	Year	%
1	0%	1	0%
2	0%	2	20%
3	100%	3	40%
		4	60%
		5	80%
		6	100%

4. Plan Loans: Michael was hopeful that his employees would not have to use their 401(k) funds for loans because his primary intention

was that his employees would develop their retirement savings, and allow the money to grow and compound. Yet, Michael realized that life's vicissitudes sometimes required emergency measures, so he authorized his company's plan to allow loans based on each employee's individual account. This was another way the plan could be friendly and flexible; in exchange, Michael would strongly encourage his employees' financial education to focus strenuously on building an emergency fund and creating short-term, midterm, and long-term investment goals to diminish the need for loans.

5. <u>Changing Investment Accounts</u>: Michael thought it would be helpful if the plan participants were allowed to change their investment accounts when they chose. Even though it's not recommended that the accounts change very often, this fit into the plan's underlying philosophy of being friendly and flexible. This way, if an employee felt he or she really needed to move their money from one fund to another, the employee had the ability of going online with the third-party administrator and custodian to make whatever changes they wanted, and whenever they chose.

6. <u>Adjusting Employee's Contribution Amounts</u>: If an employee wanted to adjust the amount of funds being diverted from their paycheck to their 401(k) retirement account, they would be allowed to do so monthly. Once per month was very reasonable, considering that all changes impacted the company's business office. The employee could file the proper paperwork in a timely manner, and the request would be processed on a monthly schedule.

7. <u>Rollovers</u>: As mentioned, when Michael met with his employees to discuss the idea of establishing a company 401(k) plan, the employees agreed they would help with the initial funding of the new company plan by rolling over their IRAs. The amount of funds in the IRAs, plus the first year's employee contributions, and the company's 3% matching contributions, would result in a projected end-of-year balance of $4 million.

8. <u>Employee Education</u>: It was clear to Michael that retirement education was an important part of the company's plan. Once his employees knew what he knew, hopefully with a lot less emotional pain and aggravation than he and Mary had gone through, the plan participants could wisely position themselves to benefit from the steady growth of a significant retirement resource. Michael's employees were a mix of multiple ages and educational backgrounds; he knew his employees looked to him for leadership and advice, and they believed he knew a lot more about finance and investing than they did. This was a typical employee bias, and Michael keenly felt his responsibility and obligations to serve them the best way possible.

Because financial education was so important, Michael decided to invite the plan's advisor to meet with the staff every quarter, and Michael would make a room available with refreshments and an hour or two of paid time to attend the meeting as a way of encouraging their education about investing for retirement and inspiring them to stay on track. Michael also wanted the plan's advisor to be available throughout the day and after the workday for one-on-one meetings with staff members who set appointments. Michael agreed with the advisor that the group meetings should focus on a general economic overview followed by a brief market update, and then a presentation with a discussion on plan-specific asset allocations and investments. Michael felt this would be a reasonable and helpful workshop to guide his employees toward a greater awareness of how the company plan could create individual success for each participant. Michael was very excited that he was able to give back to his employees in such a significant way.

Note:

It's always wise to do your due diligence and solicit several 401(k) plan proposals from professional providers so you can compare and select the proposal with the best combination of services and least expenses.

Comparing 401(k) Plans

When Michael studied the 401(k) fees and expenses information
the original financial advisor had provided, Michael realized he did
not yet have any way of knowing whether the cost was standard or
exorbitant. The proposal was from a salesman who could only provide
his own company's proposal; Michael didn't necessarily think this
proposal was bad, but he didn't know what his other options were.
That's when Michael contacted an independent financial consultant
and hired them to conduct a fees and expenses comparison. Because
they were an independent financial consulting company, the company
Michael chose explored a variety of combinations, such as TPAs and
record keepers as separate entities, and also as combined entities.
In addition, a variety of custodians were considered, ranging from
insurance companies to single mutual fund companies to discount
brokerages, providing a good assortment of choices for a proper
analysis.

The comparison abstract appears as Figure 6: 401(k) Plan
Comparison. This is an example of the form used to quote the costs of
401(k) plans. In reality, each of these four options would be the result
of an administrative review of three or four pages; a proper analysis
would result in about 15 to 20 pages, which we will abbreviate in the
narrative that follows.

Figure 6: 401(k) Plan Comparison.

401(k) Plan Comparison

Plan Data as of: Analysis Date
Participants: 15
Assets: $4,000,000

	Current %	Current $	Option 1 %	Option 1 $	Option 2 %	Option 2 $	Option 3 %	Option 3 $
Plan Characteristics								
Set Up & Conversion	NA	NA	NA	NA	NA	NA	NA	NA
Investment Advisory Fee								
Asset Break Points %								
First $5 million 0.750%								
Over $5 million 0.500%	1.00%	$40,000	0.750%	$30,000	0.750%	$30,000	0.750%	$30,000
Total		$40,000		$30,000		$30,000		$30,000
Recordkeeping & Administration Fees								
Base Fee				$400				$427
Participant Fee				$600				$675
Form 5500 Filing								$250
Market Value Fees				$800	Flat Fee			
Total	0.20%	$8,000		$1,800		$3,600		$1,352
Custodial Fees/Brokerage Fees	0.07%	$2,800	0.03%	$1,200	0.03%	$1,400	0.030%	$1,200
Special Services								
Plan Distributions and Tax Reporting (may be paid by participant)	NA		NA		$60 each		NA	
Loan Initiation Fee (paid by participant)	NA		NA		$100 each		NA	
Annual Loan Maintenance Fee (paid by participant)	NA		NA		$40 Each		NA	
Plan Audit Support (in excess of 5 hours/year)	NA		NA		$175 Each		NA	
Special Projects	NA		NA		$175 Each		NA	
Investment Management Fee (Mutual Funds avg) Estimate	0.72%	$28,800	0.72%	$28,800	0.72%	$28,800	0.72%	$28,800
Audit Fee (not applicable < 100 participants)								
Fee Reductions (Mutual Fund revenue sharing)	0.36%	($14,400)	0.36%	($14,400)	0.36%	($14,400)	0.36%	($14,400)
Estimated Cost		$65,200		$47,400		$49,400		$46,952
Percent of Assets		1.63%		1.19%		1.24%		1.17%
Total Annual Dollar Savings		$0		$17,800		$15,800		$18,248

All data to be independently verified via each service providers quote.

At the top of the chart, we can see there are 15 participants consisting of Michael and his 14 employees; and the 401(k) plan's assets are $4,000,000, which is the amount of money in this plan at the end of the first year, giving us a hypothetical value with which to illustrate the comparisons. In this example, the analysis does not disclose the actual names of the plan providers, but the fees are extracted from real scenarios to lend authenticity to this example. The purpose is to present the layout of what a 401(k) plan comparison may look like. Of course, always ask your advisor to compare all your viable options, and not just the one they may sell.

 Important:

Fees and expenses are necessary, providing the benefits and services your company desires. However, it's also important to make sure the fees and expenses are competitive with other providers, and that your plan is purchasing the benefits and services you believe are truly important for your company and employees.

Also note there are five columns; the first column labels the fees and expenses; the second column represents the proposal of fees and expenses provided by the original financial advisor who was referred by Michael's friend and offered a bundled 401(k) plan; the three remaining columns represent the options provided by the independent financial advisor referred by Michael's CPA.

Set Up & Conversion: On this row, the setup and conversion fees are not available for comparison because we are assuming that all the providers have waived them. This is because the plan was targeted to have $4 million in assets by the end of the year, and everyone was willing to be paid later based on the year-end performance. If Michael's new plan had started with no assets, we would expect to see setup fees; however, on the other hand, there would then not be any market value fees or any other fees based on assets under management (AUM), and therefore there would also not be any fee sharing, since fee sharing is based on assets. Because Michael's new plan was projected to have $4 million in assets by year-end, all the service providers were happy to delay their compensation now for a better reward later. In passing, remember that setup fees are negotiable, so always discuss the price.

Investment Advisory Fee: This row shows the fees of the financial advisor. The first column indicates that the fee is variable based on the amount of money in the 401(k) plan. The fee is 0.750% if the account has under $5 million in assets, and the fee drops to 0.500% when the account exceeds $5 million in assets. Typically there are three tiers, but because this is a startup plan with only $4 million, only two tiers are listed. The tiers in this chart apply only to the options made available in columns 3, 4, and 5, managed by the independent advisor offering unbundled plans. The investment advisor, such as the RIA or the broker, is the recipient of the investment advisory fee.

Further review reveals that the original financial advisor is charging 1% as his fee for managing the account's $4 million; this results in an annual fee of $40,000. The lowest fee is 0.750% because the account is under $5 million, and is $30,000 for any of the three options, a fee reduction of $10,000.

Recordkeeping & Administration Fees: Here we see the fees of the record keepers; usually the TPA and record keeper is the same service provider, so it's assumed the fees for both are combined as one. A Base Fee is the fee for simply being engaged by the plan; as you can see, Option 1 and Option 3 are very similar in cost, at $400 and $427.

- A Participant Fee is a cost per participant for working on the plan; at $600 and $675, Option 1 charges $40 for each of the 15 participants, and Option 3 charges $45 for each of the 15 participants; again, they are very similar in cost.

- To file Form 5500, the record keeper in Option 3 charges $250 for this annual filing.

- The Market Value Fees are calculated from basis points; these fees are based on a percentage of the assets managed. In this case, the provider for Option 1 has been calculated at $800 based on the $4 million in the plan.

In column 2, the record keeper's fees are based on 20% of the plan's end-of-the-year balance, which comes to $8,000. In Option 3, the record keeper charges a flat fee of $3,600. Here you can see the wide range of fees charged by different record keepers, emphasizing how important it is to get several quotes and negotiate prices.

Custodial Fees/Brokerage Fees: These are the fees charged by the investment companies that are holding the money, such as Vanguard, Fidelity, etc. The custodial fees in column 2 are the highest, while the fees for the other three options are very similar. It is interesting to note there are sometimes subtleties that have an impact on fees. For example, it may be that both Option 2 and Option 3 have the same custodian, but because of this custodian's relationship with the record keeper of Option 3, the custodian's fee is a bit lower. The lesson here is that even with the same custodian there can be different fees based on the record keeper and the TPA relationship; every factor is separately calculated.

Special Services: In this area of the chart, you can see that some plans will charge for every particular service, and others will not. These are services that trigger a billing only when a participant uses that service.

Investment Management Fee (Mutual Funds avg) Estimate: For this category, we're keeping it simple and assuming that the same selection of mutual funds is being used in each of the four plan options; the mutual fund company receives the investment management fee.

Audit Fee: There is no audit fee because the plan has less than 100 participants.

Fee Reductions (Mutual Fund revenue-sharing): This category illustrates the fee reductions which will reduce the total of the preceding costs. Based on the selection of funds that are available to the plan participants, there will be an estimated kickback from the funds of $28,800. In this case, the reduction is the same (0.72% /$28,800) because the lineup of funds is the same for each option; this would not normally be the case, except we want to keep this example simple.

Revenue sharing is normal; this is standard operating procedure in the investment industry, and everyone knows about it and uses it in their calculations.

The important detail to know is that your advisor may be receiving some revenue in this manner, and that he or she discloses it to you so you can accurately assess your plan's fees and expenses.

Estimated Cost: This row shows the total of fees and expenses. The services offered by the initial advisor, whom Michael had originally contacted on the advice of a friend, has the highest cost at $65,200. The other three options are similar in cost, but Option 3 has the least total costs, coming in at $46,952, and the highest total annual dollar savings. Assuming the quality of all services is the same, Option 3 is the most cost-effective and the best choice for Michael.

Percent of Assets: Option 3, which is the most cost-effective choice, shows a cost of 1.17% of the plan's assets. Option 1 was a very close second. The costs of the initial financial advisor are the highest of all, so it was wise of Michael to request a cost comparison.

Total Annual Dollar Savings: Here we see the total amount of money that would be saved when compared with the initial financial advisor's proposal. A savings of $18,248, as evidenced in Option 3, is significant!

Conclusion: In this plan comparison example, several conclusions became clear. The first lesson is that it is always a good idea to gather several quotations and make a comparison. The second lesson is the variety of services and range of fees available from an assortment of providers. The third lesson is that it pays to take the time to find the right investment advisor for your company; the best choice will be an advisor who can guide you when making the selection of a TPA, a record keeper, and custodians of the funds; you're also selecting the best advisor for your 401(k) plan because of this person's ability to reduce fees, increase returns, manage the assets expertly, and provide a meaningful employee education program.

Summary

The foregoing case study was a fictitious scenario of a business owner's inquiry through the initial steps of establishing a 401(k) plan. Michael carefully selected four goals that had value for his company, his employees, and his personal retirement planning. Seven plan features such as eligibility, loans, rollovers, etc. were discussed as choices Michael could incorporate in his company plan, and the study concluded with a comparison of the costs of the plan when served by different combinations of financial advisors, TPAs, record keepers, and custodians...to provide a reasonable picture of a real-world experience you might soon have.

In the next chapter, we'll examine the evaluation and selection of two important 401(k) service providers, the TPA and the record keeper.

Chapter 2 Review Questions:

1. The main reason a company plan would restrict eligibility for employees who have less than one year of service or less than 30 consecutive days of employment is because the plan sponsor wants to reward steadily employed staff.

    A. True

    B. False

2. A company's matching contribution has to be dollar for dollar.

    A. True

    B. False

3. Even though a company's 401(k) plan could allow employee loans, why is this not a good idea for the employee?

    A. Borrowing against the 401(k) account may limit growth of the account.

    B. The fees and penalties for borrowing could be costly.

    C. The loan might not be repaid, so the advantage of having a 401(k) account is diminished.

    D. All of the above.

4. It is important to select a financial advisor to help you select a TPA, a record keeper and fund custodians.

    A. True

    B. False

Answers

1. Answer: A. Most employers want to offer the 401(k) as a benefit for their regular workforce, and save the burden and costs the office would otherwise have if every employee was included.

2. Answer: B. The matching contribution can be any amount, or none.

3. Answer: D. While employees may have a need to borrow against their account, it might be in their best interest to discourage them from doing so.

4. Answer: A. The best choice will be an advisor who can guide you when making the selection of a TPA, a record keeper, and custodians of the funds; you're also selecting the best advisor for your 401(k) plan because of this person's ability to reduce fees, increase returns, manage the assets expertly, and provide a meaningful employee education program.

Chapter 3:
Interviewing and Hiring the Right Financial Advisor for You

When you have finished reading this chapter, you will:

- Know whether you want to share the fiduciary responsibility, or transfer the full fiduciary responsibility to your plan advisor

- Have a strong understanding of the 12 key categories for evaluating financial advisors

- Understand the significance of the Investment Policy Statement (IPS)

- Recognize the importance of employee 401(k) educational services

- Realize the importance of hiring a financial advisor who performs benchmarking services

- Know the right questions for determining your advisor's investment philosophy

Selecting a financial advisor is one of your most important responsibilities as a plan sponsor. The financial advisor you hire will make recommendations on investments that will have a significantly powerful impact on your employees' retirement money, affecting their ability to retire well or not, and you must be assured that the investment advice you and your employees receive is prudent, unbiased, and will result in decisions that help your employees' retirement funds grow in safety.

It's not just a matter of picking a financial advisor that's savvy enough to make good investment recommendations, but it's also necessary that your financial advisor is well educated about IRS regulations affecting your company's retirement plan. One of the biggest problems about 401(k) investment advisors in recent years is the issue of whether or not the selected financial advisor is making biased investment recommendations. When an influential consultant such as a financial advisor has relationships or alliances with the money managers of investment funds, the opportunity for a conflict of interest becomes a concern. It is a violation of IRS Code if your investment advisor is recommending investments in funds and then receives payments from the managers of those funds. When interviewing an investment advisor, it's important to establish the objectivity of the advisor's recommendations.

Sharing Fiduciary Responsibility: Fiduciary responsibility is another big issue that needs insightful resolution. Because of the extreme nature of responsibility that's placed on your shoulders as the plan sponsor, it's wise to either share fiduciary responsibility with a professional who possesses expert experience and knowledge, and can provide you with astute advice on all the elements of your company's 401(k) planning, or perhaps even better, transfer the full fiduciary responsibility to your advisor. There are many investment advisors who will happily accept responsibility for the fiduciary advice they offer; they are trained, experienced, capable...and this is their job.

 Important:

Sharing fiduciary responsibility with a professional who is a trained and experienced expert with 401(k) plan management provides a compelling advantage because this reduces your concerns and saves a lot of time otherwise spent managing the plan.

There are two types of financial advisors that can serve you and your company's plan.

a)   Shared responsibility: ERISA 3(21) defines a fiduciary that is a paid professional providing investment recommendations to the plan sponsor or to the trustee, who then can accept or reject the investment recommendations; the fiduciary responsibility is shared between this type of advisor and the plan sponsor/trustee.

b)   Full responsibility: ERISA 3(38) defines a fiduciary with the full authority to make investment decisions, subject to the plan's documents and investment policy statement, and upon whom rests the full fiduciary responsibility.

Many plan sponsors prefer hiring a 3(38) advisor because the responsibility is shifted away from the company's owner and into the capable hands of an investment professional. Considering the frequency of litigious arguments in the courts, combined with the increasingly rigorous reviews by the IRS, this may be a very wise choice for you. Many investment brokers will not accept fiduciary responsibility for the services they perform, so it is probably in your best interests to hire a financial advisor who will.

Retirement Financial Advisors: You might also consider hiring a consultant to help you select a financial advisor. Retirement financial advisors specialize in helping plan sponsors sort through the intricacies of initiating a new 401(k) plan. For first-time plan sponsors, selecting a financial advisor is a momentous decision because this person's effect on your company's plan and plan participants is so significant; for this reason, some plan sponsors choose to hire an expert who can advise them during the selection process. Depending on your ability to understand the complexities of interviewing and evaluating financial advisors, it may be a very wise choice to hire a retirement financial advisor. If you already have a 401(k) plan, a retirement financial advisor could also help evaluate the performance of your current financial advisor and many elements of your company's plan, such as complying with new regulations, evaluating the cost of the fees and expenses your plan is currently paying to ensure they are competitive, and reviewing the quality of your employees' retirement fund education, the investment advice they are receiving, and the quality of the recommended investments that are available through the plan.

Whether or not you choose to use the services of a retirement financial advisor in your selection process, this chapter will analyze the 12 key features inherent in evaluating financial advisors and selecting the professional that will best serve your company's needs.

Key:

Take the time to carefully interview and select your retirement plan advisor. This professional is your 401(k) plan's key man. Your plan's advisor will become your trusted partner, and will guide you with dozens of decisions, making your engagement pleasant, productive, and rewarding.

1. Background and Experience

As you know from your experience when working with professionals of any type, there is often a wide range of background and experience among the applicants; because you want the best financial advisor possible, you and your interview committee, or you and your retirement financial advisor will need to conduct a sophisticated filtering and analysis process to determine which of the financial advisors interested in working with you will be your best choice.

When investigating the background and experience of a financial advisor, there are five categories to consider:

General company overview: You will want an overview of the financial advisor's company so you can be assured the company is substantial. Find out who owns the company, and ask for the professional biographies of the principals. Determine how long the company has been in business and learn about the company's history. Has the company always served retirement plan clients, or are there other services and interests of the company? Ask for documentation of this company's history with servicing retirement plan clients to confirm the company's degree of experience. Inquire how many employees the company has, and how many of them are investment advisors. If the company uses subcontractors, find out who they are and what services they provide.

Client experience: Request information about the company's clients, and determine how many of their clients' companies are similar to your own. By knowing the number of clients they have, the dollar value of the investments under their advisement, how many new clients they've gained in the last two years as well as how many they've lost, and the recognition this company has recently received from independent professional associations, the better you'll be able to assess the value of this company's services to you and your employees. The financial advisor's company should list the types of services it offers other companies with 401(k) plans, and be able to refer to examples of the company's ability with guiding and contributing their clients through various government audits, compliance activities, plan terminations and mergers, as well as any corrective action that was required. In this category, it will also be valuable to find out what the financial advisor believes is their "secret sauce", adding value to their services and distinguishing them from the services offered by other firms.

Legal status as a registered investment advisor: You'll need to determine the current legal status of the financial advisor's company by asking for a list of all the federal, state, and other regulatory agencies that have issued or registered the company's licenses. It's important that you also find out if the financial advisor's company has ever been disciplined by a government agency for unethical behavior, or sued by an unhappy client; the details may reveal whether there was any wrong doing. Equally revealing would be a discovery that the company was found guilty of any violations or was required to pay fines because of an ERISA or a securities regulation violation.

Fiduciary services: Similarly, you'll want to know if the company is bonded and insured, and by how much. It's also important to establish if this company works on an advisory basis; if so, request a copy of the company's most recent Form ADV from the Securities and Exchange Commission, both Parts 1 and 2. Form ADV is a disclosure document that requires information about the investment advisor's company, business practices, and any disciplinary events imposed on the company's employees. The company's Form ADV is also available online by conducting a search on the Securities and Exchange Commission's website. You'll also want to inquire if the company performs its services on a commission basis. It's also necessary to review a list of the company's clients and require references from four clients whose size is relevant to your own.

Investment and consulting services: It's important to understand how the investment advisor intends to meet his or her responsibilities to you and your employees. Find out who will be your company's primary contact, and this person's experience with serving employer-sponsored retirement plans. A professional biography of this person detailing his or her areas of expertise, credentials, number of years with the company, the number of plans and the average size of these plans with which this professional is currently working is information you will want to know. There are also the details of how often this advisor will meet with your employees, and if that will be one-on-one or in employee workshops, and if this person is available for conference calls. You also need to find out what the scope of the consulting services will be, the research capabilities of the company, and any other members of the financial advisor's company that will be available to support the work that will be done on behalf of you and your employees.

A careful investigation of all these different factors should give you a very good idea about the background and experience of the financial advisor's company. As you can see, it may be a good idea to engage the services of a retirement financial advisor who can help you review the many proposals your company will receive from financial advisor companies applying for your 401(k) business.

2. Acceptance of Fiduciary Responsibility

As mentioned in the introduction to this chapter, it is essential to determine if the financial advisor will accept fiduciary responsibility, and to what degree. Most plan sponsors are quite busy with the daily business of managing their company, and do not have time for the extra diversion of becoming proficient with the regulations and many details of offering a 401(k) plan to their employees. Considering the implications of the fiduciary responsibility that will otherwise default to you, unless you are well versed in retirement plans, IRS Code, ERISA regulations, and investment strategies for the range of your employees' financial needs, you'll want to have a 3(21) investment advisor sharing partial fiduciary responsibility with you, or a 3(38) investment advisor taking the full burden off your shoulders. Finding the right financial advisor for your company's plan is very important!

When you're interviewing a financial advisor, you should find out if the advisor's company will accept the legal responsibility and become a fiduciary for your plan, and whether as a 3(21) or a 3(38). In addition, you should expect your financial advisor to access resources that help meet IRS compliance; inquiring about the nature of these resources will help you decide if your company will be sufficiently represented when compliance issues arise. Considering that your company may have a 401(k) committee, it would be wise to inquire if the financial advisor is capable and willing to offer training, education and support to your committee. Also important is asking about potential conflicts of interest that might occur between the financial advisor and money managers with whom the financial advisor is currently conducting business. It would be helpful to find out if the financial advisor's company has a written conflict of interest policy, and how strict it is. It will also help you to sleep at night if you were to find out, should you consider hiring this financial advisor, that none of his or her clients have ever been the subject of an investigation by the IRS or the Department of Labor, or if they have, that matters were settled with positive outcomes which do not reflect on the poor performance of this advisor.

3. Development of Plan Architecture

When considering which financial advisor is best for your company, it's important to know whether or not the advisor has experience with the type of plan architecture you want for your company. An open architecture 401(k) plan means the plan can select and invest in any assortment of investment types, such as mutual funds, stocks, bonds, ETFs, etc. A closed architecture 401(k) plan means investment choices are limited to the investment types offered by the 401(k) provider, which is typically a single mutual fund family or an insurance company. Regardless of which type of plan architecture you've selected for your company, you must make sure the financial advisor you hire is familiar with working within this architecture.

 Definition:

"Open architecture" means that your financial advisor is not restricted from selecting investment choices for your company's 401(k) plan.

"Closed architecture" represents that your financial advisor is restricted from selecting investment choices for your company's 401(k) plan.

---

4. Development of Investment Policy Statement

The Investment Policy Statement (IPS) is an essential part of the 401(k) plan, and developing the IPS is one of the most critical activities performed by the fiduciary. The IPS is the business plan for the 401(k) and the primary management tool for administering the plan. This policy statement reduces liability for the fiduciaries when investments either fail or perform poorly. The IPS, when written correctly, will clearly reflect the 401(k) plan's mission and investment objectives.

Note:

An IPS is the roadmap for your company's 401(k) plan.

A well-written IPS should be the foundation for your plan's compliance with regulations, outlining the investment objectives for your 401(k) plan, the selected asset classes, how performance will be monitored and how investment choices can be added and deleted from the plan. The IPS also identifies the guidelines for selecting individuals to manage various aspects of the plan including maintaining the effectiveness of the plan to meet compliance issues, especially as circumstances change. When interviewing a financial advisor, you'll want to know how the advisor provides guidance in developing a customized IPS for your company. Ask to see other clients' Investment Policy Statements, and inquire how these IPS came to be, and the role the financial advisor played in developing and finalizing these statements.

Figure 7: Fiduciary Suitability.

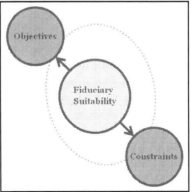

5. Investment Philosophy

When choosing a financial advisor, it's important that the advisor you select has an investment philosophy that is prudent. Your investment advisor should advocate diversification among a variety of investments so the performance of a single investment type does not weigh unduly on the value of the portfolio. The advisor should also advocate for using funds with low expenses, because expenses can diminish the value and performance of your 401(k) funds over time. Positioning investments for the long term, and avoiding short-term market influences, is another important part of a healthy investment philosophy. You'll want an advisor who carefully studies investment risk and continually monitors fund performance so you can be assured that the funds in your company's 401(k) are well-suited for selection by your employees. It's also important that your financial advisor has analyzed the demographics of your employees so an appropriate mix of investment styles is available. Lastly, your financial advisor should be an expert when it comes to being up to date on the benchmarks for investment performance, and the benchmarks on fees; this way your advisor can assess and recommend the funds that are most appropriate for their value and cost. Of course, these elements of an investment philosophy should be included in your company's Investment Policy Statement.

6. Investment Selection Process

The investment selection process is another fundamental element to review when selecting a financial advisor. It's important that your advisor has sufficient research resources available to analyze and monitor investment performance; asking about these investment tools should give you an idea of how the advisor determines which funds and which managers are a good choice for your company's 401(k). Some of these research tools could be proprietary, or they may be from a third-party provider; this will provide added information about the performance you can expect from the advisor. It's important to assure yourself that the research your advisor uses comes from independent databases, and not from biased sources, and that the discussion about the funds the advisor would include demonstrates knowledge about the type of assets contained you want in your Investment Policy Statement. Part of this conversation should also reveal how the advisor determines investment benchmarks.

How often does this advisor conduct performance review meetings, and how frequently are reports issued about the performance of the funds? Does the advisor maintain a list of investments on a "watch list" as a method for adding potentially desirable investments? What can you expect from the advisor when an investment is not performing well, and what is the advisor's process for terminating such investments?

7. Employee Meetings, Education and Services Commitments

Keeping your employees informed about the plan is a very important element of your responsibilities, for several reasons. First of all, you want to make sure your employees understand the value of the 401(k) plan and the impact their investment will have on their future. Second, you will want your employees to know how to make smart choices based on their financial needs, particular to their age and resources. Third, you want to avoid liability and ensure that an employee education program is available; employees may claim they were uninformed due to your failure to convey timely information and disclosures, which is one of your plan's compliance requirements.

 Important:
Your employee education program is critical for the success of your employees' retirement plans. When your employees truly understand the value of the 401(k) plan, they will be able to make informed decisions that can positively affect their financial future.

Ideally, you want your financial advisor to develop an annual education strategy with your 401(k) committee, designed for the particular needs of your employees. Once your employee demographics have been determined and their needs identified, appropriate educational goals can be established; then the education program can be created and conducted to help your employees comprehend the importance of the 401(k) plan and how they can benefit from active participation. This educational program should be ongoing, and could consist of a series of workshops that provide your employees with not only the basics, but also with a more detailed program that develops their understanding and acumen as investors. The availability of an employee education program will also assist with communicating changes to your company's 401(k) plan as time and opportunity necessitates.

8. Capabilities with Plan Design and Technical Issues

Plan design: You'll need to consider how capable the financial advisor can be with designing a plan that's suitable for your company and for your employees. As the plan sponsor, your company's 401(k) plan should serve your company's goals when it comes to tax relief and rewarding your employees.

Coverage and Eligibility: Coverage test rules are different from eligibility rules. Eligibility rules, at their strictest, require an employee to be 21 years old, and have 1,000 service hours with the company. Coverage test rules function by identifying a control group by looking at all employees of all related business-type employers. After the plan has determined both the coverage testing group and non-excludable employees, it must then determine who is benefiting from the plan. The benefiting determination is made separately for highly compensated employees and for non-highly compensated employees by using a ratio formula. If this ratio is at least 70%, the plan satisfies the coverage test.

Contributions, Vesting and Forfeiture: Will rollovers from other plans be welcomed; and, as the plan sponsor, will you participate in matching contributions, and if so, what will your contributions be? At what point will employees be vested in the 401(k) plan and entitled to own 100% of the employer's contributions? Will employees who are dismissed prior to being vested have to forfeit employer contributions their account has received?

Regulatory Compliance: Your financial advisor must have the experience to design your plan so all regulations are satisfied and your plan is managed in a manner that assures continued compliance.

Investment Options: Your company's 401(k) plan must delineate the investment fund choices, and should be designed so the demographic range of your employees can be satisfied with appropriate options.

Hardship Loans and Withdrawals: A plan sponsor does not have to offer either loans or hardships, but if offered, policy language will need to be included describing the nature of a hardship loan, and what will occur if the loan is not paid back within time restrictions. The plan also has to describe the process for withdrawing funds from the company's plan.

Employee Education Program: The plan should express its intentions for educating your employees about the purpose and value of the company's 401(k) plan so they can be served as completely as possible.

Technology: Your financial advisor must assure that the technology you'll need to support your 401(k) plan's investments and record-keeping is available and reliable. There should be a policy and plan that addresses data recovery in case of a security breach; and the financial advisor should be able to describe how data will be secured and kept confidential. Privacy and confidentiality are key issues in our society today, and your financial advisor should have safeguards and contingencies in place, should a disaster threaten.

9. Reporting on Trends in the 401(k) Marketplace

It's important to stay up-to-date on pending regulations, and aware of concerns that are current in the news, such as the recent disquiet about participant fee disclosure. You will want your financial advisor to be aware of the issues that may affect your company's plan, and be able to advise you on making adjustments in a timely manner so you have time to plan ahead for the changes that may be coming, and stay ahead of concerns that may embroil you. Your financial advisor should schedule quarterly meetings to advise you, your 401(k) committee, and your employees about investment and regulatory issues that are developing and have the potential for impacting the performance of your plan.

10. Benchmarking Services

The value of having a financial advisor who performs benchmarking services is that you'll now be able to determine if your fees are commensurate with industry standards. This is valuable information because it determines whether or not the stated and hidden expenses and fees paid by your company or employees are appropriate; you'll also learn if there are services you should be receiving for these fees that ought to be provided or improved.

Expense analysis should be conducted at quarterly intervals to protect you and your plan's participants from excessive payments that reduce their retirement funds' growth. Remember, too, that you have a fiduciary responsibility to assure that funds in the plan are serving the plan participants in the most efficient manner possible. When your financial advisor reports the quarterly findings to you and your employees, this information is documented for compliance review and the plan participants know that the fees being paid are reasonable and appropriate.

11. Fees

As just noted, fees are a significant issue that require careful review. In 2012, the Department of Labor revised its guidelines regarding fee disclosures so there would be more transparency for plan participants to understand the purpose and the cost of fees being paid out of their retirement accounts. Plan participants who are paying these fees can now more clearly see the costs associated with managing their retirement accounts; making these fees visible to participants has recently been a very significant issue in the investment industry.

Note:

Your plan's 401(k) fees and expenses are necessary, of course. Just make sure the fees and expenses are competitive with other providers, and your plan is purchasing the benefits and services that best serve your company and employees.

In supporting this intention, your financial advisor must be able to explain how his or her company is being compensated for the services provided. Part of this inquiry should focus on assuring yourself that your financial advisor is making unbiased recommendations to you and your employees, so no conflict of interest can exist between the advisor and the fund managers with whom your advisor is making investment purchases. Your advisor should have a policy statement that explains the source of compensation or benefits from the companies with which he or she works, and which also explains how funds received from the fund managers are allocated. Ideally, they should be used to offset some of the fees being paid by your company's plan for the financial advisor services you are receiving. As mentioned above, a periodic expense analysis will help determine whether or not the fees are properly benchmarked to industry standards, confirming that the expenses and fees are appropriate and reasonable, or that there is now an opportunity for a fee reduction and additional savings for your plan's participants. You will also want to be kept informed about any potential changes in the retirement industry's expenses and fees so you can make appropriate plans for timely adjustment.

12. Implementation Strategy

Another critical element when interviewing a financial advisor is to ask questions about the implementation strategy that will be employed when setting up your company's 401(k). The financial advisor should explain there will be an initial meeting to discuss the goals and objectives of the plan for the initial and subsequent years. The financial advisor should also describe his or her experience with starting first-time plans, and express their intention for being active with helping you and your 401(k) committee evaluate and select a third party administrator (TPA), the record keeper, and the custodians. Your financial advisor should commit to helping you and your committee write your company's plan, help with the paperwork, and be the intermediary who responds to inquiries from the 401(k) committee and your employees. Your financial advisor should also reassure you that your employees will receive timely plan information so they will know their eligibility and can join the plan when it's ready to receive them.

Summary

This chapter focused on the 12 key elements requiring careful consideration when evaluating the services of a financial advisor. The success of your company's 401(k) plan depends, in large part, on the effectiveness of this professional, and for this reason, it was suggested that you hire the services of a financial financial advisor whose experience with 401(k) regulations and professionals can be a strong and helpful influence on acquiring the advisor who will best serve your company's and employees' needs.

Insight was also provided regarding the liability of fiduciary responsibility and your choice of sharing that responsibility, or divesting yourself of it by assigning it into the care of an experienced 3(38) financial advisor.

In the next chapter, we'll discuss the process for setting up your company's new 401(k) plan, which includes building and preparing your internal team, issuing a request for proposals (RFP), and rolling out your new plan!

Figure 8: Steps to Success.

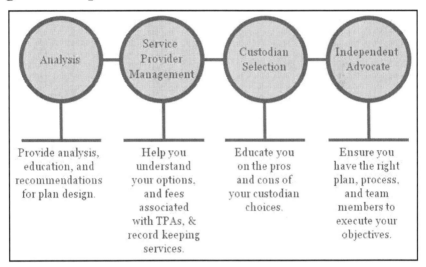

We'll end this chapter with a convenient list of 30 questions you might want to use when interviewing financial advisor candidates.

30 Interview Questions to Ask a Financial Advisor

Q1: Why should I use you as my financial advisor?

You should seek an advisor, and his or her company, who personifies the following key tenets:

Independence: The advisor is an unbiased third party who provides an objective point of view without the distraction of conflicts of interest.

Relationship Management: The advisor strives to achieve a deep understanding of your situation and, by working together, a mutual respect. His or her relationship with you is the first priority, and a strong relationship is fundamental to success.

Proven Expertise: You and your company will benefit from the collective experience of all the professionals on the advisor's team. The team-based approach provides you with access to the specialized expertise of each one of the company's professionals.

Perspective: You want an advisor who has provided financial services for clients through a wide range of market conditions, and will provide a prudent approach and long-term perspective.

Depth: Your advisor will first determine your goals, tolerance for risk, and time horizon. These factors will be measured against the advisor's extensive knowledge of investments, only then considering asset allocation and diversification with your best interests in mind.

Education and Training: The advisor's educational background is among the highest in the industry. Carefully study the biographies of the advisor and his/her team.

Experience: Knowledge is incomplete without experience. Seek an advisor who has successfully navigated his/her clients' financial planning and investing needs through several economic and market cycles.

Q2: How long have you been in business?

You'll want an advisor who has at least a decade (or two!) of experience.

Q3: What is your educational and professional background?

As mentioned above, carefully study the advisor's and team members' professional resumes.

Q4: What services do you provide?

You'll want to closely review the variety of services that are available because you may require support in other areas of your business; having an advisory firm that knows you as a client in one area may be an important value for you in another. It would be highly beneficial to work with an advisor with a strong background in both investment management and comprehensive financial planning.

The advisor can help you assess your current portfolio and investment management strategies compared to your goals and objectives to determine if you are on target. The advisor can also evaluate different portfolio management strategies and help you select and implement a strategy that will give you the best chance of meeting your goals.

An advisor with a strong planning process will help assess your current financial situation, identify specific needs, goals, and concerns and help evaluate your options and strategies for addressing them. A good advisor will help you with a variety of quality financial planning alternatives. Whether you are working on a retirement plan, tax plan or estate plan, your advisor must have the expertise you need to reach your goals.

Q5: Will you look at my overall financial picture?

You want an advisor who can also review your company's financial circumstances and recommend improvements for increased efficiency. The financial planning process should be performed in a comprehensive fashion, covering many financial planning needs, or as a modular plan, covering just one or two pieces of the financial puzzle. Your advisor should be able to tailor the financial planning to meet your particular needs.

Q6: Do you have training in comprehensive financial planning?

Be sure to check your advisor's professional degrees and credentials, and also note his or her professional affiliations.

Q7: Do you use Monte Carlo Simulation for retirement planning?

The Monte Carlu Simulation is a stringent processes for evaluating, monitoring and adjusting investment and financial planning strategies. An advisor with advanced education and training, should be familiar with the utilize Monte Carlo simulation as well as most all other advanced statistical tools, techniques and methods for their financial planning and investment management processes.

Q8: Who is your typical client?

When you hire an advisor having expertise with a variety of clients, you are likely to have an expanded array of services which can aid your company, your executive staff, and your other employees. It may be valuable to have an advisor with expertise in serving individuals seeking investment management and financial planning expertise, as well as trusts and estates, for example.

Q9: Do you have inactivity fees?

You don't want to employ an advisory firm that charges you for their inactivity!

Q10: Do you have account minimums?

This is a good question because you want an advisor and a team who is in the business of helping people solve their financial planning and investment management problems, and willing to evaluate anyone's individual facts and circumstances with a free financial assessment. The assessment should determine if the advisor is able to provide value.

Q11: Why do you want me as a client?

Expect an answer like this one: "You are the reason we are in business, and we want you to work with smart, honest, ethical people who truly care about what is important to you and your family."

Q12: What kind of people don't you want?

Again, look for an affirmative response such as this: "We enjoy working for clients who appreciate our hard work, dedication, service and our continued commitment to excellence."

Q13: Will anyone else be working with me?

You want an advisor who believes in an internal and external team approach to addressing comprehensive financial needs.

Internally, the team should provide a full-service, a 360-degree approach to serving you. Each team member, having a specialized role to play, will interact with you as appropriate at various points in time. The relationship manager will act as the quarterback of the team, supporting your work with the client service team member, the financial planning team members, the investment team members, and the reporting team members.

With your external team, the advisor will act as the quarterback and assemble the professionals whose services may be required to help you meet your needs.

Q14: Do you have discretion to act without my approval?

You may choose to have your advisor act as a fiduciary, whose primary responsibility is acting on behalf of and for the benefit of the plan participants. If this is the case, then you should find an advisor who manages discretionary investment portfolios per a written investment policy state (IPS). The advisor should not manage your ability and willingness to take risk because your risk objective function is uniquely yours, and you must communicate any changes in your risk tolerance to your advisor immediately.

Many clients assume that because the advisor is the expert, the advisor should be able to tell which portfolio is best for the client. However, the advisor only knows which portfolio is the right one for you once the advisor understands your goals, objectives and your ability and willingness toward taking risk. As there will inevitably be changes to your situation over time, your advisor must be informed to better advise you.

Q15: Can you provide client references?

You should acquire the references and then do your due diligence.

Q16: Do you have or have you had any unhappy clients?

This is another good question to ask because the response will provide you with a lot of information you can assess to better decide if this advisor/candidate is a good match for you. Here are two examples of how the advisor you're interviewing might explain any disappointed clients he or she has had.

The purpose for the investment policy statement (IPS) is to establish guidelines that will govern the investment activities between you and your advisor regarding the investment goals, objectives and management policies applicable to your investment portfolio. Your advisor should dynamically monitor your every changing lifestyle...

- Your ability and willingness to take risk
- Your income needs
- Your taxes
- Your savings
- Etc.

...with the dynamic movements of the global markets and the world economic environment. Additionally, your advisor should overlay the geopolitical environment into the decision making process. However, there are times in which there is a disconnect with what a client is feeling and what has been communicated in the IPS. When that happens, it is possible for the client to become unhappy. For example, the IPS might call for a moderate growth portfolio, but after several years of upward market movement, the client is feeling like taking more risk and would prefer the aggressive growth model. However, because the client did not communicate his change in risk temperament, the advisor follows the IPS and does not change to the more aggressive model. A miscommunication like this will result in unhappiness. Communication is a two-way street and the client and the advisor must work together to ensure that the current portfolio strategies are matched to the client's current willingness to take risk.

It is also possible to become unhappy because of the differences in terminology. For example, your advisor may use the term "moderate" to describe a particular asset allocation model, however not all "moderate" models are equal. Moderate growth models can all have significantly different risk and return profiles, none of which is right or wrong; they just have different approaches to taking risk. These differences can come from labeling issues or benchmark mismatches. Benchmark mismatches are, for example, when the client is looking at the S&P 500 benchmark, but the advisor's benchmark is a custom-made, multi-asset class benchmark that better matches the manager's IPS mandate, as opposed to the S&P 500 index.

These are two examples illustrating how a client can become disappointed with their advisor.

Q17: What made them unhappy?

This is a continuation of Q16. As discussed above, the principal reason for developing a long-term investment policy and for putting it in writing is to enable you and your advisor to protect your portfolio from ad hoc revisions of sound long-term policy. The written investment policy will help you maintain a long-term perspective when short-term market movements may be distressing and your investment strategy might otherwise be questioned.

Q18: Have you ever been disciplined?

"No!" is the best response. If the advisor has been disciplined, you'll want to find out why.

Q19: May I review samples of material you give to your clients?

The advisor should be delighted to share this information with you.

Q20: How often will I hear from you, and what will prompt your calls?How often do you reevaluate or change my portfolio? Under what conditions would you change my portfolio?

As a matter of course, your advisor should keep you apprised of any material changes in economic outlook, recommended investment policy, and tactics. In addition, the advisor should meet with you no less than annually (preferably quarterly) to review and explain the portfolio's investment results and any related issues. The advisor's entire planning team should welcome your phone calls and be available on an ongoing basis for your convenience.

From time to time, market conditions may cause the portfolio's investment in various strategies to vary from the established allocation. To remain consistent with the investment objectives established by your Investment Policy Statement, the advisor should continuously review the portfolio and each strategy in which the portfolio is invested. If the actual weighting differs from the target weighting by an unacceptable amount from the recommended weighting, the advisor should inform you and recommend rebalancing the portfolio back to the recommended weighting.

In general, the advisor should follow an investment strategy monitoring process which is dynamic and follows a basic five-step process:

1. Evaluate investor and economic environment

2. Determine optimal strategy allocations

3. Update IPS

4. Measure, evaluate, and communicate performance

5. Monitor circumstances dynamically

Reporting

1. Your advisor, via the custodian, may provide you with a report each month that lists all assets held in your accounts, values for each asset and all transactions affecting assets within the portfolio, including additions and withdrawals.

2. You should receive no less frequently than on a quarterly basis and within 40 days from the end of each such quarter the following management reports:

   a) Portfolio performance results over the last quarter, and from inception

   b) Performance results of each individual investment for the same periods

   c) Performance results of comparative benchmarks for the same periods

   d) Performance reporting on a basis that is in compliance with GIPS standards

   e) End of quarter status regarding asset allocation

   f) Any recommendations for changes of the above

Q21: How and how much are you paid? If you are a Registered Investment Advisor, may I have a copy of your form ADV II?

All fees received should be clearly communicated in your client agreement and ADV II. Copies should be promptly provided at your request.

Q22: Do you or does your company have a vested interest in any financial products and are you required to sill them even if they do not meet my personal needs?

The answer should be no, unless you are interviewing an advisor representing a bundled (closed architecture) investment portfolio through a single mutual fund family or an insurance company.

Q23: Do you use a trading platform and or technical trading software packages?

Your advisor-candidate should use a variety of institutional research and trading tools to better manage your portfolio. The following are a sample of some technology systems:

- Bloomberg Terminal
- Morningstar Direct
- Zacks Research Platform
- OneSource Market Information
- Tamarac (trading and rebalancing)
- Applied Finance Group (AFG) Tools
- Portfolio Center (accounting and reporting)
- Standard & Poor's Research

Q24: Do you have an investment philosophy? If so, what is it?

Your advisor-candidate should be able to provide you with adaptive portfolios built for all market conditions that maximize long-term portfolio values through dynamic allocations.

Here is an example of a dynamic allocation investment philosophy:

- Concentrated stock (equity) satellite seeks a return in excess of the Russell 3000
- Concentrated bond satellite seeks a return in excess of the Barclays Aggregate index
- Two core asset allocation models:

◇ Dynamic Risk Models (DRM) seeks to maximize long-term portfolio values through participating in less downside volatility.

◇ Strategically Designed-Tactically Dynamic Models (SDTD) seeks to maximize long-term portfolio values through participating in more upside return capture.

Q25: Do you believe that you can time your entry and exit points? In other words, do you wait for the right time/conditions to enter or exit a trade?

Your advisor-candidate should state that the best way to manage portfolios is through a rigorous research and management process that incorporates both strategic and tactical strategies. Duplicative controlled systems breed success, and therefore, it's best to follow time-proven strategies for managing money. Here is an example of an exceptional research process:

Figure 9: A Model Research Process.

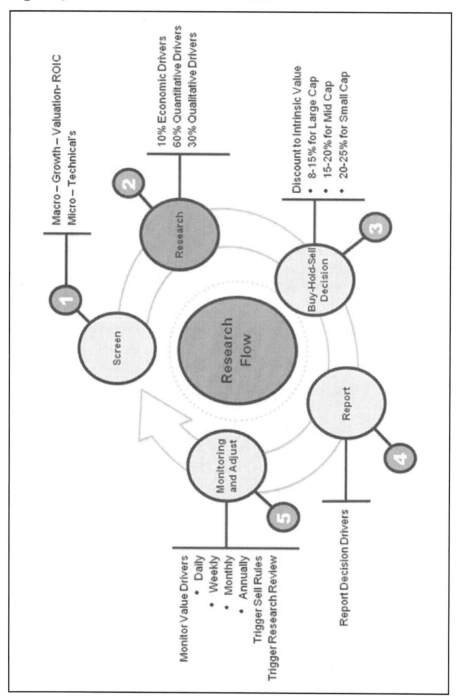

Q26: Do you have a clear exit strategy for taking profits?

This, of course, is a critical question. You'll need to carefully review your advisor-candidate's response so you can be assured that your portfolio will grow efficiently.

Q27: In addition to my personal financial planning needs, what other factors do you base investment decisions on?

Your advisor-candidate should claim that he/she will integrate both your qualitative and quantitative lifestyle protection goals with a dynamic economic and market research process to optimize your probability of success. The first step is gaining an understanding of your life goals by applying a required rate of return analysis (RRR). The second step should be building your portfolio with strategies that provide you with a high probability of obtaining your RRR. Finally, your portfolio should be monitored dynamically to fit your changing circumstances with the changing global market conditions, making adjustments as necessary to keep your portfolio on track.

Q28: What products do you have available and or use?

Here's an excellent answer: "As an SEC Registered Investment Advisor, we have a fiduciary duty to make recommendation and use products that are in your best interest, and that are not biased on how we get paid. Because we are fee-based and independent, we have all financial products at our disposal. Therefore, we have no product limitations that would prevent you from receiving the very best advice possible."

Q29: What are your views on load funds vs. no load funds and management fees?

You'll want to employ an advisor who believes that fees matter, and thus will use the lowest cost funds available for your circumstances.

Q30: Please tell us about your company's performance with meeting the needs of its clients.

a. Do you beat the market? What benchmark do you use?

b. What annual return should I expect?

c. How did you perform in the downturn of 2000 and 2008?

d. How did you perform in the last 12 months?

e. Have you or will you go to cash?

f. Under what conditions should I leave and seek service elsewhere?

Here are some good responses; your candidates' answers will probably vary, but you can see the value of the following information:

a. We do not try to beat the market. We build a custom required rate of return and then design a portfolio that gives you a high probability of obtaining your required rate of return. Therefore, the benchmark is customized for you and based on your lifestyle protection plan.

b. You should expect, on average, to earn a long-term return that is in line with your required rate of return.

c. We performed well. Our motto is to make more money not by chasing returns, but by not losing it to begin with. Remember, what goes down 50% must go up 100% to break even.

d. Since every client portfolio is custom designed for the client's individual and unique circumstance, it is hard to compare how we did with a broad stroke. In general, each of our separate core-satellite portfolios compared favorably with their specific benchmarks.

e. Absolutely, as long as it is permitted in the investment policy statement (IPS).

f. We would hope you would never need to leave, however, as described in this document, if communication breaks down and we are not able to effectively communicate, it may be wise to find another advisor with whom you may be more compatible.

 ## Chapter 3 Review Questions:

1. The demographics of your employees is important because:

   A. The demographics indicate the appropriate mix of investment funds for your employees.

   B. The demographics indicate the possible interest of your employees with wanting to rollover their other tax-free investments.

   C. The demographics indicate the anticipated costs for matching contributions as employees become vested.

   D. All of the above.

2. Which one of the following choices is not true about the value of keeping employees informed about the plan?

   A. Employees need to learn about the financial opportunity represented by the 401(k) and how it can benefit them in retirement.

   B. Employees need to know how to choose from among the investment funds in the plan.

   C. Most employees understand how to invest in a 401(k) and will not require a company-sponsored educational program.

   D. An employee education program meets one of the fiduciary obligations.

3. As the plan sponsor, you should receive reports from your financial advisor:

   A. Monthly

   B. Quarterly

   C. Semiannually

   D. Annually

4. It's important that fee disclosures are kept transparent because:

   A. Plan participants have the right to know how much they are paying.

   B. Plan participants should understand the purpose of the fees they are paying.

   C. When plan participants are informed, the plan advisor cannot be accused of fiscal irresponsibility related to fees and expenses.

   D. All of the above.

Answers

1. Answer: D. (a) An older demographic is likely to prefer more
    conservative investments; a younger demographic is likely to
    prefer more aggressive funds. (b) Older employees are likely
    to have a number of other tax-delayed investments they might
    choose to roll into the company's 401(k). (c) If a company has
    a staggered vesting schedule, knowing the details about the
    employees' timing will be helpful with planning the company's
    budget.

2. Answer: C. Most employees require a carefully planned
    educational program designed for adults. Also, the educational
    component is a requirement for compliance.

3. Answer: B. Quarterly reports are frequent enough to stay
    informed.

4. Answer: D. Plan participants must be informed because the
    fees are being paid from their 401(k) accounts.

Chapter 4:
Interviewing and Evaluating the Right TPA and Record Keeper for You

When you have finished reading this chapter, you will:

- Understand the tasks your Third Party Administrator (TPA) will perform for your plan

- Discern the important details to consider when evaluating a record keeper and a record-keeping system

- Know what to ask about the services your financial advisor can offer your employees

- Identify who is responsible for compliance testing, required participant notices, and fee disclosures

- Recognize the advantages of investing through a managed account, or a self-directed brokerage account

This chapter discusses the important details involved with selecting your 401(k)'s third-party administrator (TPA) and record keepers. Both these roles are key functions in supporting your company's 401(k) plan. Your TPA's responsibility is to administer the plan, calculate and allocate the employer's contributions, prepare for compliance testing, file the annual 5500 forms, track employee eligibility and complete all necessary government documents. The TPA's value is in understanding the many requirements of plan administration, and taking important tasks and legal responsibilities off your shoulders.

The record keeper is also an essential functionary of your company's 401(k) plan, because the record keeper is typically the custodian of the plan assets, or the platform used for investment transactions, and

keeps track of the flow of dollars in and out of the various funds as
determined by your employees' choices, your company's matching
dollars, and the fees and expenses that those exchanges generate.
The record keeper also may perform such other activities as valuing
the fund's investments, providing account statements to the plan
participants, and processing distribution checks, etc.

Hiring the right TPA and record keeper for your company will spell
the difference between aggravation and appreciation.

Record-Keeping Systems

Not all record-keeping systems are created equally. Some record-
keeping systems are much more technologically advanced than others,
employing the latest technology for record-keeping and allowing
the record-keeping process to perform daily accounting of net asset
values (NAV), while some can't. Some record-keeping systems can
perform accounting activities with mutual funds, ETFs and a variety
of securities, while some can't. A TPA with a superior record-keeping
system will provide better service for your company's plan than a TPA
whose software has become outdated.

 Note:

Don't allow your 401(k) plan to be limited by
selecting a record-keeper with outdated technology.

A TPA with a superior record-keeping system can provide the financial
advisor with more flexibility, more capability, and more latitude in
selecting the investments the advisor believes are appropriate for
the range of the employees' expressed aspirations. Depending on the
investment desires of the employees and the financial advisor's ability
to respond to those intentions, there may be times when the advisor
might prefer the value of using an ETF and time-traded funds instead
of selecting a mutual fund; but if the TPA's record-keeping system
cannot accommodate the accounting for that type of security, then
investment decisions are being based not on the availability of a good

portfolio or proper financial theory, but instead by the limitations of a weak record-keeping system, thus delaying performance instead of advancing it. Therefore, working with a technologically appropriate record-keeping system is necessary for optimal implementation.

Processing Plan Transactions

Processing transactions within the plan's investment funds is essential to the record-keeping system because the ability of one controls the efficacy of the other. Here's an example to illustrate the point. Mutual funds trade on net asset value (NAV) as recorded at the end of the day. Electronically traded funds (ETFs), however, trade throughout the day like a stock. If the record-keeping system is incapable of recording intraday trades, then obviously the financial advisor is restricted on his or her ability to invest because the system will not allow the necessary pricing capability. Some record-keeping systems will allow the financial advisor to use stocks and bonds, mutual funds, ETFs, certificates of deposit, and a variety of investment types, and some will not. The ability to select investments, of course, also depends on whether the plan is founded on closed architecture (a limited choice of investments) or open architecture (a wide choice of investments).

Of course, from the financial advisor's perspective, and from the employer's perspective, the less limitations due to technology or the inability of a team member to perform, the better. The ideal situation is when team members are able to make decisions for the right reasons, and not because they are hampered by limitations. While it's true that not all transactions require a universe of choices, it's better to have the availability of the choices; your financial advisor would much rather have the option of selecting out of the many choices... instead of the many choices being selected out.

Plan Sponsor and Participant Websites

A critically important feature of your company's 401(k) is setting up a system for you and your employees to access information about your company's 401(k) plan and each participant's individual account. This technology platform will be the hub of communication between the custodians of the funds and the plan participants.

The responsibility for building this platform and ensuring its operation belongs to either the TPA or the record keeper, or both, depending on how this was decided during contract negotiations, and as recommended by your financial advisor.

The value of having an effective and efficient technology platform becomes clear when you consider that your financial advisor might be planning to set up your company's 401(k) plan by selecting, for example, an investment portfolio of 40 different mutual funds from 40 different families, a dozen EFTs, and certificates of deposit from three different banks. It would be quite disadvantageous for plan participants to access and understand their investment portfolio if they had to go to a large group of websites to see how their funds were performing. Because this would be so unwieldy, the TPA or the record keeper, or both, must build a customized website portal that accommodates the range of investment funds in your plan's portfolio, and makes this information available through a link on your company's website.

Some 401(k)-related websites are more functional than others and can be very user-friendly, resulting in a good user experience. Quality is measured by how well the plan participants can find and understand their information. The TPA, the record keeper, and the custodians must all communicate well and link their software programs so the plan participants have a seamless experience.

Whether the technical responsibilities belong to your TPA, record keeper, or both, they need a good technology team to set up the system on your company's website. This is why technological capability is an important factor when interviewing and evaluating these service providers. As you know from your own experience, there's a whole lot of backend that has to be functional to make the transactions, accounting, and plan participant services efficient and pleasant to use!

Customer Services

Customer service is very important, so with good technology the employees can get onto the website and do most of the things right there on the platform. They can change their beneficiary, make investment selections, and acquire the administrative services they need through the customized website. Should anything happen to the website, such as a crash, the TPA is responsible for fixing it. The TPA is also responsible for ensuring there are multiple ways for plan participants to acquire the information they need, and typically a customer service line is also established.

When it comes to customer service, the financial advisor should be called for investment advice; however, the investment advisor cannot make any changes to the plan participants' accounts. A participant can contact the financial advisor and talk about their account, and of course, advise the participant about their investments, about which funds would be appropriate, and can recommend an investment model, but the financial advisor cannot make any changes for the participants. The employees would have to go to the customized website and make their own selection, or they would have to call the customer service line and have the TPA perform the transaction.

 Key:

The financial advisor is critical for expert investment advice, but it's the TPA who connects all the pieces and manages the plan.

It's the TPA who is the glue that makes all the pieces work together; they are the customer service contact, provide support to the plan sponsor, and work with the financial advisor, the record-keeper, and the custodians.

Plan Sponsor Support

We've touched on this briefly above, but it's worth repeating here. The TPA helps the plan sponsor understand their legal responsibilities and ensures that the company's 401(k) plan is compliant with all regulations. Because the TPA is at the hub of the 401(k) wheel, the TPA needs to be responsible and responsive to all parties; the last thing the plan sponsor wants to hear about are problems with the 401(k) plan's operations; one way the TPA can support the plan sponsor is by assuring that all the plan's spokes are well coordinated and performing their functions properly.

Employee Education and Communications

The financial advisor and the TPA share the responsibility for employee education and communications. Both providers usually educate the employees on the legal specifics in the plan's design. This includes such information as eligibility, being vested, and being able to borrow or withdraw funds. The financial advisor's area of expertise is with educating the employees on how much money they should be saving, how much risk is acceptable, and which investments are the best choices for each individual account. Employees will be receiving monthly statements which will be available either electronically or on hard copies mailed to their address. Every year, employees will also be receiving the summary plan description. An effective employee investment education program could be a considerable aid with helping plan participants develop their investment acumen so they can monitor their funds' performance and make appropriate choices for building their retirement resources.

The Client Relationship Team

The TPA will sometimes assign certain employees to work with your company's plan, so you always know you can call Steve and Janet, or Emily and Debbie, when there is an issue that needs to be resolved. Your TPA contacts should have a strong background in 401(k) plans, finance, and account management. They should be well-informed on fee disclosures, fund transactions, and be able to respond to technical issues and call in the cavalry when it's necessary to do so. In addition, they should have strong collaborative, written and verbal communication skills, with the ability to articulate complex issues concisely and effectively.

Compliance Testing and Form 5500 Preparation

Compliance testing is one of the primary duties of the TPA and record keeper. This is also a very standard task, so the expectation is that this work will be done quite well.

One of the more important tests that are required annually by the IRS is meeting the nondiscrimination requirements. Nondiscrimination testing is conducted to determine that highly paid employees are not being benefited more than non-highly paid employees. Also known as Highly Compensated Employees, these individuals are defined by the IRS as owning a specific percentage of the company, and/or by the amount of their annual monetary compensation. (Check with the IRS for current figures.) Passing these tests is essential for the 401(k) plan to retain its viability, and also for maintaining healthy employee relations. Another aspect of compliance testing is to analyze operational practices against the 401(k) plan's provisions to assure synchronicity. If there is an inconsistency, adjustments must be made to either the plan, or the plan's processes.

Some TPAs may be able to do more fancy compliance testing, such as cross-tested plans, Social Security integrated plans, cash balance plans, and integrated defined-benefit plans with a defined contribution plan. As you can see, the capabilities of your TPA can either enhance or limit plan facilitation. Compliance testing results are reported to the plan sponsor and the IRS.

Form 5500 is the Annual Return/Report of Employee Benefit Plan, which is required by the IRS, the Department of Labor, and the Pension Benefits Guarantee Corporation. The filing date for calendar year plans is July 31 of the following year, or you may file an extension. Failure to submit Form 5500 in a timely and accurate manner could result in severe penalties. This form is required no matter how many employees are in your company plan. If your plan has over 100 plan participants, you must also conduct an annual audit of your plan's assets by an independent accounting firm. Form 5500 is not intimidating, but does require a careful review of participant categories for an accurate accounting of eligible employees.

Hiring a competent TPA who is capable of properly managing compliance testing and accurately filing forms so the 401(k) plan retains its tax qualification status is critical.

Drafting and Distributing Required Participant Notices and Fee Disclosures

Based on the different elements of your 401(k) plan, there will be a number of participant notices that will require distribution to employees at specific times of the year, or upon specific triggering activities. Your TPA should be knowledgeable about the requirements of your plan, be able to draft or acquire language that's necessary to keep your plan compliant, and transmit the notices in a timely manner to those who are required to receive them. Of course, one of the more important and visible participant notices is the notice for fee disclosures.

Investment Platform

We've mentioned the investment platform before, explaining that some plans may have the option to invest in stocks, bonds, mutual funds, and ETFs, while other plans are limited by their investment platform to only the mutual funds offered by Vanguard, or only the investments that are available through the insurance company's platform. The investment platform is a critical element in the availability of choice, and either your investment opportunities are limited to a narrow set of selections or they offer a wide range of alternatives to satisfy the capacity of your financial advisor's expertise.

Managed Account Services

Normally, the plan provides a list of available investment vehicles composed of mutual funds and, if the technical ability of your TPA allows it, exchange traded funds (ETFs).

A plan participant can then choose any one of these available investment options or any combination they want. All the plan participant has to do is complete the paperwork and the amount of funds they choose to allocate will be distributed among their chosen investments. In this manner, each participant can select for themselves how they want the money invested.

However, those plan participants who are especially astute and have sufficient funds in their retirement account may be wise to choose a portion or all of their funds invested in a managed account. A managed account is a customized investment account designed at a level of risk that's appropriate for each individual participant, and which is then managed by the financial advisor.

Definition:

A "managed account" is a customized investment account designed at a level of risk that's appropriate for each individual participant, and which is managed by the financial advisor.

The advantage of investing through a managed account is that the plan participants who choose to do so are benefited by the expert services of a professional investment advisor. Whether the account has $50 or $50,000, the advisor chooses the investments that are best suited for the participant and then the account is set on autopilot with the financial advisor managing it for the participant. The expectation is that the invested funds will grow more rapidly and more safely when selected by a professional investment advisor rather than when chosen by a participant who is not educated or experienced with picking investments.

Self-directed Brokerage Accounts

Self-directed brokerage accounts are mostly designed for the owner of the company and the key executives who typically have more funds in their retirement account. The account holders choose their own investments, with the investment advisor being available for recommendations.

With a self-directed brokerage account, the universe of investments is available for selection through such companies as Charles Schwab or TD Ameritrade. The financial advisor can pick stocks, bonds, mutual funds, and manage the money as he or she would normally do with any other client.

A self-directed brokerage account is not a good choice for everybody, especially if the amount of money in the account is limited. A self-directed account is appropriate for a high paid executive because, for example, they are able to purchase a higher quantity of stock. It's not appropriate for a lesser paid employee to have a self-directed brokerage account because the fees are higher and usually diversification is weaker. Remember, too, that the financial advisor has a fiduciary responsibility to guide participants with making good decisions. Employees with small accounts cannot be refused access to a self-directed brokerage account because discrimination is not permitted; but neither is it necessarily the best financial choice for them, given the design of this plan and their limited resources. It's not suitable because you can't purchase very much stock with $50 a month, and the brokerage charges an annual fee in addition to the commissions it would make on individual trades. So while it would be quite expensive for employees with small accounts, it could be worth the cost for the executives who have a larger account with which to work.

Transition Services

This is simply a service for the flow of plan participants into the plan, out of the plan, and rolling over their funds into other retirement investment vehicles. This is a standard service expected of the TPA and record keeper.

Fees

The issue of expenses and fees is a very sensitive one because these costs eat away at the value of the funds over time. You wouldn't think that a few fees here and there wouldn't add up to much, but given the Law of Compounding, we all know that little drops gathered together can make an ocean. In recent years the IRS has taken special interest in how fees are assessed and how they are disclosed to plan participants. Therefore, since the purpose of a 401(k) is to provide a means for retirement monies to grow and accrue, spending too much money on expenses and fees defeats the purpose.

Then again, services are needed to manage the 401(k) plan. All of this costs money; TPAs and record keepers have to be paid for their time and the quality of their service. Even though the cost for the services of the TPAs and record keepers are disclosed at the beginning, it must still be determined how they are paid. Are these fees paid by the plan sponsor, or will the expenses come from the employees' retirement funds? It can be both or either.

 Important:

As the plan sponsor, you must be informed and knowledgeable about the fees and expenses of your company's 401(k) plan, confident these fees and expenses are reasonable, and satisfied that the fees and expenses are purchasing beneficial services for your company and employees.

Some of the time it's the employees who pay the fees pro rata from the plan, and then the plan pays the TPA and record keeper. Other times there are rebates from the mutual fund families which can then be used to offset these fees; often, the TPAs will bid their plan so he revenue sharing from the mutual fund families will cover the fees. This particular method is a bit like a no-upfront cost loan; a home buyer visits a lending institution to acquire a mortgage and the deal sounds and feels good because all the costs are built into the loan. With a 401(k), your funds may have a little higher internal fee that allows the TPAs to get a rebate, and therefore some TPAs will credit your account, and this will either cover or reduce your expenses. Yes, this is a bit of a game, but it's not so bad as long as everybody plays fairly. This arrangement is something to know about, and most people find it acceptable because they don't want to pay upfront; this way the funds pay for some of the cost, but because everything is disclosed at the beginning, everybody knows what's going on and are willing to go along with it.

Summary

For all the preceding reasons, acquiring a TPA and record keeper who can provide your 401(k) plan with the most options and the best service is clearly in the best interests of your company and employees.

There are a lot of moving parts for your TPA and record keeper to monitor and control, and the more capable they are with the newest technology, professional experience, their ability to stay informed and responsive to IRS compliance issues, and their adaptability to changing circumstances, the more value they'll contribute to this very complex assortment of financial and human components. Find and hire the best!

 ## Chapter 4 Review Questions:

1. A record-keeping system can either inhibit or allow investment fund choices.

   A. True

   B. False

2. A self-directed brokerage account is designed for everybody.

   A. True

   B. False

3. The TPA helps the plan sponsor understand the legal responsibilities and ensures the 401(k) plan is compliant with all regulations.

   A. True

   B. False

4. The advantage of investing through a managed account is:

   A. The participants in the managed account have the advantage of a financial expert making investment decisions on their behalf.

   B. The plan participant can stop thinking about his or her 401(k) investments.

   C. The investments are now on auto-pilot and will stay the same until the plan participant exits the 401(k) at retirement.

   D. The account manager does not have to report his or her activities to the plan participants more than once per year.

 Answers

1. Answer: A. The more flexible the system, the more varied investments that are possible.

2. Answer: B. A self-directed brokerage account is mostly designed for the owner of the company and the key executives who typically have more funds in their retirement account.

3. Answer: A. It's critical to have a TPA who is always informed about legal changes and compliance issues.

4. Answer: A. The plan participants who choose to do so are benefited by the services of a professional investment advisor.

Chapter 5:
Creating Your New 401(k) Plan

When you have finished reading this chapter, you will know:

- The process for issuing a Request For Proposals (RFP) for interviewing financial advisors

- The value of having an investment plan advisor assist with the RFP process

- The three components for conducting a successful RFP

- A method for determining the membership of your retirement plan committee

- How to decide your plan's financial, human resource, and structural goals

- The best questions to ask when interviewing and selecting a financial advisor

- The four elements of crafting your company's 401(k) plan

- If your company's 401(k) employee education plan will be effective

- The best way to analyze a 401(k) plan

- The five simple steps for transferring your existing plan

Up to now, we've focused on the key educational pieces you needed to know for building a strong foundation of knowledge about 401(k)s. In this chapter we'll review the full spectrum of the key pieces needed for establishing your company's new 401(k) plan.

You are now familiar with open architecture (a wide choice of investments) and closed architecture (a limited choice of investments), the roles of the various players who will be managing your company's 401(k) plan, possess a conversational background about ERISA and fiduciary responsibilities, recognize the common features and benefits of a 401(k) plan, and grasp the basics of evaluating and selecting a third party administrator, record keepers, and the all-important financial advisor, and you will soon see how all these elements come together and form the complete mosaic of your new 401(k) plan.

Key:

One of the best ways to select a financial advisor for your 401(k) plan is by requesting proposals from companies in your area that create and manage 401(k) plans.

The first essential topic is the process you will use to identify and select the best financial advisor for your company's 401(k) plan. The current standard for selecting a financial advisor is issuing a request for proposals (RFP).

The RFP process is a good tool for screening service provider candidates for your company's plan; after advertising your interest for acquiring the services of qualified candidates, surveying the respondents, and selecting those professionals who meet your standards, a predetermined list of questions is distributed to which the candidates must reply in order to be selected for an interview.

This process is regarded as an unbiased method for demonstrating the responsible activity of the plan sponsor's fiduciary duty, as well as an effective way to assure the alignment of your plan's goals with the services of your future financial advisor. The RFP process, however, can be lengthy and confusing, especially for a plan sponsor who already has a burdened desk.

The solution is to hire an investment financial advisor who is an expert in the process of establishing company 401(k) plans, to assist with the many tasks which lie ahead. Most plan sponsors are not prepared for the variety of activities involved in setting up a company 401(k) plan, and quickly see the wisdom of hiring a professional to help with the details of:

- Developing the company's retirement plan committee

- Identifying the company's 401(k) goals and objectives

- Interviewing and selecting the TPA, record keeper, and financial advisor

- Drafting the contents of an RFP request

- Responding to the RFP candidates' inquiries

- Determining which candidates to interview

- Conducting the finalists' interviews

- Following up with committee members' requests after the interviews

- Making the final selection for hiring

- Beginning the plan implementation process

This enterprise is more likely to be a successful and productive event when managed by an experienced professional.

There are three components to conducting a successful RFP.

Figure 10: The RFP Process.

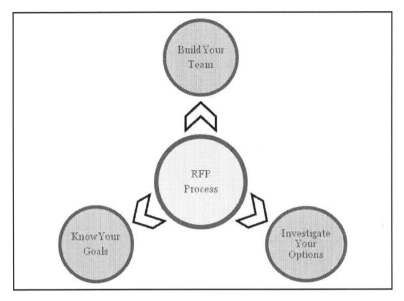

1. Building Your 401(k) Team

The initial step of preparing your plan is selecting the members who will serve on your company's 401(k) team. Unless you are a very small company, or self-employed, it could be in your best interests to create a retirement plan committee. The reason is quite simple; when a committee is involved in the recommendation process and the discussions and motions that lead to the committee's recommendations are documented, the burden of liability is lessened. This is also true for decisions about selecting funds for the plan's portfolio, as well as selecting the company's financial advisor. In addition, a committee's recommendations may result in the increased likelihood of improved decision-making and employee participation.

To begin, the size of the retirement plan committee needs to be determined. A small organization needs only a few members, whereas a bigger company may benefit from a greater number of members; of course, while more members may benefit the committee with more human resources and a wider range of opinions, too many members can also complicate the decision-making process. Upon reflection, you'll know the right number of committee members for your company, at least to start. In general, a committee of five members could be sufficiently broad-based and also reasonably-sized for making effective and efficient decisions.

Note:

When selecting members of your staff to serve on your company's 401(k) committee, you should consider a diversity of demographics so all members of your staff feel represented.

The diversity of the committee's members will also desire resolution, and your experience with the demographics of your employees will likely suggest a good combination. Your committee will need members who substantiate validity in the opinions of your employee population, so you're looking for a range of ethnicity, gender, age, education, and financial and human resource skills. The selected members should have good communication skills and be willing to share their unique perspectives to facilitate discussion and build consensus.

Because of the sensitive issues this committee will face, the idea of engaging an investment financial advisor to counsel, and even to lead this group could be an opportune decision empowering your committee and resulting in their successful performance. The value of having an experienced person advising or leading your committee, especially given the increase in regulations, the multitude of choices they'll face, the realistic concern for meeting employee expectations, and the magnitude of the committee's fiscal decisions cannot be understated. An investment plan consultant can facilitate the committee's discussions, reassure them on matters of compliance and regulations, and can be a worthy resource for guiding and supporting the committee's good intentions with results that satisfy your interests and the interests of your employees.

2. Know Your 401(k) Plan Goals

Your plan will only be as good as the goals and objectives you set, so having a strong sense of purpose is a key factor in building your plan's success.

Once your 401(k) committee members have been selected, understand their charge and have received some training, their first task is establishing the retirement plan's goals. This doesn't have to be an arduous task because the goals are rather standard; we offer a short list a few paragraphs below. However, having the committee review and confirm these goals is a very important step; now the committee members have a clear focus for employing these goals as the structure for assessing the merits of the financial advisors they will soon be interviewing in the RFP process.

Your company's new investment financial advisor will be a comforting resource for suggesting plan goals, and working with the committee to refine the goals so they are particularly applicable to your organization. The advisor will be able to recommend suitable goals based on other companies similar to your own in industry, geographic region, and financial size.

An important second task, if you can, is writing a solid draft of the investment policy statement (IPS) prior to the interview process, because this will serve the committee with a set of plan attributes which will be helpful during the interview process. This will also guide the financial advisors who respond to your RFP with the ability to use this information as a means for highlighting their capabilities and past performance in achieving your plan's aspirations. Given your circumstances, it may be best to wait until you've hired an advisor, or ask your newly hired advisor to review and improve the IPS before beginning the screening and hiring process for the other plan service providers.

Note:

Setting your 401(k) plan's goals does not have to be a difficult process. Here are some helpful suggestions...

You'll need to draft three sets of goals: financial goals, human resource goals, and structural goals that serve the smooth performance of your plan.

Financial Goals:

1. Meet your fiduciary obligations as the plan sponsor.

2. Offer a variety of investments so your employees can select quality assets.

3. Reduce corporate taxes while benefiting employees.

4. Provide maximum pretax savings so all highly compensated employees can invest the maximum annual amount if the choose to do so.

5. Determine the annual amount of matching funds the company is willing to afford.

6. Decide how the plan's fees and expenses will be paid.

Human Resource Goals:

1. Guide employees by preparing their finances for retirement.

2. Provide a quality retirement education program.

3. Secure accurate and helpful financial reporting for participants.

4. Provide a plan that attracts and retains employees.

<u>Structural Goals</u>:

1. Keep fees and expenses low.

2. Meet all legal requirements.

3. Establish a schedule for plan review and renewal.

4. Limit administrative overload.

Now that you and your 401(k) committee have established the plan's goals and drafted an IPS, your committee is ready to begin the task of soliciting financial advisors to compete for the advisor position with your company.

3. Investigate Your Options Through the RFP Process

The best way to find, evaluate, and select a financial advisor who is best suited to help you achieve your company's 401(k) goals is by issuing a request for proposals (RFP). Here are some of the benefits of conducting a formal RFP search:

- A significant educational value will be gained by sifting the responses

- The risk of the plan sponsor's fiduciary obligation will be mitigated; a search of this type demonstrates a deliberate process for selecting a financial advisor

- Considerable savings of fees and expenses may result when emphasis is placed on hiring an advisor whose fees represent current benchmarks

- A greater understanding of current trends or issues in the 401(k) marketplace can be achieved

RFP questions: When developing your RFP document, there are a number of questions requiring responses by each of your financial advisor candidates. These questions should be organized in categories, as you see below.

<u>Simple Company Data Questions</u>: When you create your RFP response document, you'll include a number of standard questions:

- Company name

- Address

- Contact information

- Ownership of the company

- Key individuals in the company

- The main lines of business

- Years the company has been in business

- List of the company's licenses and registrations

<u>Basic Company Questions</u>: These are examples of the questions your RFP document should ask; your investment financial advisor will provide these questions and more:

- Brief description of the company's history

- The total number of the company's employees

- The total number of the company's Investment Advisory Representatives (IAR) who will be working on the company's plan

- Number of new retirement plan clients gained in the last two years

- Number of retirement plan clients lost in the last two years

- Percentage of company's revenue from advisory services for retirement plan investments

- Number of clients receiving retirement plan advisement

- Dollar amount of retirement plan assets under advisement

- Provide a reference list of four clients whose companies are similar in size to ours

- Company Services: The answers to these questions will help you understand the basic service relationship.

- Explain your company's experience with serving clients who were being audited and/or undergoing compliance reviews

- Provide a professional biography of the primary person your company would assign to work with us

- Describe your company's differentiation from other investment consulting companies

- Explain your service model for a company of our size

- Investment Services: These questions will provide good performance information.

- Explain how you help a company create its Investment Policy Statement (IPS)

- Indicate the research tools your company uses that are proprietary.

- Explain your corrective process for investment funds that are not performing

- Discuss the tools your company uses to evaluate fund managers and investment funds

- Describe your company's resources for researching investments

- Explain how your company determines investment benchmarks

- Describe how often your company will hold performance review meetings, and how information will be conveyed

<u>Participant Services</u>: These questions will provide insight to how the financial advisor will work with your employees.

- Describe the services your company provides to plan participants and explain why you believe these services are effective

- Explain how your company establishes educational goals and learning outcomes for plan participants

- Discuss how your company would create allocation models that would serve our company's employees

- <u>Provider Services</u>: In this set of questions, the financial advisor is asked how his or her company works with the broader 401(k) team of third party administrators, record keepers, and trustees.

- Explain your company's process for reviewing the benchmark services and fees of 401(k) service providers

- Describe how your company locates, evaluates and recommends 401(k) vendor service providers.

- Discuss how many 401(k) service provider searches your company has performed in the last two years, and whether any of these searches resulted in a vendor replacement

- Given the current number of clients your company has, explain how many different service providers are working with you in providing service to these clients

<u>Fiduciary Relationship and Compliance Issues</u>: This is where you'll get a clear picture about the fiduciary relationship the financial advisor would like to establish, and more information about the advisor's experience and performance with compliance matters.

- Discuss your interest in becoming our company's 3(21) or 3(38) investment advisor

- Explain the resources your company has available for addressing compliance issues

- Explain any conflicts of interest you foresee in working with our company

- Describe your company's conflict of interest policy

- Describe the training and support your company could provide to our investment committee

- As a 3(21) or 3(38) fiduciary, discuss the services you would provide to our plan participants

- Discuss your company's response to a regulatory concern experienced by one of your clients

Fees: Conflict of interest regarding fees and fee disclosure has received a lot of attention from the IRS in recent years, so these questions are particularly timely.

- Explain how your company is compensated for the services you provide

- Discuss your company's policy about receiving any form of compensation or benefits from providers whose products or services you recommend to your clients

- Indicate the percentage of revenue your company receives from commissions, and from consulting

- Explain all the fees your company will charge for its services to our plan

- Explain your company's intentions to offset fees to our companies plan with fees embedded in our plans investments

- Discuss your company's willingness to guarantee your fees for a specified term

<u>Technology and Data Security</u>: The security of confidential information is an important priority, and you'll want to be assured that your employees' investment data is secure, and that all the information is redundant in case of a technological breakdown.

- Discuss the technology available to your company and explain how this technology serves your company's plan

- Describe how your company's data is securely maintained

- In the event of a security breach or a system crash, explain your company's data and operations recovery plan

These questions and others that may be suggested by your investment financial advisor should provide you and your committee with enough information to select the financial advisor who is best suited to work with your company and for your employees.

 Important:

The RFP process is an excellent way for you and your committee to understand how a 401(k) can benefit your company and its employees, as well as ensuring that fees and expenses are reasonable for the services provided.

The U.S. Department of Labor's ten questions: In May 2005, the U.S. Department of Labor published a fact sheet titled "Selecting and Monitoring Pension Consultants-Tips for Plan Fiduciaries". This document was released to provide plan sponsors with a set of questions designed to reveal information that could lead to serious conflicts of interest between financial advisors and vendors whose products and services were recommended by the advisors. The intention was that these conflicts of interest could be avoided once the plan sponsors were aware of relationships that could be tainted, because either steps could be taken to immediately adjust any improper business activity, or the plan sponsor could refrain from entering into a contract with a financial advisor whose company was incapable of restricting this improper behavior.

Here are the 10 questions from the Department of Labor, with brief commentary.

1. Are you registered with the SEC or a state securities regulator as an investment advisor? If so, have you provided us with all the disclosures required under those laws (including Part 2 of Form ADV)?

Form ADV is the form used by the U.S. Securities and Exchange Commission to register investment advisors with both the SEC and state securities authorities. Part 1 requires basic company information in a simple check-box and fill-the-blank format. Part 2 requires registrants to submit narrative essays explaining the advisory services offered, a schedule of fees, potential conflicts of interest, disciplinary actions, and the professional backgrounds of management and key personnel; this section of Form ADV is the primary disclosure document advisors provide to their clients, and is available to the public online on the Investment Advisor Public Disclosure website.

This is a good tool to use, because you can search the SEC's database for information about any financial advisor you choose. If you're unable to find a listing for a financial advisor, contact your state securities regulator.

2. Do you or a related company have relationships with money managers that you recommend, consider for recommendation, or otherwise mention to the plan? If so, describe those relationships.

Financial advisors may have business relationships with money managers, and with companies that provide the services your 401(k) plan may need. Knowing what these relationships are will provide you with insight to the potential for conflicts of interest, furnishing you with the information you need to protect your fiduciary responsibilities.

3. Do you or a related company receive any payments from money managers you recommend, consider for recommendation, or

authorize mention to the plan for your consideration? If so, what is the extent of these payments in relation to your other income (revenue)?

Question 2 inquired about the relationships; this question asks if there is any money involved in that relationship. If money managers are paying the investment advisor, this could be a conflict of interest; you need to find out if this is so.

4. Do you have any policies or procedures to address conflicts of interest or to prevent these payments or relationships from being a factor when you provide advice to your clients?

It's important to know that the financial advisor has a company policy to address the expectations of its clients, and a plan of action in case there is a breach in professional behavior.

5. If you allow plans to pay your consulting fees using the plan's brokerage commissions, do you monitor the amount of commissions paid and alert plans when consulting fees have been paid in full? If not, how can a plan make sure it does not over-pay its consulting fees?

It's always better to make sure the proper amount of payment is made and overpayment does not occur. You'll want to make this a feature of your contractual relationship with the financial advisor. Having overpayments monitored and returned only increases paperwork, office time, and unnecessary aggravation.

6. If you allow plans to pay your consulting fees using the plan's brokerage commissions, what steps do you take to ensure that the plan receives best execution for its securities trades?

This is an important detail because the overall costs of transactions can increase depending on where and how orders are executed. Fees and expenses eat into your plan's bottom line, and your fiduciary responsibility is to ensure that all the retirement funds are used for the purposes intended, one of which is helping your employees grow their retirement funds. Every dollar that is saved in fees and expenses can become that much more in your employees' accounts.

7. Do you have any arrangements with broker-dealers under which you or a related company will benefit if money managers place trades for their clients with such broker-dealers?

This question focuses on the financial advisor's relationship with broker-dealers who may have relationships with money managers whose purchases then may benefit the financial advisor. Just because the purchasing activity is one step removed doesn't mean the financial advisor is free of the conflict of interest.

8. If you are hired, will you acknowledge in writing that you have a fiduciary obligation as an investment advisor to the plan while providing the consulting services we are seeking?

Investment advisors have a fiduciary obligation whether or not they are registered with the SEC. Their fiduciary obligation requires them to disclose information about a conflict of interest. Having this understanding in writing is one layer of protection for you as the plan sponsor.

9. Do you consider yourself a fiduciary under ERISA with respect to the recommendations you provide the plan?

When a financial advisor acknowledges they are a fiduciary under ERISA, if they receive fees from vendors due to their recommendations, they are in violation of the regulations; this is a prohibited transaction unless the fees they've received are used to offset their consulting fees.

10. What percentage of your plan clients utilize money managers, investment funds, brokerage services or other service providers from whom you receive fees?

The answer to this question may be helpful with evaluating the nature of the financial advisor's relationships with third-party service providers, and will help further define the advisor's fiduciary behavior.

As you can see, the U.S. Department of Labor became aware of the impropriety of the way in which some financial advisors were conducting business; this new awareness on the importance of objectivity and unbiased recommendations and other professional services provided by financial advisors came under intense scrutiny, the result of which was the advisory, above, issued by the Department of Labor. All of this must evidently be a filter through which you interview financial advisor candidates, ultimately selecting one with whom to work. Care must be exercised so your fiduciary responsibilities are not compromised.

Communicating with your RFP candidates: Once your RFP has been distributed, you'll find there will be a steady flow of inquiries of various kinds. Because there will likely be a lot of financial advisors interested in working for you, they will, being professionals, want to make sure they exactly understand your intentions, and therefore you can expect to receive phone calls requesting clarification on various parts of the RFP no matter how well you drafted the RFP. This is actually a positive event because the financial advisors who do submit their company's proposal will have a refined and more accurate idea of what you want, assuring that you will more likely receive proposals that are attractive and relevant to your purpose. Based on our experience, it's normal to expect that these inquiries will create new issues that were unanticipated when the RFP was written; this is also positive, because clarity is valued. As these new issues come up, it's important to inform all inquiring advisors about the new information so everyone is on the same page and the RFP and its application process will be regarded as fair.

Depending on the size of your company, it may be a good idea to hold a conference call for all provider candidates. A group presentation with questions and answers might be an excellent way for the candidates to all hear the same information directly from the plan sponsor or investment financial advisor, as well as hear each other's questions and the responses. This might also eliminate multiple conversations that you or your investment financial advisor might otherwise have to conduct. It may also be a good idea to have the call recorded and subsequently provided to the candidates, and to the candidates who are unable to attend the conference call. If you already have an incumbent provider, it's generally more efficient not to include this individual in the call.

Evaluating the RFP responses: In this segment of the RFP process, you and your RFP committee, will be examining the RFPs to determine which of the candidates are most likely to be the best fit for your company. Your evaluation of the candidates should focus on determining if there is an alignment between your company and the financial advisor's company in three key areas.

Philosophy: Are your two companies compatible with the performance model offered by the advisor's company? For example, are you expecting a high degree of customer service, or more interested in program customization? Will the cultures of your two companies be able to work together in harmony?

Product: Will the candidate's company offer you a highly satisfactory range of products, outstanding third-party administration, an exceptional record keeping system, and state-of-the-art web-based services?

Interpersonal: How easy or difficult is it to communicate with each other? How compatible are you with understanding each other clearly and easily? Are collaboration and problem-solving skills similar, and is there a personal and human connection that establishes an ease with relating to each other?

These are the three categories with which you should evaluate each of the financial advisor candidates. The first two, philosophy and product, appeal to the rational mind because they are quantitative factors. The third category, interpersonal, is an emotional and subjective factor because it is qualitative. Your satisfaction with the first two categories will be a great filter for deciding which candidates to invite to an interview, and during the interview you will then have the opportunity to assess the value of the third category and its potential effect on your company.

Initial Review and Evaluation of the Proposals: Once the deadline arrives and the proposals are in, it then becomes the duty of your committee to review the RFPs with the specific focus of determining how the candidates have addressed your company's stated goals. Most RFP responses are likely to be written in such a manner that you and your committee will be overwhelmed by an excess of information, a large part of which has little value to the specifications of your RFP. Therefore, careful sorting is necessary. You'll find that there are many excellent financial advisor companies available, and your challenge is to filter your respondents to identify which companies are the best fit for yours. These, of course, become your finalists. Under the leadership of your committee's foreman, or your investment financial advisor, it may be helpful to review the RFPs of all the providers and identify the strengths and weaknesses of each in a written summary that's generally accepted by your committee members. Thereafter, a simplified similarity/differentiation table can be created that permits the comparison of the companies.

Presentations by the Finalists: Once those companies have been identified that most fit the specifications of the RFP, invitations should be sent for interviews. While much information can be gained by reviewing the candidates on paper, the experience of meeting with the candidates face-to-face will more closely indicate the potential for a productive alliance. The interviews of the finalists should focus on confirming the candidates' abilities to meet the mandates of the RFP, and also resolve the question of the interpersonal compatibility of the candidates with your company's culture and human environment. Before making a final decision and awarding the contract, we recommend your committee conduct a site visit of the leading two or three firms, if feasible, so company counterparts may meet each other and determine the potential for productive interaction; these impressions should be documented and filed for future reference, as well as the entire decision-making process so there is a written record of how and why your new financial advisor was selected. After a final review, the candidate that best fits your company's philosophy, product requirements, and personal chemistry should be awarded your company's contract. An important concluding task is providing feedback to both the candidates who applied and those who received interviews so all candidates can understand the basis for your decision. This should be documented as well.

The next step in this process is to issue a contract to your selected advisor, and prepare for the implementation of your plan.

Craft Your Plan

Now that you've selected and secured your financial advisor, it's time for your new consultant to work with your 401(k) committee on finalizing the IPS and developing your company's new 401(k) plan. This project is almost completed! This is the time to keep the engine running and drive your race car across the finish line!

Figure 11: The Four Elements of Crafting Your Plan.

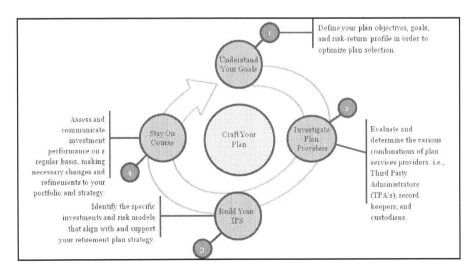

Up until now you and the 401(k) committee have been formulating the various elements of your company's IPS and 401(k) plan. Now that you have a financial advisor on board, it's time to finalize the plan and fit all the pieces together. In a sense, you and your committee have selected the architect...and now the final blueprints need to be drawn up.

Your financial advisor and 401(k) committee will review the details of the investment policy statement (IPS) once more, and confirm that your IPS is a prudent policy that safeguards the retirement interests of your employees. With your new investment financial advisor at the helm, the services of a third-party administrator (TPA) and record keeper can now be acquired; these services will be based on the needs of your plan, providing the most latitude available through the specifications you and your committee have chosen. Next, your financial advisor will recommend a list of investment funds, and possibly a set of model allocations from which your employees may choose. All the necessary paperwork will be completed in a timely manner, with everything continually being documented, and finally your plan will be ready for employee education and enrollment.

Rollout Your Plan

Now that all the background work has been done by your company's 401(k) committee, and with your investment financial advisor and financial advisor working together and leading the team, it's time to unveil your company's new 401(k) plan and begin educating your employees about the value of becoming plan participants.

Participant Education: If you should ever conduct a little research on the effectiveness of employee 401(k) education, you would quickly see that one of the biggest obstacles to educating your employees about the value of the investment tool they could now possess is that most companies' education programs are not effective for adult learners. Typically, there is a great fanfare about the company's new retirement program; this is accompanied by a whirlwind of employee workshops that include a large data dump of information about the plan, the investment fund opportunities, details about eligibility and legal considerations, and the imperative to take action at once.

However, in most cases this is an insufficient way for employees to fully understand how they can make use of their new program. The financial industry is beginning to realize it may be wiser to employ the skills of instructional designers and professional teachers, rather than rely on the information provided by people who are experts in finance. This is similar to the experience most students have in college: their university professor is regarded as an expert in his or her field, but the professor has probably had no formal instruction on how to be an effective teacher, and thus only roughly conveys the course's information in a manner that eludes good instructional practices and fails to support the different modes of learning...limiting the comprehension and use of the material by the people who need it.

A better way to support your employees' education is by developing an education plan with clearly stated objectives, such as these:

Plan participants will learn about:

- Financial risk, and identify their personal risk tolerance

- The value of time, and assess the value of the investment time they have until retirement

- The different asset classes available in the plan, and the potential risk and return of these asset classes

- The value of diversifying their investment funds

These are just a few examples of learning objectives which can help your employees make good investment decisions. You'll want to hire an investment advisor company that has an outstanding 401(k) employee education program with these and other significant education objectives that will motivate your employees to participate in your company's 401(k) plan and receive the maximum benefits from their ongoing investments.

The key to knowing if your company's education plan is effective is whether or not you see a change in your plan's participants' behavior; as the plan sponsor, you know the program has value and can make a significant difference in the lives of your employees; this is the message your employees need to have, and your company's education plan will only be effective if your employees know it, too, and take action on behalf of their financial future.

<u>Enrollment Process</u>: Your plan's enrollment process must be clear, and easy to do. Employees should be informed if they are eligible, or are ineligible because they must wait until they are a certain age, have worked for the company for a stated length of time, or must be full-time employees. Eligible employees will be asked to register online with an easy application process.

Because approximately 30% of all eligible employees do not participate in their company's 401(k) program, some companies choose to establish an automatic enrollment plan. An automatic enrollment plan means that all eligible employees are enrolled in a basic investment plan unless they file a form to withdraw. Once enrolled, of course, plan participants have the option of adjusting their investment plan, or staying with the basic investment plan. An automatic enrollment plan is effective in reducing employee nonparticipation to about 15%, or half of the typical amount. This has the potential to improve the future of those employees who are slow to act, and also benefits your company with increased tax deductions if your plan matches employee contributions.

<u>Investment Selection</u>: As stated previously, employees will need to become familiar with the variety of choices available in your company's 401(k) plan, achieve a sufficient level of education to know which choices are the best for their financial situation, understand the risk and reward those investment choices represent, and also grow comfortable with understanding the performance of their choices over time.

Once your employees are educated in the value of the 401(k) plan, are enrolled, and have been guided in the selection of their investments, your plan is operational. From this point forward, your education program should continue to inform employees on important topics, and your 401(k) plan should be reviewed at least annually to review the investment plan statement, the performance of the funds, suggested changes to the investment menu, and a review of the fees and expenses that have occurred and are projected.

Analyzing and Transferring Your Plan

If you currently have a plan and are not satisfied with it for some reason, or you believe your costs are too high, you can always have your plan analyzed and compared with other options; if you determine that other choices are more appealing and will save your plan participants' money, you can then transfer your existing 401(k) plan to the new providers.

How to analyze a plan: This is a task best performed by a financial advisor whose experience will ensure that the conclusions are accurate. Hiring an advisor to complete this task would be a sensible choice, as opposed to asking your current 401(k) advisor.

Most investment advisor companies will conduct a cost comparison analysis report such as you saw in Figure 6: 401(k) Plan Comparison, to properly illustrate the various fees of the service providers. The 408(b), which is the official fee disclosure form, will be reviewed in tandem with the Balance by Funds Report so calculations can be conducted to determine all costs. These reports are generally filed with the plan administrator, which may be the CFO, the company owner, or a charter office manager. Once this analysis has been finalized, the consultant can then discuss the comparisons so you completely understand the various fees and their costs, allowing you to then make the best business choices for your company's 401(k) plan.

Now that you can determine which plan providers are best, and can see the potential savings to your plan's participants, you can set the transition in motion. You now have sufficient information to choose your best course of action, which is namely to select a new advisor or retain your current advisor, and make a decision on the combination of service providers who represent the best quality and cost-efficient choice. Once you've made your decision, your financial advisor can refine the details and begin the transition process.

How to switch your plan: Transferring your plan can occur at any time during the year, and it will probably take about 90 to 120 days. There is no restriction on the time of the year to make a transfer, but conducting this activity at the end of the year might require extra diligence because of all the other end of the year activities occurring.

There are five simple steps for transferring your existing plan:

1. Select the investment advisor, TPA, and record keeper. The 408(b) is the official fee disclosure form identifying the fee expenses of your service providers. Once you have chosen these service providers, your team will be in place to complete this task. Also, once your new investment advisor has been selected, you can rely on your advisor to work closely with you to set up your new plan and direct the other providers.

2. Identify the objectives for the 401(k) plan design, the 401(k) investment philosophy, and the 401(k) contribution budget. These are key elements of your company's existing plan, and since you are now transferring to a new provider, check to make sure that these accurately portray your intentions. The Balance by Fund Report contains the information on the dollar amounts of each of the investment funds in your company's 401(k).

3. Notify prior providers and all enrolled employees about the impending change. Obviously, you'll need to tell the prior providers that you are terminating their service, and you also need to alert the plan participants to expect the adjustments. There will be a blackout period during the transition during which there can be no account adjustments by the plan participants. Your TPA will initiate the paperwork and set the transfer in motion.

4. Educate and enroll the participants. The plan participants need to be made aware of any new elements to the company's plan, and then the plan participants need to be enrolled in the new plan.

5. Transfer the assets to the new 401(k) retirement plan. After all arrangements have been made and completed, the funds can be transferred securely.

That's it! You've now transferred to your new plan.

Summary

This chapter considered the essential elements of setting up your company's new 401(k) plan. We've discussed the details of selecting your company's 401(k) planning team, and walked you through the RFP process so you could see the types of information you'll need to acquire to make the best choice of a financial advisor. After your advisor has been selected, he or she can help you and your 401(k) committee finalize your 401(k) IPS and plan, initiate the employee education program, and then enroll your employees and guide them in selecting their investment choices.

The next chapter will explain, from the financial advisor's perspective, how your new 401(k) plan is being established, providing you with insight about how your advisor is thinking, planning, and building a collaborative relationship with you.

Chapter 5 Review Questions:

1. The three components to conducting a successful RFP are:

    A. Having a good 401(k) team

    B. Knowing the goals of your 401(k) plan

    C. Carefully considering your hiring choices through the RFP process.

    D. All of the above

    E. None of the above

2. Which one of the following IPS financial goals is incorrect?

    A. Provide a plan that attracts and retains employees.

    B. Determine the annual amount of matching funds the company is willing to afford.

    C. Decide how the plan's fees and expenses will be paid.

    D. Reduce corporate taxes while benefiting employees.

3. Which one of the following IPS human resource goals is incorrect?

    A. Provide a plan that attracts and retains employees.

    B. Offer a variety of investments so your employees can select quality assets.

    C. Guide employees by preparing their finances for retirement.

    D. Provide a quality retirement education program.

4. Which one of the following IPS structural goals is incorrect?

   A. Meet all legal requirements.

   B. Secure accurate and helpful financial reporting for
       participants.

   C. Limit administrative overload.

   D. Establish a schedule for plan review and renewal.

5. The purpose of the U.S. Department of Labor's publication,
"Selecting and Monitoring Pension Consultants - Tips for Plan
Fiduciaries" was to provide plan sponsors with a set of questions
designed to reveal information that could lead to serious conflicts of
interest between financial advisors and vendors whose products and
services were recommended by the advisors.

   A. True

   B. False

6. Which one of the following is not one of the four elements for
crafting your plan?

   A. Understand your goals.

   B. Build your Investment Policy Statement (IPS).

   C. Stay on course.

   D. Delegate fiduciary responsibility whenever possible.

7. What is the biggest obstacle to the effectiveness of employee 401(k) education?

   A. Most companies' education programs are not effective for adult learners.

   B. Many employees are not interested in learning about retirement funding.

   C. Too many employers do not want their employees meeting with the financial advisor on break times.

   D. There is just too much information to share with employees in an efficient manner.

Answers

1. Answer: D. When you have a solid team, know your 401(k) goals, and select the best professionals available, the RFP process will be rewarding.

2. Answer: A. Providing a plan that attracts and retains employees is a human resources goal, not a financial goal.

3. Answer: B. Offering a variety of investments so your employees can select quality assets is a financial goal.

4. Answer: B. Securing accurate and helpful financial reporting for participants is a human resource goal.

5. Answer: A. The intention was that these conflicts of interest could be avoided once the plan sponsors were aware of relationships that could be tainted, because either steps could be taken to immediately adjust any improper business activity, or the plan sponsor could refrain from entering into a contract with a financial advisor whose company was incapable of restricting this improper behavior.

6. Answer: D. The missing element is to investigate plan providers.

7. Answer: A. Professional finance experts are not always the best choice for instructing adult employees; professional and content-trained teachers may be a more effective choice.

Chapter 6:
How We Help You Set-Up a New Plan

When you have finished reading this chapter, you will understand how your company's 401(k) plan advisor will:

- Finalize your plan's goals

- Investigate and recommend plan providers

- Complete the details of your plan

- Implement your plan

- Monitor your plan

- Help you improve your company's existing 401(k) plan, if applicable

Now that you and your 401(k) committee have selected your plan's financial advisor, we think it's important you see the task that lies ahead from the viewpoint of your new advisor. An experienced professional will have previously established a number of 401(k) plans for a variety of companies of all different types and sizes. You can expect your financial advisor to quickly set project goals and begin work immediately.

 Note:

After your financial advisor has been selected, it's time to finalize all the details of your 401(k) plan, with the guidance of your new advisor.

Also, while it's true that a lot of information has been communicated during the RFP process, not everything that was discussed in the RFP process was in its final state. The financial advisor you selected through the RFP process has a good idea about the expectations of your company's plan, but now the intentions are to bring all the pieces together and draft the final ISP and plan with your new financial advisor.

Figure 12: New Plan Set-Up.

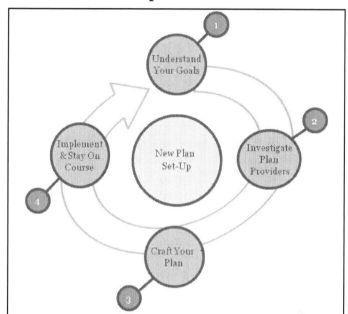

Understanding Your Goals

Assuredly, your financial advisor has been introduced to your company's 401(k) goals during the RFP process, except now, as a confidante, there should be a further discussion that more completely defines the goals that you, as the plan sponsor, have in mind. Generally speaking, there are two main reasons an employer will create a 401(k) plan.

The first reason is that the 401(k) plan is good for business. By establishing a 401(k) plan, significant tax benefits are realized; also, the plan sponsor can increase his or her retirement funds with pretax savings which will multiply through managed investments; and thirdly, a 401(k) plan is a strong instrument for recruiting, retaining, and rewarding valued employees.

The other reason a company will establish a 401(k) plan is because the employer loves his or her employees and, now that the company is doing so well, the owner wants to reward the employees for the company's success, and wants the employees to have the best chance for retirement because the owner cares about their lives, and their children, and is so thankful for the years of labor and loyalty that he or she wants to make sure everyone has a chance to have a decent retirement; the cost in terms of extra time, trouble, and expenses isn't a concern...as long as the people who have helped the company now also have the same opportunity to grow and succeed.

Of course, in most cases the discussion will incorporate both these reasons for desiring a 401(k) plan, and will reveal information the financial advisor will need for establishing the objectives that lead to achieving the plan's goals. When the plan sponsor says he or she wants to take advantage of the tax savings available through a company retirement plan, further review will likely lead to the supporting objective of including a self-directed brokerage account for the highly paid executives. Or, when the plan sponsor and the financial advisor discuss the value of rewarding the employees' hard work, the financial advisor will hear the employer's willingness to include matching funds.

So, now is the time when the goals and objectives are set and become the foundation for the rest of the plan's organization and personnel choices.

Investigate the Plan Providers

The financial advisor should be the key individual involved with helping you select the TPA and record keeper. Think of your financial advisor as the quarterback of the 401(k) team, coordinating the players and the plays so the ball moves downfield and scores. Since your financial advisor has been in business for a number of years, he or she probably already knows a number of reliable professionals who will provide excellent service for your company's plan. Now, a different conversation should occur with you and with your 401(k) committee in which the financial advisor proposes several candidates for these positions, explaining why these particular professionals would be a good fit for your company.

 Important:

Your company's financial advisor should be involved in selecting the TPA and record-keeper because your advisor will be working closely with these professionals.

Once a short list has been established, requests should be transmitted to these providers inquiring about their interest and availability, and your financial advisor should set a schedule for your committee to interview the candidates. Of course, the committee will need to review the applications, and be prepared for the interviews. Once the interviews are concluded, then the committee, with the financial advisor supporting the decision-making process, can recommend its selections. Thereafter, contracts can be signed and your new providers can begin their preparations.

Crafting Your Plan

During this time, the details of the plan can be finalized. The Investment Policy Statement (IPS) should now have been finalized; here are some of the examples of items which will need to be determined:

- Eligibility to participate in the plan

- Process for entry into the plan

- Transfer to or from the ineligible class

- Return to the plan after ineligibility

- Elective deferrals by plan participants

- Employer matching contributions

- Contributions from rollovers

- Contributions from transfers

- Allocation limitations

- Vesting and forfeitures of employer contributions

- Distributions to participants

- Loans to participants

- Investment funds in the plan

- Expenses and fees

As you can imagine, your 401(k) plan will likely wind up being about 50 pages and will include many more categories than just the few listed above. Rely on the skills and expertise of your financial advisor to guide your company, your 401(k) committee, your employees, and the other providers through this process. Your financial advisor undoubtedly has a wealth of resources from which to draw, and you'll find that these tasks will be handled expertly.

Implementing Your Plan

Once your company's plan has been drawn up and finalized, which is likely to consume about four weeks, it will then take about six to eight weeks longer to set up your company's 401(k) plan. During this time, your financial advisor will be working with your newly hired TPA and record keeper, monitoring and supporting their work as the employees' website gateway is constructed. At the same time, your financial advisor will be selecting funds which are appropriate to your plan so your employees have funds through which they can invest. While these two wheels are turning, the employee education program will be prepared, and workshops scheduled. Publicity about the program will begin so employees have a chance to start learning about their new financial opportunity.

Staying on Course

The long expected day has arrived and your company's new 401(k) plan is now operational!

The TPA and record keeper have prepared all the behind-the-scenes tasks, such as setting up record-keeping systems for eligible employees, building the company's webpage gateway and investment platform enabling employees to access the company's 401(k) system online, preparing and distributing the required participant notices, etc.

Your financial advisor has selected and prepared the funds and managed accounts which will be included in the plan, and they are ready for your employees to begin making steady contributions.

In addition, all the eligible employees have had their initial orientation to the company's 401(k) plan, possess at least a basic understanding of how the 401(k) works and how to engage with the plan, and are excited and grateful for the opportunity to build their retirement funds to ensure a safe and comfortable retirement.

Key:

Your 401(k)'s educational program is extremely important. Since your company wants to save money on taxes, and if you are providing matching funds, one of the best ways to help your company with its taxes is by encouraging your employees to make contributions...for their benefit, and your company's benefit.

Remember that most of your employees do not know much about the value of a 401(k) plan. A strong adult education program will make a significant impact on their understanding and on their financial future.

All that's left is monitoring the plan, being prepared to set into effect any necessary remedies, measure and report on the plan's effectiveness with achieving its objectives and goals, following through with the employee education program, and meeting the requirements of compliance testing.

Working with an existing plan: If your company already has a 401(k) plan and you've hired a new financial advisor to make improvements, the task is normally much easier than starting from scratch.

Taking an existing plan and fixing it is a lot different than figuring out what to build. It's just like speaking with a contractor about your house. You could tell the contractor you want him to build a house, but then the questions start to fly: What kind of house? A big house, or small house? How many rooms? How many bathrooms? But if the house is already built, and you ask your contractor to remodel the house, the questions and the tasks are a lot more contained. Your contractor can open up walls, add windows and eliminate doors, or whatever it is you want. Your financial advisor will be very capable of making the changes, or advising you on how to improve the plan you already have.

The same is true if you want to switch from one plan to another, such as shifting from a pension plan to 401(k) plan. An experienced financial advisor can examine what you have, and build a bridge from your existing plan to the plan you would like to have instead. This presupposes that switching between plans is a good idea, because your financial advisor will also provide an opinion about whether it's better to keep things as they are, or recommend a change. It's much easier if a plan is already in existence and you don't have to build a plan from the beginning.

Summary

The process of establishing a new 401(k) plan for your company is complicated with many moving parts. The process involves tax issues, legal issues, compliance issues, your employees' welfare, the employees' education program, working with a number of specialized professionals, selecting appropriate investment funds, establishing a committee and validating their work, etc. None of this is easy, but neither is it hard for a seasoned professional.

Most of this project will depend on the skills and qualities of your financial advisor. In Chapter 5, we reviewed the entire process...from the plan sponsor's desire to establish a 401(k) plan, and through the many steps to the end when employees are enrolled and begin their investment selection. The majority of this work should be done under the guidance of your financial advisor, which now you've seen from the perspective of your financial advisor.

Chapter 6 Review Questions:

1. Why is it a good idea to wait on finalizing many of the elements of the 401(k) plan until after the financial advisor is selected?

    A. There is no point making decisions on details that will all be changed once the advisor is chosen.

    B. The advisor will not want any team members making decisions.

    C. The plan sponsor's fiduciary responsibilities prevent finalizing many of the 401(k) plan's elements until the financial advisor is selected.

    D. The advisor's experience and expertise is desirable during the decision-making process.

2. The financial advisor should be the key individual involved with helping you select the TPA and record-keeper.

    A. True

    B. False

3. About how long will it take to set up your company's 401(k) plan, after it has been finalized?

    A. 4 – 6 weeks

    B. 6 – 8 weeks

    C. 8 – 10 weeks

    D. 10 – 12 weeks

Answers

1.   Answer: D. The advisor has the range and depth of experience to guide the company's decisions with skillful and knowledgeable recommendations.

2.   Answer: A. The advisor will be working closely with the TPA and record-keeper, so it's important that the advisor has a good team with which to work.

3.   Answer: B. Once the 401(k) plan is finalized, it should be operational in about 6 – 8 weeks.

Chapter 7:
Interview Insight:
The Top 10 Questions You Want to Ask

When you have finished reading this chapter, you will:

- Know what your plan's fees and expenses are

- Understand how to compare your plan's fees and expenses with the fees and expenses of other plans

- Be able to consider ways of reducing your plan's fees and expenses

- Realize how to increase your employees' participation in the plan

- Identify how to be certain you are meeting your fiduciary responsibilities

In our experience, there are 10 questions which are most often asked by plan sponsors. We believe most of your initial questions will be answered on the following pages.

1. Fees and expenses can be costly, and will cost my company money if my company pays the fees and expenses, or they will reduce my employees' retirement funds' growth if they pay the fees and expenses. I want to reduce fees if I can, so how do I know what the fees and expenses are, in total?

Your company's 401(k) fees and expenses can be determined by looking at three documents. The first document is the 408(b) Fee Disclosure Form; the 408(b) requires 401(k) service providers to disclose information about their compensation. This document shows the dollar amounts and/or the percentages which the investment advisor, the TPA, the record keeper, and the custodian are charging your plan. Remember that the services for which your plan is paying are also identified in your company's investment policy statement (IPS).

If you are establishing a new plan, the service providers interested in working with you will need to show their intended fees and expenses for the services you wish to include.

The second document is the Balance by Fund Report; this report shows the total of the 401(k) funds in your company's plan, necessary to determine the actual dollar costs of certain activities based on the value of the funds in the plan.

The 5500 is the third document; it identifies the number of employees in your plan; this is important for calculating the employee-related costs of your 401(k) plan.

An analysis of these three documents will result in an accurate determination of the fees and expenses in your 401(k) plan, and how much your plan is paying for them.

2. Now that I know how much we're paying for the fees and expenses, how do I know if these fees are comparable to what other plans cost?

You can ask your plan's financial advisor to do a 401(k) plan comparison analysis. When you do, your advisor will contact several TPAs and record keepers and ask them to quote their fees and expenses so a benchmark comparison can be made with your current service providers. Your financial advisor could also contact an assortment of custodians to determine how the competitors' custodial fees compare. If you're concerned that it's your financial advisor who may be more costly than necessary, you can always ask a financial advisor from a different company to quote their fees for comparable services, or even hire the other financial advisor to conduct the entire comparison analysis. This way, when you have several different quotes for the variety of services your plan offers, you'll be able to clearly see how your current fees compare. You can then choose to negotiate the fees, or change your service providers if their fees and expenses are too high.

3. Aside from changing my plan's advisors, how can I reduce these fees?

One of the best ways to reduce your plan's fees and expenses is to negotiate with your service providers. By telling your service providers that you're looking for ways to reduce your plan's costs and are thinking about switching providers, you may find them willing to reduce their fees to retain your business. If they don't show interest in negotiating with you, then it may be time to switch providers. Another tactic would be cutting some services and, by reducing plan features and benefits, some of the fees and expenses will be eliminated. If your company is paying for certain services, a third tactic is asking your employees to share in the costs and contribute a portion to the plan's expenses.

4. I know that the 401(k) plan is important for my employees' retirement planning. How do I increase employee participation in the plan?

Education is paramount; once your employees realize the personal value of the company's 401(k) plan, they will more clearly see the importance of participating and securing their retirement future. Therefore, anything you can do to improve your employees' education about the plan will be a strong factor in increasing their participation as well.

Some of the ways you can increase their educational experience is by allowing your financial advisor to conduct quarterly meetings; this would be especially well-perceived if employees can attend these meetings during company time. The group meeting should be no longer than about one hour, followed by the opportunity for your employees to meet with the investment advisor one-on-one during lunch, break times, and on-site after the work day is over. Additional educational opportunities would include having the financial advisor's newsletter posted on the company website; having good technology partners so participants can interact with their investment account on a 24/7 basis with a user-friendly interface; ensuring that your 401(k) team members are good communicators and can get information to participants clearly and in a timely manner; and by providing matching contributions and bonuses to inspire your employees to increase their education and improve their participation in the plan.

5. I want my employees to be confident about which investments would be best for them. Of course, some investments are right for some, but not the best choice for others. How can I be assured that my employees will make the right decision for themselves?

Education is the solution, and having a clear picture about their individual financial circumstances will lead them toward taking the action specific to their needs. While it is very important that your employees understand the value of the company's 401(k) plan as a tool for augmenting and expediting the growth of their retirement funds, and also important that they understand the different purposes of the investment funds available to them, these two factors are not completely sufficient by themselves.

The first and most critical step for each of your employees is to understand their current financial situation and assess what their needs will be when they reach retirement age. What they need most now, as they begin to build their retirement, is a plan that helps them understand where they are, and where they need to be when they choose to retire. Their retirement plan will provide the roadmap for understanding how much money they will need in retirement...so they know how much to save now. The process for understanding which investments are best for them depends on their current financial circumstances, and the financial planning that will help them reach their goals.

The investment funds suggested by the financial advisor must include a range of investments appropriate for the range of your employee population. If the demographics of your plan's participants indicate your employees are in their 20s, this population may be best served by more aggressive investments; but if most of your employees are in their late 50s, perhaps conservative and balanced funds would be a more appropriate choice. Your investment advisor must provide investments that are appropriate for everybody, and the investments should be selected so nobody can hurt themselves with undue risk.

Remember also that advanced financial advisors understand that employees have certain investment biases; employees have behavioral issues around investing, such as over diversification. Many studies show that employees trust their employer with monetary matters, and believe their employer is exceptionally well-educated when it comes to making investments. Therefore, if the company's 401(k) plan has 10 different investment funds or models, employees are likely to want to put 10% of their monthly contributions into each of the 10 investments available to them. Obviously, this investment behavior may not be well suited for everyone, or even anyone.

There is also a familiarity bias. If the company's 401(k) plan offers company stock as an investment option, employees will tend to overweight their investment ratio by putting more retirement money in the company stock than in other investments which may be more appropriate for their unique circumstances.

These investment biases are further complicated by studies which demonstrate that once people have made their asset allocation decisions, they seldom rebalance their portfolio; employees will set their monthly distributions and never or seldom change their original allocations. Therefore, it's very important that employees receive sufficient education at the outset so they understand the impact their decisions will have on their investment practices, and can make the best choices early in the program and with the rationale of their unique circumstances.

You can expect the financial advisor to provide a menu of professionally managed investment models ranging from conservative to aggressive. In addition, the advisor will provide a list of about 20 individual investments used in the different models. Employees may follow their own asset allocation recipe, or they could choose one of the professionally managed and rebalanced asset allocation models. The decision is completely theirs.

Plan participants should be instructed to first establish their financial goals and financial plan based on their financial circumstances, and then allocate their contributions based on the required rate of return in the time remaining before retirement. An advanced financial advisor will ask each employee to complete a qualitative and quantitative intake form so the employee's risk tolerance can be properly estimated, and the employee can be steered toward the investment selection decisions that most support the appropriate investment path.

You and your employees can confirm that the available choices are good investment options by asking your investment advisor to provide a benchmarking analysis of the selected funds. The analysis would show the fees, the fund managers' rating, a comparison with other similar investment funds, and the short and long-term performance history of each of the funds. This information should be sufficient to assure you of the selection quality. The selection should cover a variety of asset classes, such as small-cap, mid-cap, and large-cap funds, bond funds, money market funds, and a reasonable array of different investment sectors such as technology, health care, energy, etc. If, for example, all the selected funds are large-cap funds, it's a disservice, but if a variety of high-quality investments are available, you're meeting your responsibility as a fiduciary.

6. What is a default investment option, why do we need one, and how do I know if we have a good one?

The default investment is the investment into which a participant's contributions are deposited if he or she has not designated a fund to receive the contributions. Some participants fail to take timely action, so a default investment is named to receive these funds until a designation can be made. The law says the money must be allocated to a default investment within a short and reasonable period of time, as the money cannot sit suspended without allocation.

There can only be one default investment, and the plan sponsor, as the trustee, should decide which of the plan's investments should be named as the default. Should it be a bond fund, a stock fund, or an emerging market fund? Or is a money market fund the best choice? The best way to select a default investment is by selecting one that's most suitable for the majority of the plan participants. Remember, you always want to pick the best tool for the job. In this case, if most of your plan participants are over the age of 60, your fiduciary responsibility would likely best be met by naming a bond fund, or a money market fund, or a balanced fund as the default. If most of your plan participants are in their 20s, you might consider an aggressive growth fund, or the aggressive allocation model portfolio. The ideal choice for you as a fiduciary is to carefully consider the willingness of your plan's population to take risk; then you can select the appropriate default investment.

7. What are my fiduciary responsibilities, and how can I make sure that I'm actually doing them?

The Department of Labor has clearly stated that a fiduciary for a 401(k) plan must do the following:

- Make decisions based solely on the best interests of the participants and their beneficiaries

- Make decisions with the exclusive intention of benefiting employees in the plan, and their beneficiaries, and provide money to pay reasonable expenses of the plan

- Implement all duties with the appropriate care, skill, and diligence of a prudent person who is knowledgeable with financial matters

- Act in accordance with the plan documents

- Provide investment choices that are diversified

To assure yourself that you are fulfilling your fiduciary responsibilities, and to provide documentation that you are meeting your responsibilities, we recommend you follow these best practices:

- Form a plan oversight committee that meets regularly

- Have a formal Investment Policy Statement (IPS)

- Follow the parameters of the IPS

- Always document the processes followed to monitor the plan

- Hold periodic compliance reviews of the plan

You should also avoid making these common mistakes:

- Relying on non-fiduciary service providers for investment monitoring and advice

- Untimely remittance of participant contributions to the plan

- Lack of a formal process for investment selection and monitoring

- Limited or no oversight of plan service providers

- Failing to follow the plan document

- Lack of awareness of plan fees compared to other plans of a similar nature

- Lack of communication about fees to participants. (Remember: Fees can be found in the 408(b)(2) form.)

As a fiduciary, the plan sponsor is liable for losses incurred by a plan if the plan sponsor makes investment decisions that specifically cause harm suffered by the plan.

While most employers look for the assistance of qualified financial or investment professionals, it does not completely eliminate the fiduciary's responsibility. The fiduciary is still required to review the investigative data of the consultant, and document that the fiduciary believes the decisions made were in compliance and done in good faith.

By being aware of your fiduciary responsibilities, taking consistent action to meet them, and documenting the process you used to arrive at your decisions, you will be able to satisfy inquiries and strengthen the integrity of your fiduciary role.

8. Is it difficult to switch plans if I'm unhappy with the current plan?

No, it's actually very easy to switch plans. It may take a little time, but it's not difficult to switch at all. If your plan is an unbundled open architecture plan, it's fairly easy to replace the element that's not performing properly. For example, with an open architecture plan that has an independent TPA, record keeper, custodian, and investment advisor, if the plan sponsor does not like the performance of the TPA, the TPA can be removed and another TPA can be interviewed, hired and installed. A good analogy for an open architecture plan is a machine with interchangeable parts; if one part is not performing well, it can be replaced. However, in a closed architecture plan, if one element of the plan is not working well, the entire plan will have to be replaced.

When transferring your 401(k) retirement plan to a new provider, there are a few key steps that must be made to stay in compliance. The steps begin once a contract has been signed to move your 401(k) plan to a new provider.

First, review your contract with the terminating 401(k) provider to check the notice requirement for termination of services. Next, you will need to send a termination letter to your current 401(k) provider. This will notify the company of your intent to terminate your 401(k) plan, but more importantly, it outlines what duties are expected of each party.

Your Duties:

- Informing the exiting provider that you will send liquidation and transfer instructions

- Notifying the exiting provider that you expect them to provide all year-end government filings for the year ending 12/31/XX.

Their Duties:

- Inform you of the initial date of the participant blackout period, which must be a minimum of 30 days from notification.

- Inform you of the date the funds will be transferred.

- Inform you of the anticipated date for reporting on the liquidation of assets.

Finally, you will need to send a blackout notice to all your employees notifying them that their 401(k) investment accounts will be frozen 30 days from the date the notice is sent. This notice will inform the participants they will not be able to make any changes to their accounts until the transfer is complete. Once the transfer has been completed, plan participants will be able to resume management of their individual 401(k) investment accounts.

9. Please explain the difference between a bundled and unbundled plan.

A bundled plan is a plan in which all the 401(k) provider services (TPA, record keeper, etc.) are delivered to you in one package; this is the all-in-one package. If it's bundled, you don't have interchangeable parts; you can't just cut out one part that's not working. You might love 75% of the plan provider services, but you have to live with the part you don't like or you have to change the entire plan.

If you have an unbundled plan, you can always replace the part which is underperforming without eliminating the services of the other providers.

10. Which is better, the bundled or the unbundled plan?

Answer: Once again, it's a matter of choosing the right tool for the job. The bundled plan is an easy choice because you get the whole package...but you have less flexibility. The unbundled plan is more complicated because it has more parts that need to be coordinated with each other, but you have much more freedom of choice.

It all comes down to a decision based on cost. If you're starting with a brand-new plan and there are hardly any assets in the plan, a bundled plan is going to be simpler for you. The fees are going to be higher internally, but the dollar cost will be lower because the custodian is going to absorb the fees. For a small company with a new plan, a bundled plan might be the best option. On the other hand, a more complex plan suggests you'll be better served with an unbundled open architecture plan. Both plan types are good, depending on your circumstances; again, you want to use the right tool for the job.

When making the decision to switch from a bundled to an unbundled plan, or vice versa, there is no timing restriction. You can make the switch at any point during the year. Switching from one plan to another typically takes about 90 days, though sometimes it might take six months. The complexity of the various factors associated with your plan, where the funds are, how rapidly the participants and the plan administrator sign the transfer papers, etc., will determine the transition speed. It's clear that your plan administrator will be aware of calendar dates to avoid, such as the end of the year when the annual reports are due, but there is no law keeping you in your bundled or unbundled plan, or limiting your transition to only a narrow window of time. Once you've made your decision, it's our recommendation you switch plans as soon as possible; the quicker your plan is transferred, the sooner your plan's participants will benefit.

Summary

We hope the questions that were most on your mind have now been answered satisfactorily. Your next set of questions is likely to be more particular to your company and the plan features which best fit your vision for your company's 401(k) plan.

 Chapter 7 Review Questions:

1. What is most important for employees to understand about using the 401(k) plan to their advantage?

   A. They should assess their financial needs for retirement.

   B. They are saving and investing pretax dollars.

   C. Their employer will match the employees' contributions.

   D. They should never borrow or withdraw money from their account until they retire.

2. Studies indicate that once people have made their asset allocation decisions, they seldom rebalance their portfolio.

   A. True

   B. False

3. The default investment option is established for those employees who fail to take timely action, and the default account must be suitable for the majority of the plan participants.

   A. True

   B. False

4. It's usually very difficult to switch plans once you have a 401(k) plan established in your company.

    A. True

    B. False

 # Answers

1. Answer: A. When employees assess their needs for retirement, they can then know their choices and create a plan to have what they'll need.

2. Answer: A. Most people "set and forget" when they should take a more active interest in understanding how to achieve the maximum value from their investments. An experienced financial advisor and a strong employee educational program are significant elements for attaining improved results.

3. Answer: A. Most default accounts are conservative funds that receive contributions from employees who are slow to make decisions on their portfolio allocations.

4. Answer: B. It's actually very easy to switch plans. It may take a little time, but it's not difficult to switch at all.

Chapter 8:
Summary

This section of the book was written to give you, the plan sponsor, the information you need to establish a 401(k) plan for your company.

The two main reasons to start a 401(k) plan are so your company may reduce its tax bill, and you and your employees can improve your retirement savings with tax-deferred dollars. This benefits you personally, and also is an effective tool for recruiting, rewarding and retaining employees.

We presented a fictional situation through the case study of Michael Kendall, and discussed his goals, explained his choices for his company's plan features, and also provided an example of a comparison between several 401(k) plans to give you a more comprehensive picture of the process that lies before you. Of course, this financially rewarding project is best traversed in the company of an experienced professional. We've made a point of recommending that you hire the services of an RIA, a registered investment advisor. A person of this stature is familiar with establishing new 401(k) plans, and also reviewing existing 401(k) plans with an eye toward their improvement, if such is your situation.

As you know, a project is only as successful as the members of its team, so we dedicated a significant portion of this book to explain what we believe is the best process for interviewing and evaluating your company's 401(k) financial advisor, third-party administrator (TPA), and record keeper. We also presented important details about what you should expect each team member to do efficiently and effectively so your workload is diminished and your company's 401(k) plan is in the hands of competent professionals.

Aside from the basic information you'll need as a plan sponsor and the detailed explanation of all the moving parts to a 401(k) plan, there are six key takeaways we feel are important to emphasize.

1. Your responsibilities as a fiduciary: This is the most important part of the 401(k) plan because, as the plan sponsor, you are a fiduciary responsible for your company's plan. This is why you want to assure yourself that the service providers you hire to create and manage your company's 401(k) plan are experienced professionals who will ably guide you.

2. Hire the best professionals for the job: Your situation will determine who will be the best professionals for your company's plan. It's clear that you don't need a starship captain when a capable lieutenant will do. On the other hand, given your fiduciary responsibilities, you want to hire a team of professionals who are capable of delivering the services your company requires.

3. Start your 401(k) plan as soon as possible: Given your experience, you know that time is money, and as the days turn into weeks and the weeks into months, the funds that could be saved in company taxes and the money that could be deferred into a lucrative retirement account are being used in less efficient manners. Do not delay! You now have the information in your hands that could change your personal and company's finances for the better, and quickly.

4. A good portion of this book was also dedicated to explaining the difference between open architecture and closed architecture 401(k) plans. Open architecture 401(k) plans allow your financial advisor to select from the universe of available investments, whereas closed architecture 401(k) plans limit investments to the variety proffered by brokers and insurance companies. Either type may be best for your circumstances.

5. Be attentive to your plan's fees and expenses: We've mentioned that in recent years the IRS has been very concerned about 401(k) plan fees and expenses; this is to your advantage. As you're aware, every dollar has significant value when multiplied through the years, so acquiring the services of professionals whose fees and expenses are reasonable will result in more dollar value for your retirement account and those of your employees.

6. Do your best to ensure your employees receive a good 401(k) plan education: You're providing an excellent retirement plan for your employees, but it won't help one bit if your employees don't understand the value of this retirement savings option. You may make the difference, in a very significant way, in your employees' retired life, so by permitting your company's 401(k) financial advisor to meet regularly with your employees and provide individual counseling, you will be providing a gift of both measurable and immeasurable value.

The next section, Section 3, is focused on the plan participants, which includes you and your employees. We hope you'll make this book available to your employees so they can take advantage of your company's new 401(k) plan, and by so doing, improve the value of your company and the financial security of their lives.

Section 3:
Essential 401(k) Knowledge for You, the Participant

Chapter 1:
An Eye on Retirement

When you have finished reading this chapter, you will understand:

- Why it's important to save money regularly for your future

- The value of time when saving money

- The basic mathematics of compounding interest

- The importance of repaying unessential debts quickly

- The benefit of keeping a monthly financial log book

Hello, and welcome. You are reading this book because either your company has a 401(k) plan and you want to understand how this retirement program can serve you and your family, or because you've heard about 401(k) plans and wish to know more about them before you ask your employer to start a 401(k) plan at your company. Whatever your purpose is, this book will provide you with an intelligent and perceptive overview of 401(k) plans with the details you need to develop your own personal retirement plan.

Three sections: This book has three sections, explained as follows:

Section 1: Section 1 was written for both you and your employer, and it describes the three different plan types, discusses the roles of the five key professionals needed to make a 401(k) plan work efficiently, and reviews some of the key laws and regulations that govern the legality of 401(k) plans. You will probably find this information worthwhile because it gives you some background on the 401(k) plan you have or want to have at your company.

Section 2: Section 2 was written for your employer, who is also known as the plan sponsor. A 401(k) plan is not permitted at your company unless your employer decides to sponsor the plan and performs several complicated and required tasks that legally allows your company to offer a 401(k) plan to your company's employees. You are, of course, welcome to read Section 2, which explains the details of starting a 401(k) plan at your company from the employer's perspective. As you can see from the Table of Contents, the topics of evaluating and selecting key financial advisors are reviewed, as well as the details for creating and then establishing a company 401(k) plan.

Section 3: Section 3 was written entirely for you, the plan participant. In this section you will be introduced to Linda Nelson, a fictitious company employee, and through her example you may learn what you need to know and do to make efficient use of this potentially effective financial opportunity. Along with Linda's case study, the book discusses several significant features of a 401(k) plan (Chapter 2), and also offers many important guidelines for developing your own retirement plan (Chapters 3 – 5), which can help you achieve your retirement goals and live well in your later years. The book concludes with suggestions about working with your own investment advisor (Chapter 6), and in Chapter 7 you'll find a short insightful interview that answers some of the key questions most 401(k) plan participants would like answered.

We hope you'll find this book a valuable tool for making your 401(k) plan a powerful and lucrative source for the funds you'll need so you can enjoy your retirement years. As with everything, very little happens unless you take action: a Mercedes-Benz without gas won't budge an inch; an old beat-up Ford with a tank full of gas will get you where you want to go. This book will help you see your choices, guide you on making key decisions, and show you the map that reaches your personal financial goals.

The Importance of Saving

If you've heard it once, you've heard it 1,000 times. You have to save money for your retirement, and you have to do it steadily. Living on welfare and food stamps, or other government subsidies for the poor, is not the way you want to live in your Golden Years. Most people imagine a retirement in which they can live comfortably, either in their home or a downsized apartment, have enough funds to eat well, pay the bills, possibly travel, enjoy their grandchildren, and live their last 20 or 30 years peacefully and without anxiety. Will this happen for you?

It's hard to say. The thing about the future is that no one really knows what will happen 15, 20 or 25 years from now. Did anyone expect fifteen years ago that a bag of groceries would cost $30, or that a gallon of gas would cost almost $4.00? No, of course not. And yet, given the effects of the Great Recession, the downturn in the global economy, the changes in global weather patterns, the continually increasing human population on Earth, and the ever present threat of terrorism and war, the future remains, as it always does, vastly unknown!

Figure 13: The Impact of 2% Annual Inflation on Your Purchasing Power.

Inflation Example: Value Today $50,000

Inflation   2.00%

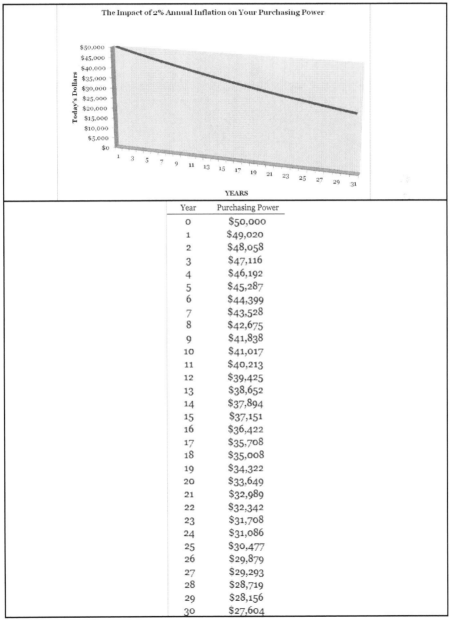

The Impact of 2% Annual Inflation on Your Purchasing Power

Year	Purchasing Power
0	$50,000
1	$49,020
2	$48,058
3	$47,116
4	$46,192
5	$45,287
6	$44,399
7	$43,528
8	$42,675
9	$41,838
10	$41,017
11	$40,213
12	$39,425
13	$38,652
14	$37,894
15	$37,151
16	$36,422
17	$35,708
18	$35,008
19	$34,322
20	$33,649
21	$32,989
22	$32,342
23	$31,708
24	$31,086
25	$30,477
26	$29,879
27	$29,293
28	$28,719
29	$28,156
30	$27,604

It's always good to live with an optimistic attitude, and it is just as wise to prepare for the future with practical and purposeful behavior. Because there are so many unknowns about the world as we will know it a decade or two from now, regularly saving and investing your money in a fund that promises the potential of prudent growth makes sense to most people.

There are the usual reasons for saving money:

- Emergencies

- Down payment on a house

- New car

- Repairs and other replacement needs

- Education

- Vacations and other luxury items

- Retirement funds to last the remainder of your life

All of these have relative merit and deserve some attention because of the value they bring to your life, but the most important reason is to fund your retirement. Yes, you might get hit by a bus tomorrow and only your heirs will benefit, but there's a more likely chance that you won't, and you'll have plenty of time to be glad you made a few sacrifices earlier in life and saved your money...or you'll have plenty of time to regret that you didn't and wish that you had.

Repay Your Debts: One very important idea to consider, as we get this conversation rolling, is that you might be served best if you repay your debts. Everyone's circumstances are different, and we're not suggesting that all debt is bad. You may have had to take out a car loan, and are paying it back with interest for 60 months or so. Your interest rate may not be very high, but every dollar you pay in interest is a dollar less you can set aside for retirement. Having no debt is actually the best situation because then you are not paying interest on your debt. When you pay money to service your debt, you're just staying in the hole you've dug for yourself. Some holes can be really deep!

Credit card debt is especially unhealthy for your financial well-being. Many people carry thousands of dollars on their credit cards and are paying very high interest rates for the privilege. In order to be financially sound, perhaps the first thing you should do is eliminate all your credit card debt and only carry the debt you can fully pay back every month. This way you are using the credit card companies instead of them using you.

Key:

Debt is very unhealthy to your financial wealth because you owe the money you borrowed plus the interest. Debt makes it that much harder to get ahead. Eliminate debt as soon as you can so you can start saving and make money work for you, not against you.

Life Expectancy: Another big consideration is that people are living longer these days than they did a generation or two ago. With the advances in medicine and public health conditions, people are now living into their eighties and nineties. A longer lifetime means you'll have to set aside even more money for the extended years of your life.

Social Security: Yet another issue to think about is the continual debate in the news about whether Social Security will be funded sufficiently when it's your turn to retire and receive this benefit. The Baby Boomers are now beginning to retire, and various projections suggest that Social Security may dwindle significantly as this generation receives its financial entitlement. Social Security was never intended to be the primary retirement income, and was always only intended to supplement a person's income in their elder years.

Save Regularly: Still another key factor in your financial success is setting aside some money from your paycheck every month. In this case, more is better, but even a little bit of money set aside on a steady basis every month will result in a better nest egg than if you did nothing at all. The reason this is so is because money grows in time. Doing nothing will probably leave you with nothing, but by being disciplined and allocating a portion of every month's paycheck to retirement savings and retirement investments, your money has the opportunity to increase every year as you age toward retirement. Don't wait until your paycheck increases; start saving now so time can be your friend.

Kick the Habits: One of the best ways to find an extra $50 each paycheck is by keeping a log book of your spending for one full month. Every day, record every penny you spend. This may seem like a foolish task, but by the end of the month you'll be amazed at how you've spent your money. Going through a normal day, we spend a dollar here and a dollar there, but once you total up these random dollars, you may find that money is pouring out of you like water from a sieve. That comforting cup of Starbucks' coffee every day will add up to $60 or more each month; having a $5 lunch at work quickly becomes $100 in 20 days. Are you still smoking? Depending on your habit, you could be burning up $100 or more between paychecks. To have more money, you have only two choices: either make more money...or save more money. Once you see some of the excesses your log book will show you, you can then make an intelligent choice about what to cut so you'll have more when you retire.

These days, a penny may seem trivial. How many of them have you stepped over when you're walking down the street? Even so, the lowly penny is a good example of the dramatic effect of how your money can increase with more mindful decisions on spending or saving. Figure 14 on the next page is an imaginative way of demonstrating how quickly money increases when you are careful with every penny you have.

Figure 14: Doubling a Penny Every Day for 36 Days.

Day	Value	Day	Value
0	$0.01	18	$2,621.44
1	$0.02	19	$5,242.88
2	$0.04	20	$10,485.76
3	$0.08	21	$20,971.52
4	$0.16	22	$41,943.04
5	$0.32	23	$83,886.08
6	$0.64	24	$167,772.16
7	$1.28	25	$335,544.32
8	$2.56	26	$671,088.64
9	$5.12	27	$1,342,177.28
10	$10.24	28	$2,684,354.56
11	$20.48	29	$5,368,709.12
12	$40.96	30	$10,737,418.24
13	$81.92	31	$21,474,836.48
14	$163.84	32	$42,949,672.96
15	$327.68	33	$85,899,345.92
16	$655.36	34	$171,798,691.84
17	$1,310.72	35	$343,597,383.68
		36	$687,194,767.36

After only 36 days...you have enough pennies to completely pay for California's 2014 drought relief plan! Drops of water can make an ocean, and pennies can add up to a vast fortune.

The Value of Time: You probably know that time is your friend, at least when it comes to your finances! A simple formula to remember is that money almost doubles every seven years when it earns 10% per year. That means that $1,000 becomes almost $2,000 if the money is left undisturbed while earning 10% interest each of the seven years. We like it when interest works for us!

 Important:

Money doubles every seven years at 10% interest.
Let money work for you! Start or continue
saving. Your company's 401(k) plan offers a
tremendous value for your future financial security.

Well, you may say that seven years is a long time, and it is, but now
think about how many seven-year periods there are in your life
between today and when you retire. Most people think about retiring
when they reach age 65, and lately, because of the Great Recession,
many people are thinking about not retiring until they are in their
early 70s, but it's different for everyone. We'll discuss this more at
length in Chapter 4, The Big Picture, but right now just casually
calculate the number of seven-year periods that remain until you
retire.

Okay, let's say you have three sets of seven years. If you're retiring at
65 that means you are now 44 years old. Let's also say you currently
have $10,000 set aside in your retirement account. If left undisturbed
while earning 10% a year, and without adding any more of your
money, that $10,000 becomes almost $20,000 in seven years; almost
$40,000 seven years later; and almost $80,000 in the final seven-
year period. There is a term for this, and it's called the miracle of
compound interest. You can see that time can be your friend, if you
will allow it. This is why steady saving every month, starting now if
you haven't yet done this, can result in your financial security.

Figure 15: Compound Interest for 21 Years at 10% Per Year.

Year	Beginning Value	Ending Value
1	$10,000.00	$11,000.00
2	$11,000.00	$12,100.00
3	$12,100.00	$13,310.00
4	$13,310.00	$14,641.00
5	$14,641.00	$16,105.10
6	$16,105.10	$17,715.61
7	$17,715.61	$19,487.17
8	$19,487.17	$21,435.89
9	$21,435.89	$23,579.48
10	$23,579.48	$25,937.42
11	$25,937.42	$28,531.17
12	$28,531.17	$31,384.28
13	$31,384.28	$34,522.71
14	$34,522.71	$37,974.98
15	$37,974.98	$41,772.48
16	$41,772.48	$45,949.73
17	$45,949.73	$50,544.70
18	$50,544.70	$55,599.17
19	$55,599.17	$61,159.09
20	$61,159.09	$67,275.00
21	$67,275.00	$74,002.50

Pretty astounding, isn't it? This is an example of the power of compound interest, and the value of saving over time.

Don't Buy a Refrigerator: Well, yes, we are being facetious, but there is a method to this madness. What does a new refrigerator cost these days? A quick check will reveal that refrigerators sell within the range of $600 to about $2,500. Okay, let's consider a refrigerator that costs $1,000.

In seven years, that $1,000 at 10% will have grown to $2,000. Seven years later, the sum is $4,000. Again, seven years later, now we have $8,000. Add another seven years, and that $1,000 that we started with has grown to $16,000. In 28 years, $1,000 became $16,000. Doesn't that seem incredible to you? This is the power of money's growth through time. You can have the same dynamics working for you once you start saving every month for the rest of your working life. As we said earlier, a little bit of belt tightening now could result in throwing the belt away when you retire.

Review Your Accounts Regularly: Another good piece of advice is to be aware of what's happening in your retirement accounts. It's not a good idea to just park the money and walk away. This is your retirement we're talking about, and an active interest is better than a semi-active interest, and a semi-active interest is better than just ignoring everything and assuming you'll be okay. We're not expecting you to become a Wall Street expert, but being generally aware of how your investments are doing will help you see if your funds are on track. As with anything, the more you know, the more you are likely to achieve. When it comes to your finances, there are a great many choices, and you should have a general understanding of what's available and which ones are the smartest for you.

Professional Advice: Because there are so many choices, perhaps the wisest thing you could do would be to hire the services of a professional financial advisor. Later in this book, in Chapter 6, we'll discuss some of the advantages and details of working with a financial advisor. You'll be surprised to know the costs are not as high as you might believe, and the benefits could be astronomical.

Key:

Because your financial future is so important, you should seriously consider hiring the services of a financial advisor now and then. Your advisor can work with you on developing your financial goals, and start a plan for achieving those goals in the time remaining before you retire.

The key point in this chapter is to emphasize the importance of saving, and saving on a regular basis. Though it may seem far in the distance, we all know how elusive and illusive time can be; turnaround, and your child is suddenly a teenager; turnaround again, and you are attending your child's wedding; one more twirl and suddenly you're a grandparent. Use time to your advantage and make time and money work for you.

401(k) Plan Alternatives

A 401(k) is only one of several different types of retirement plans that are available to you, and you should know what they are and a little bit about them. In Section 2, Chapter 1, there is a short list of about a dozen alternatives with a brief description of each. Even though these alternative retirement plans exist, they may not be available through your company.

The only reason the 401(k) exists at your company is because the owner has decided to accept the responsibilities of offering a 401(k) to the company's employees. This is why, if your company does have a 401(k), you should take advantage of it. It's one more tool you can use to help you reach your retirement funding goals. A 401(k) can be an exceptionally powerful method for accelerating the growth of your retirement monies.

Note:

While there are a number of alternative retirement plans, your company's 401(k) might be the best choice if your employer is offering matching dollars. No other retirement plan offers this key advantage. It's like receiving free money.

In Chapter 4, you're going to meet Linda Nelson. Even though she's fictitious, her story may be similar to your own. Linda's experience will offer you many key insights to the importance of investing for retirement, and the value of making good use of your company's 401(k) plan.

Summary

In this introductory chapter, we discussed the importance of saving, and saving earlier rather than later, using the example of the refrigerator with the miracle of compounding. In Chapter 4, "The Big Picture", we'll present even more astounding mathematical evidence to support this opinion. For now, however, in the next chapter, we'll describe the amazing investment tool known as a 401(k). If your company has one, you're very fortunate. If your company doesn't, you might want to give a copy of this book to your employer. Your employer will benefit as well, and in several significant ways; you just might get a big thank you!

 Chapter 1 Review Questions:

1. Using Figure 13 as a reference, what will be the purchasing power of $50,000 in today's dollars 30 years from now, assuming a 2% inflation rate?

    A. $50,000

    B. $30,477

    C. $27, 604

    D. $25,000

2. Which of the following statements is incorrect?

    A. Every dollar you pay in interest is a dollar less you can set aside for retirement.

    B. Having no debt is actually the best situation because then you are not paying interest on your debt.

    C. Only carry the debt you can fully pay back every month.

    D. Credit card debt is a healthy type of debt because interest rates are reasonable.

3. Social Security was always intended to be the primary retirement income.

    A. True

    B. False

4. Saving money from your paycheck before it's taxed is a really good idea.

    A. True

    B. False

Answers

1. Answer: C. $27,604. This is just about half of today's purchasing power, showing how inflation affects the value of money over time. 2% is considered a normal inflation rate, so this indication is relevant!

2. Answer: D. Credit card rates are extremely high. Many credit card companies will offer low initial rates, and then raise the rates when a payment is tardy. Credit card debt is very unhealthy to your financial goals.

3. Answer: B. Social Security was intended only as supplemental income, meaning that retirees were expected to have investments or savings as their primary resource in retirement.

4. Answer: A. This is good for two reasons. First, you won't be paying taxes on the funds being deposited in your 401(k) account until you withdraw them, hopefully many years later. Second, your monthly payroll taxes will be less than usual because you are receiving less taxable income each month.

Chapter 2:
Understanding the Importance of Having a 401(k)

When you have finished reading this chapter, you will:

- Realize the financial advantages of having a company 401(k) program

- Be able to explain why a 401(k) is called a "defined contribution plan"

- Know several possible reasons why your employer decided to establish a company 401(k) plan

- Possess enough information to tell if your company's 401(k) plan is a good one

- Realize the impact of taxes on retirement earnings

- Be familiar with the common features of a 401(k)

- Understand the roles of the plan's fiduciaries

- Know how to find out if you are eligible to join your company's 401(k) plan, and the maximum annual contribution you can make

- Identify the biggest risk to the money in your 401(k) account

A 401(k) can either be another very good investment tool for you, or it can be an exceptional investment tool. It really depends on the details of the plan that's been approved for your company. We'll get into the details of that in a moment, but for right now the important thing to know is that your company's 401(k) allows you to legally set aside and invest money from your paycheck every month before it's taxed by the U. S. government.

This is a tremendous benefit for you because it allows you to build your retirement fund more rapidly. If you were restricted from using pretax dollars and could only save money that had first been taxed, you might lose between 15 – 25% or more to Uncle Sam. By investing pretax dollars, your retirement savings and investments have an even greater potential for growth.

Figure 16: Rate of Return Comparison.

Tax Rate	10.00%	20.00%	25.00%	30.00%	40.00%
Gross Return	10.00%	10.00%	10.00%	10.00%	10.00%
Net Return	9.00%	8.00%	7.50%	7.00%	6.00%
Difference	-1.00%	-2.00%	-2.50%	-3.00%	-4.00%

As you can see, as your tax rate increases, your net return diminishes.

In the figure below, using the assumptions listed in the first section, you can see that in 10 years the amount of $10,000 will grow to $19,671.51 with the net rate of 7%.

Figure 17: Value of $10,000 at Various Returns and Taxes.

Assumptions:	
Present Value	$10,000.00
Gross Rate of Return	10.00%
Tax Rate	30.00%
Net Rate of Return	7.00%
Years of Growth	10
Value	$19,671.51

		Value of $10,000 in 10 Years at Various Returns & Taxes				
				Tax Rate		
		10.00%	20.00%	25.00%	30.00%	40.00%
	3.00%	$13,052.82	$12,676.51	$12,492.03	$12,309.98	$11,953.02
	5.00%	$15,529.69	$14,802.44	$14,450.44	$14,105.99	$13,439.16
Gross	7.00%	$18,421.82	$17,244.05	$16,680.96	$16,134.48	$15,089.58
Rate of	10.00%	$23,673.64	$21,589.25	$20,610.32	$19,671.51	$17,908.48
Return	12.00%	$27,886.73	$25,009.53	$23,673.64	$22,402.31	$20,042.31
	15.00%	$35,477.96	$31,058.48	$29,040.24	$27,140.81	$23,673.64

In this chapter we're going to explore the common features and various details of a 401(k) so you know the basic rules of the game, allowing you to become a much better participant in this retirement funding opportunity. By the end of this chapter you'll have a strong basic working knowledge of the value of having a 401(k) through your company.

What Exactly Is a 401(k)?

A 401(k) is a profit-sharing plan that allows employees to deposit some of their salary in a retirement account before receiving a paycheck. Your paycheck is less because you've deducted money for your retirement account, but you're saving that money for retirement and don't pay taxes on it until you withdraw it.

Setting aside retirement funds from your paycheck before taxes are taken out is the hallmark of 401(k) plans, and an important part of the current trend of employers helping their employees save for retirement. Known as deferrals, and also as contributions, deposits in your retirement account can be made on a pretax basis, but they can also be made on an after-tax basis when designated as Roth contributions.

Contributions to your retirement account can be either fixed or discretionary. If the contribution is fixed, the deposits are set at the percentage you choose, and the contribution stays the same until you decide to change it. If the contribution is discretionary, that means you are permitted to add additional funds to your retirement account when the opportunity arises, as it might if you received an inheritance.

It's also important to know that contributions can be made by either the employer or employee, or both.

The first great thing about a 401(k) is that you are allowed to make regular contributions to your retirement account before you pay the tax on your salary, meaning you don't pay taxes on the funds you now defer to your retirement account...allowing you the opportunity to build your retirement account more rapidly. Yes, you pay taxes on this money when you withdraw it, but by not paying taxes now, you have more money to build your retirement nest egg and can use the value of time to your benefit.

The second great thing about a 401(k) is that in many cases your employer will make matching contributions to your retirement account. The word "matching" does not mean dollar-for-dollar. Your employer's match is usually a percentage of the amount you are contributing to your retirement account. In addition, there is a limit to how much your employer is permitted to match. As an example, your employer may decide to match 2% of your monthly retirement contribution, not to exceed $2,000 per year.

Well, this is great news because your employer is helping you build your retirement fund. It's almost like free money...and everyone can use some of that!

Note:

"Matching" does not always mean dollar-for-dollar. Your employer may only match one of your dollars with $.50 of the company's dollars, or maybe $.25 to one of your dollars. Your company may even choose not to offer any matching dollars; it all depends on how your company is planning to save taxes.

Definition:

Tax-deferred: Whether or not your company offers matching dollars, a 401(k) is an excellent retirement savings program because the money you put in your 401(k) account is "tax-deferred". This means you don't pay taxes on the money until years later when you withdraw it. Your money will grow faster without the burden of taxes.

When we use the word "matching", we don't mean that your employer is matching you dollar for dollar; however, your company's 401(k) plan defines the amount that your employer will match. For example, your employer may match every dollar you contribute with a match of $.10; or your employer may match every dollar you contribute with $.25, or even $.50. Your employer is under no obligation to contribute any matching funds to your retirement account; however, most employers do. The company's plan specifically states your employer's matching portion. The good news is that if your employer does provide matching funds, the more you set aside in your 401(k) account, the more "free money" your employer will also contribute to your retirement fund. This is like a no-brainer!

The beauty of the 401(k) is obvious; your employer recognizes the value you and your fellow employees bring to the company, and has chosen to reward you with this special opportunity to help you prepare for retirement. Yes, the employer also benefits by reducing company taxes by providing matching funds, but how nice it is that your employer has found an elegant way to save both the company's money ... and yours! With a 401(k), everybody can benefit.

In the tables below, we present an example of an employee's 401(k) account. This person has a net payroll of $50,000 per year, and has decided to invest 8% of the $50,000 in their 401(k) account, which is $4,000. The company has decided to match their employees' contributions at a rate of 50%, which in this case is $2,000. The result is that this account now has a balance, based on contributions from both the employee and the company, of $6,000. Your company may not have such a high matching contribution rate, but as you can see, any matching contribution is additional money in your retirement account. In essence, the government and your company are both contributing to your ability to accelerate your retirement savings.

Figure 18: Example of the Growth of a 401(k) Savings Account with Company Matching Funds.

Assumptions:	
Wages (Net of Payroll Tax)	$50,000
401K Contribution %	8.00%
Company Match	50.00%
With Company Match	
401(k) Annual Savings	$4,000.00
Company Match	$2,000.00
Total Contribution	**$6,000.00**

In the table below, you can see how a 401(k) account would increase based on the combination of various employee and company contributions. For example, if an employee contributed 6% of their $50,000 net annual payroll, which is $3,000, and the company contributed a match of 10%, the employee's account will be $3,300, which is based on the combined contributions of both the employee and the company for that year.

Figure 19: Examples of Employee and Company Contributions.

		Total Contributions				
		Company Match				
		0.00%	3.00%	10.00%	25.00%	50.00%
	0.00%	$0.00	$0.00	$0.00	$0.00	$0.00
	2.00%	$1,000.00	$1,030.00	$1,100.00	$1,250.00	$1,500.00
Employee	4.00%	$2,000.00	$2,060.00	$2,200.00	$2,500.00	$3,000.00
401k	6.00%	$3,000.00	$3,090.00	$3,300.00	$3,750.00	$4,500.00
Contribution	8.00%	$4,000.00	$4,120.00	$4,400.00	$5,000.00	$6,000.00
	10.00%	$5,000.00	$5,150.00	$5,500.00	$6,250.00	$7,500.00

Once your money is in your individual 401(k) account, and as you and possibly your employer make regular contributions throughout the months and over the years, the funds in your account are invested as you direct. This means you have a choice about how your funds are invested, and your money will grow based on the investment choices you make. In Chapter 5, we'll offer some guidance on how you might invest your funds, but for now we just want you to understand why a 401(k) is important to you.

The words "401(k)" are based on the Internal Revenue Code, Section 401, paragraph (k). This section of the Code was made legal by the Employee Retirement Income Security Act of 1974 (ERISA). Our country's lawmakers saw a way to reduce a company's taxes while also helping employed citizens increase their retirement saving potential.

As far as you're concerned, a 401(k) potentially provides you with three benefits:

1. Since your contributions are deducted from your paycheck, your income is less, allowing you to reduce your income tax.

2. All the money in your 401(k) retirement account grows tax-free, so you won't have to pay taxes on any of your gains for many years, until you begin to withdraw the money when you are retired.

3. If your company's 401(k) plan allows it, your employer will make matching contributions into your retirement account.

Remember, saving more money now could provide you with the ability to spend more money later.

Why Is a 401(k) Available Through My Company?

As we've mentioned in passing, your employer saw a good opportunity for the company, and took it. With a company 401(k), the company will save money on its taxes while also benefiting the company employees with an exceptional retirement plan. This is what you would call a win-win. The company reduces its taxable income and rewards its employees at the same time. In fact, it's a win-win-win because your employer can also participate in the company 401(k), so he or she is now also able to build a tax-deferred retirement fund.

Is My Company's 401(k) Any Good?

Your company's 401(k) must meet the requirements of the Internal Revenue Code, so just as a starting point, your company's plan contains the minimum features. Now, beyond that, the way to judge the further quality of your company's plan is by considering the following:

1. Does your employer match your fund contributions, and if so, by how much?

2. How long must you wait before you're eligible to join the company's 401(k), or can you enroll immediately?

3. Are there more than just a few investment choices in your company's 401(k) plan, or are choices limited?

4. If you wished, can you find out your account balance by phone or online, and transact other account business?

5. Does your company's 401(k) plan allow you to roll over (transfer) money from your previous employer's 401(k) into your current employer's 401(k)?

6. How often does your company hold workshops or invite 401(k) specialists to educate you about your participation in the plan and increasing the value of your 401(k)?

If you don't know the answer to these questions, then you should meet with somebody from the front office and begin to gather the answers. A 401(k) can be a very important part of your retirement's full potential, so the sooner you know this information and understand your choices, the more time you'll be able to use to your advantage.

What This Opportunity Means to Me

Mostly it means that you now have another way of setting aside money for your retirement. In this case, you are stashing pretax dollars, so you're saving money there. Then, this money is going into a retirement investment fund, so now the money is growing tax-deferred throughout the years and maybe a few decades. Then, on top of that, it's likely that your employer is also contributing to your retirement fund account, so this free money from your employer is also growing tax-deferred throughout the years. Then, when you're old enough and begin to draw on this money in retirement, you'll likely be in a lower tax bracket than in your working years, so the taxes you'll pay in the future may be less because your tax rate will be less.

In the tables below, we demonstrate the effect of having and not having a 401(k). The assumptions are intended to keep the example simple. This person is single, has no dependents or itemized deductions, has an annual net payroll of $50,000, decides to set aside 8% of the net payroll, and the company is matching with a 50% contribution. As you follow the calculations, you'll see that the person with the 401(k) has less spendable income, but has saved $975 in taxes, has $6,000 in their 401(k) account from personal and company contributions, and has an almost 2% lower tax rate (9.91% vs. 11.86%). The benefits are apparent.

Figure 20: Comparison of Having and Not Having a 401(k).

Assumptions:	
Filing Status	Single
Dependents	0
Itemized Deductions	0
Tax Rates	2013
Wages (Net of Payroll Tax)	$50,000
401K Contribution %	8.00%
Company Match	50.00%

	401(k) Option	No 401(k)
Total Income	$50,000	$50,000
Employee 401(k) contribution	$4,000	$0
Adjusted gross income (AGI)	$46,000	$50,000
Standard deduction	$6,100	$6,100
Personal exemption	$3,900	$3,900
Taxable Income	$36,000	$40,000
Estimated Tax	**$4,954**	**$5,929**
Net Income	**$31,046**	**$34,071**
Plus standard deductions	$6,100	$6,100
Plus personal exemption	$3,900	$3,900
= Spendable Income	$41,046	$44,071
401(k) Tax Savings	**$975**	$0
Decrease in Spendable Income	**$3,025**	$0
401(k) Annual Savings	**$4,000**	$0
With Company Match		
401(k) Annual Savings	$4,000	$0
Company Match	$2,000	$0
Total Contribution	$6,000	$0
Effective Tax Rate	**9.91%**	**11.86%**

Next, let's look at the power of tax-deferred savings. In the table below, an annual tax-deferred contribution of just $4,000 over a 30-year period at 10% results in almost two-thirds of a million dollars ($657,979.09). By contrast, just setting aside $4,000 a year for 30 years without compounding interest would result in only $120,000, or about one-fifth of the money...which is quite a difference! It's clear that starting a tax-deferred savings account is a major step toward financial security.

Figure 21: Example of Compounded Interest of $4,000 Annually for 30 Years at 10%.

Assumptions:	
401(k) Annual Savings	$4,000.00
Gross Rate of Return	10.00%
Tax Rate	0.00%
Net Rate of Return	10.00%
Years of Growth	30
Value	**$657,976.09**

		Taxes 0.00%
	3.00%	$190,301.66
	5.00%	$265,755.39
Gross	**7.00%**	$377,843.15
Rate of	**10.00%**	$657,976.09
Return	**12.00%**	$965,330.74
	15.00%	$1,738,980.59

As you look at the chart, you can see the debilitating effect of taxes over time! If your $4,000 earned 7% for 30 years, you can see that your gross rate of return would diminish by over $100,000 between the extremes of the 10% tax rate and the 40% tax rate ($333, 441.09 - $231,983.74 = a difference of $101,457.35.) Clearly, taxes can deplete your savings potential, which is why saving tax-deferred money in a 401(k) is such an incredible benefit for you.

Figure 22: $4,000 Annual Deposits for 30 Years at Various Returns and Taxes.

		$4,000 annual deposits for 30 Years at Various Returns & Taxes				
				Tax Rate		
		10.00%	20.00%	25.00%	30.00%	40.00%
	3.00%	$181,317.04	$172,839.33	$168,781.06	$164,838.33	$157,285.68
	5.00%	$244,028.28	$224,339.75	$215,196.95	$206,490.71	$190,301.66
Gross	7.00%	$333,441.09	$294,831.44	$277,451.51	$261,236.61	$231,983.74
Rate of	10.00%	$545,230.15	$453,132.84	$413,597.61	$377,843.15	$316,232.74
Return	12.00%	$766,172.85	$610,119.87	$545,230.15	$487,757.29	$391,715.77
	15.00%	$1,293,499.01	$965,330.74	$835,223.67	$723,525.98	$545,230.15

In the next chart, you can see that $10,000 will grow more than 2½ times its size, to $25,937.42, with a 10% net rate of return and no taxation over a 10-year period.

Figure 23: Value of $10,000 in 10 Years at Various Returns & Taxes

Assumptions:	
Present Value	$10,000.00
Gross Rate of Return	10.00%
Tax Rate	0.00%
Net Rate of Return	10.00%
Years of Growth	10
Value	$25,937.42

Here is a chart that shows the effect of several gross rates of return on $10,000 over a 10-year period with no taxation.

Figure 24: Gross Rates of Return of $10,000 in 10 Years with No Taxes.

		Taxes
		0.00%
	3.00%	$13,439.16
	5.00%	$16,288.95
Gross	7.00%	$19,671.51
Rate of	10.00%	$25,937.42
Return	12.00%	$31,058.48
	15.00%	$40,455.58

In this final chart, you can see the effect of taxes on $10,000 at various gross rates of return and varying taxation rates:

Figure 25: Value of $10,000 in 10 Years at Various Rates and Taxes.

		Value of $10,000 in 10 Years at Various Returns & Taxes				
		Tax Rate				
		10.00%	20.00%	25.00%	30.00%	40.00%
	3.00%	$13,052.82	$12,676.51	$12,492.03	$12,309.98	$11,953.02
	5.00%	$15,529.69	$14,802.44	$14,450.44	$14,105.99	$13,439.16
Gross	7.00%	$18,421.82	$17,244.05	$16,680.96	$16,134.48	$15,089.58
Rate of	10.00%	$23,673.64	$21,589.25	$20,610.32	$19,671.51	$17,908.48
Return	12.00%	$27,886.73	$25,009.53	$23,673.64	$22,402.31	$20,042.31
	15.00%	$35,477.96	$31,058.48	$29,040.24	$27,140.81	$23,673.64

Again, the impact of taxes seriously effects the potential of your retirement earnings, so being able to save pretax dollars whose earnings remain tax-deferred until you withdraw them during your non-working retirement years is a significant financial benefit for your future security.

Of course, you can also choose not to pay attention to what's happening in your 401(k) account, and if you do so, you'll probably have less success than if you became educated about what it can do for you. As we said earlier, you can park the money and let it ride, and it will increase or decrease based on the limits of the choices you made. However, you can also take an active interest, educate yourself about the various options your plan offers, and ride this pony at a gallop instead of a trot. Just because you have a company 401(k) does not mean your funds will perform well; the opportunity to do well does exist, but only if you're aware of the choices available to you in your company's plan.

There is something that we've sort of said, or maybe implied, so here's a good place to be very clear: Yes, when you decide to join your company's 401(k), monies will be deducted from your paycheck, and you'll have less each month now because the amount of your contribution will diminish your take-home pay. For this reason, think carefully about how big your regular paycheck contribution should be. Weigh both sides of the ledger; how much less can you live on now, so you have more to live on later? Remember our earlier discussion about cutting back on unnecessary expenses, because you may be surprised that with a bit of thoughtful adjustment, you can enhance your future lifestyle.

Most of us are going to live in the future. What kind of future do you envision?

Common Elements of 401(k)s

The 401(k) Plan and Summary Plan Description: The first thing to know about your company's 401(k) is the plan document. Every 401(k) has to have one, and it's loaded with a lot of information. This is also why every 401(k) plan has a summary plan description (SPD), because this way all the features of your company's 401(k) are presented clearly and in one place. Some of the details you'll find in the SPD identify who is eligible to be in the plan, the benefits of being in the plan, the available investment funds from which you can choose, etc. It's also required by the IRS that employers regularly update the SPD, especially when there are major changes to a plan, which are called "material" changes. When you inquire to acquire your company's SPD, find out if it's current or if there have recently been material changes; if so, find out when the newest version of the SPD will be available and be sure to circle back and get a fresh copy, and read it.

The Fiduciaries: Your company's 401(k) plan may have five key people called fiduciaries who manage the plan on behalf of the company and the employees. A fiduciary, in this case, is a person who is responsible for making decisions about the 401(k) plan.

Definition:

Fiduciary: A fiduciary of a 401(k) plan is a person who is legally responsible for the plan's assets, and acts on behalf of other people's financial interests.

Here is a brief introduction to the fiduciaries of your company's 401(k) plan. Remember, there may not be five fiduciaries; there may be less depending on how your company's plan has been set up. Even so, here are the roles being filled.

First is the plan sponsor; this is the company owner who is choosing to sponsor the plan at your company because of the benefits he or she foresees will occur.

Next is the plan trustee; this is the person or investment company entrusted to safeguard the funds in your 401(k) retirement account.

The third fiduciary is the plan administrator; this is the person in the company's business office who manages the plan by making sure the rules are being followed.

Then there's the record keeper, which is the person or company that keeps track of the flow of money in and out of your retirement account, and issues you a performance report, usually every quarter.

The fifth fiduciary may be the investment advisor. This is the person available to advise you on ways to improve the investment safety of your funds, and increase the speed of your account's growth.

Each of these fiduciaries is important in their own way, but perhaps the fiduciary with whom you should spend the most time is the investment advisor. You will see the value of the financial advisor in Linda Nelson's case study in Chapter 5, and will have the chance in Chapter 6 to more completely understand how your own personal financial advisor can help you.

Eligibility: You can't participate in the company 401(k) if you're not eligible, so you need to find out how your plan defines eligibility. It used to be common that employers restricted employees from becoming plan participants until they were 21 years old, or until an employee had worked for the company for at least one year, and sometimes both. These days, however, most 401(k) plans do not have any restrictions on the waiting period or the employee's age, although eligibility requirements may be restrictive for employees who only work part-time. Also, sometimes the plan might state you are eligible right away and can begin contributing to your account, but the company's matching contributions may be delayed for six months or a year; this is because the company may choose to reward employee loyalty, and not provide the benefits of the plan to employees who come and go too soon.

Actually, you may be immediately enrolled because automatic enrollment has become a popular feature in 401(k) plans. Some automatic enrollment requirements state that you must be enrolled within 45 days of your hiring, that your paycheck will be deducted by a certain percent for your contribution, and may even determine which investments will hold your funds. Of course, you have the option to adjust these terms, and may withdraw from the 401(k) if you filed the paperwork, but your best choice might be to go with it or modify the terms slightly, especially if your employer is matching your contributions. In any case, find out what the eligibility rules are, and if you are eligible and not automatically enrolled, seriously consider enrolling.

Contribution Rate: For a 401(k), this is the amount you agree to contribute into your account every pay period. These funds are deducted based on your pay period's gross, and the value for you is that you have not yet paid taxes on this sum. For example, if your monthly gross is $3,000 and you have selected a 10% contribution rate, that means $300 in pretax money will be transferred into your 401(k) account every pay period, leaving you with $2,700 which is taxable.

Key:

How much money can you afford to contribute from your paycheck every month? This is a critical question. On the one hand, you want to have as much money available every month for your bills, or for the activities you enjoy. On the other hand, you want to take advantage of your 401(k) plan as much as possible so you have a comfortable retirement.

This might be a good time to hire a financial advisor to help you figure out your long-term goals and calculate how much money you can contribute every month in pretax dollars (tax deferred dollars) to your 401(k) plan, especially if your employer is offering matching funds.

This is much better than if you were contributing after-tax dollars. Assuming you are in a 25% tax bracket, that $300 would diminish to $225. It's obvious that pretax dollars have much more value to you than after-tax dollars. Thankfully, the U. S. government is willing to reduce its tax dollars so you can keep more funds for yourself in retirement. It would only be decent of you to take advantage of this!

On this subject, you need to know there is an annual limit to how much you can contribute to your 401(k) account. This annual limit changes from year to year because of inflation. You should also know that you may be able to contribute additional after-tax dollars as well. Employees who are older than 50 can contribute as much as another $6,000 annually. Check with your plan administrator to learn the current year's allowable contribution.

You can see how important it is to know what the rules are for your company's 401(k) plan...and how you can benefit the most from it.

Company Match: The company match is the amount of money your employer contributes to your 401(k) account. As mentioned above, the company match may not begin right away, and there are some 401(k) plans that do not provide any company match. However, over 80% of all 401(k) plans do have some degree of employer contribution. The most typical match is 50% up to 3% of the employee's annual salary, or $.50 for every dollar you contribute up to 3% of your annual salary. Federal regulations determine the limit.

 When you set aside $300 a month, your company would match your contribution with $150, for a total of $450. If this was the case, you would have $5,400 in your retirement account for the year; $3,600 is your own pretax contribution, and $1,800 is free money contributed by your company. Not bad, huh? Of course, the calculations for your company and your account depend on your own personal circumstances, but now you can see how compelling this feature is and how much you stand to gain.

Also, most plans allow you to adjust your paycheck contribution either daily, monthly, or quarterly. Again, it's a matter of knowing what the rules are. You can typically make these changes through an automated system using your computer or phone, or by visiting the front office and filing the appropriate papers.

Vesting: Vesting is another issue about which you should be clear. The word "vesting" means having an entitlement, in this case to the money contributed to your 401(k) account by your employer. Some 401(k) plans dictate that any funds contributed by your company will be held for a set period of years, not to exceed six years. For example, your company may have a three-year graded plan, which means that for every year you stay with the company, you are entitled to one third of the company's contribution to your account. At the end of three years, you are entitled to 100% of the company's contribution. This is one method your company may use to retain its employees, at least through the vesting period. The company knows you're less likely to leave when your retirement account will retain the funds contributed by the company only after a set period of years. By the way, the money you have contributed from your paychecks is always your money; vesting only refers to the company's contribution to your account.

Please look at Figure 26, Matching Contribution Vesting Table. You can see that with a company match at 50%, the total annual contribution is $6,000. The employee is contributing $4,000 and the company is matching at 50%, resulting in an additional $2,000 for the employee's retirement plan. The extra $2.000 provided by the company match is a very powerful addition to this employee's 401(k) savings.

Figure 26: Matching Contribution Vesting Table.

Assumptions:	
Wages (Net of Payroll Tax)	$50,000
401K Contribution %	8.00%
Company Match	50.00%
With Company Match	
401(k) Annual Savings	$4,000.00
Company Match	$2,000.00
Total Contribution	**$6,000.00**

These are some of the more common features of 401(k)s. In the next part of this book, we'll consider what happens if you need to borrow from your 401(k) account, or if you decide to withdraw completely.

Borrowing

Most 401(k) plans allow employees the option of borrowing from their 401(k) account. We all know that sometimes serious events can occur which require the need for extra cash. Most Americans are so poor at saving, they seldom have any reserve they can use, so naturally they turn to their investment accounts, but sometimes they only have the funds they've been setting aside for retirement. It's terrible to be in this position because borrowing from your 401(k) will be painful. When you borrow, it means you intend to repay, and repaying your retirement fund means using after-tax dollars to restore your account, so it's more expensive! This means you'll borrow the money for whatever desperate purpose you have, then repay your loan using after-tax dollars, and then later when you're in retirement, you'll pay taxes again on the amounts that you withdrew. This is double taxation on the amount that you borrowed, but if this is your only choice, you'll have to bite the bullet.

 Important:

Do not erode your future financial security. When you borrow from your account, you are depleting your investment of time, creating monetary penalties you'll have to pay, and missing out on your employer's matching dollars.

When you put money in your 401(k) account, you should do everything possible not to touch the money until you retire.

The process for borrowing from your 401(k) account is that you'll first have to complete a promissory note stating your pledge to repay the loan. The promissory note records the loan amount, the interest rate, and the length of the loan's term.

Loan Amount: You are allowed to borrow up to only half of your retirement account's balance, and the law says you may not borrow more than $50,000. It's likely that your company's 401(k) will limit you to only one loan at a time, and usually the minimum amount you can borrow is $1,000. You will probably also not be allowed to borrow any of the money contributed by the company unless you are 100% vested.

Interest Rate: The interest rate most often used is the prime rate plus 1%. The prime rate is the lowest rate of interest banks are allowed to loan commercially; this rate fluctuates based on economic influences. If the prime rate is 6%, then your loan rate will be 7%. This rate stays the same for the entire time your loan is unpaid.

Term of Loan: Your loan's term is capped at five years, though you may decide to pay back the loan faster; your promissory note will record your selected term. In some instances you may be able to have a second loan from your 401(k) account, but usually this loan is restricted for use only in purchasing a primary residence. A residential loan can have a term of 10 to 20 years. The promissory note will allow you to pay back the loan faster than the full term, but you may not be allowed to pay it back faster by increasing your periodic principal payments; that's because doing so may create administrative problems. You may have to pay back the loan faster using larger sums. Be sure to look into this before you sign the promissory note.

Grace Period: Should your financial woes continue and you can't repay your loan by the deadline, there is a 90-day IRS grace period. You may not have this option available to you, and your administrator may say no; it depends on what your company's plan allows.

Hardship Loans: Your company's plan may allow you to borrow from your 401(k) account for hardship, and the nature of a hardship will be defined by the plan. Some of the more common hardship loans are for paying education expenses for yourself or members of your family; to retain your home if you are threatened with eviction; to purchase your primary residence; and to pay medical expenses. You may also want to pay back the debt on your credit cards if the total is exorbitant and you're being crushed by the interest rate, though this may not be included in your company's plan as a hardship. As an alternative, if you own your own home, you might consider refinancing your mortgage or taking out a second mortgage.

Loan Fee: And then there's the matter of the loan fee. We said this wasn't going to be easy. And neither should it be, because these funds are intended for your use during your retirement years. Still, life sometimes has some dark surprises and you may have no other recourse. The loan fee isn't very large, thank goodness. You can expect to pay a setup fee, and an annual administration fee. The total should be no more than $200. Given these potential amounts, your loan fee for a five-year period might be somewhere around $300.

Remembering our earlier calculation about how money doubles every seven years at 10%, this $300 could actually represent almost $5,000 in 28 years...money you'll never be able to spend.

And then you'll also be paying back your loan with after-tax dollars... and being taxed again on the monies you borrowed when you withdraw them once more during your retirement. The lesson here is that you should never take out a loan from your 401(k) unless you have no other choice. The penalty is too severe.

Withdrawing

Instead of a loan, you can withdraw some or all of your funds and sacrifice these retirement monies. There will be a penalty if you are under 59 ½ years of age because these funds were set aside as pretax dollars. You are legally allowed to withdraw your funds for four reasons:

Hardship: A withdrawal for hardship can be allowed for several reasons, one of which is an urgent and serious financial need. Most plans restrict the nature of the hardship, which can include the purchase of a primary residence, or the repair of that residence if damaged by a serious event. Your company's plan may also allow a hardship withdrawal for imminent eviction or foreclosure, expensive medical bills, certain types of funeral expenses and education expenses, paying your income tax, and paying the penalties that are due on your having withdrawn the monies for a hardship in the first place.

A hardship withdrawal may not be available until you've consumed all other options offered by your company such as depleting the funds in other company retirement plans you may have. Many 401(k) plans also restrict your participation for six months after you've withdrawn your funds, which means you'll miss out on your employer's contributions during that time.

In addition you will also have to go through the loan process before you can withdraw any money for hardship, and you will pay a 10% penalty for early withdrawal, plus federal and state income taxes on the withdrawn funds. Not a pretty picture!

Age 59 ½: Hooray! You've made it past the early retirement penalty age! You are now entitled to withdraw funds, though you should think twice about emptying out your pot of gold a little too soon. Your employer is required by the IRS to withhold 20% of the amount you withdraw and hold that money until tax time...but at least now you no longer have to worry about the 10% penalty.

In-Service: This is also available only if your company's plan allows it. The idea is that since you are still in service to your company, you could be allowed to withdraw the funds for a non-hardship reason, but this type of withdrawal might result in a tax liability and if you're under the age of 59 ½, you may also be required to pay a 10% early withdrawal penalty. Be sure to check and double check with your company's 401(k) administrator.

After-Tax: You're company's 401(k) plan may allow you to contribute after-tax dollars to your account, as well as your pretax contributions. Consider carefully if this is a good option for you, because once your money is in your 401(k) retirement account, there are a lot of limitations placed on accessing these funds, as you now know.

Limits on Contributions

There are annual limits on contributions to your 401(k). The government is happy to help you increase your retirement fund, but they also don't want you to sock away everything and leave them without the taxes they need. The annual limitations on your contributions are identified in IRS Code section 415. In 2014, your contribution was limited to $17,500. If you are over 50 years old, you can throw in an extra $5,500. As for the combined contribution from both you and your employer, in 2014 the limit was the lesser of 100%

of your salary or $51,000 plus $5,500 if you are over 50 years old. This dollar amount is on all contributions, pretax and after-tax, made by you and your employer, into all defined contribution plans. And, you can still contribute to IRAs once you've reached your maximum 401(k) contributions for the year.

Note:

There is an annual limit on how much money you can contribute to your 401(k). In 2013, the limit was $17,500. If you are over 50 years old, you can contribute a little bit more. Check with your company's financial advisor to find out what the current year's contribution limit is.

Investment Options

Once your money is in your 401(k) account, these funds must be distributed into investments that will hopefully grow over time. The most popular type of investment in 401(k)s are mutual funds because people are familiar with them and they spread out the risk. Many books have been written about investing money, and in this book we can only provide a general overview, but here are some of the key elements you should know about investment options.

Keeping it simple, there are stocks, bonds, and cash investments. When you purchase stock in a company, you are purchasing a piece of that company's value. A bond is different, because you are purchasing that company's debt so they can raise money to advance their company. A cash investment is also known as a money market fund, and this means your investment remains in cash that's based on short-term government bills and bonds, and adjusts slightly depending upon the fluctuating value of cash.

There is also an investment called an exchange-traded fund (ETF). An exchange-traded fund (ETF) is an investment that typically has an objective of striving to match the return of a particular market index or basket of securities, similar to a traditional index fund. The ETF will invest in either all or a representative sample of the securities included in the index it is seeking to track. An index mutual fund is a fund that tracks a particular index and attempts to match its returns.

In the table on the following page, a reference is made to passive investing and active investing. Passive investing is when an investor purchases an investment that represents the market index; by doing so, the investor attempts to match the market's performance, not exceed the market's performance. Active investing is when the investor tries to obtain better results than the market by actively selecting the stocks the investor thinks will outperform the market.

In the subsequent table "Pros and Cons of ETFs", a reference is made to cash-drag. Cash-drag is when a portfolio's cash slows down the portfolio's performance. This usually happens when the market is doing well; the cash in the portfolio is earning less than the other elements of the portfolio.

Figure 27: Exchange Traded Funds and Mutual Funds.

Comparing ETFs with Index Funds and Mutual Funds

	ETFs	Index Mutual Funds	Mutual Funds (actively managed)
Ownership	▸ Purchased on the exchange	▸ Purchased directly from the fund	▸ Purchased directly from the fund
Management Style	▸ Typically passively managed; some are actively managed	▸ Passively managed	▸ Actively managed
Pricing	▸ Traded throughout the trading day ▸ Limit orders, short selling, margin buying and options trading available	▸ NAV once per day after market close ▸ May require a minimum initial investment	▸ NAV once per day after market close ▸ May require a minimum initial investment
Cost	▸ Ongoing management fees ▸ Brokerage and trading costs	▸ Ongoing management fees ▸ Possible sales charges and redemption fees	▸ Ongoing management fees ▸ Possible sales charges and redemption fees
Transparency	▸ Underlying holdings disclosed daily	▸ Holdings generally disclosed monthly or quarterly	▸ Holdings generally disclosed monthly or quarterly
Taxes	▸ Fund shareholders generally not affected by tax liabilities related to the redemptions of other shareholders	▸ Fund shareholders face tax consequences related to the redemptions of other shareholders	▸ Fund shareholders face tax consequences related to the redemptions of other shareholders

Comparing ETFs and Stocks

	ETFs	Stocks
Ownership	▸ Ownership of ETF shares; no ownership of the underlying securities	▸ Partial ownership of an individual company
Trading	▸ Traded throughout the trading day ▸ Limit orders, short selling, margin buying and options trading available	▸ Traded throughout the trading day ▸ Limit orders, short selling, margin buying and options trading available
Liquidity	▸ Number of shares available flexible	▸ Limited number of shares available
Diversification	▸ Diversification within broad markets or sectors	▸ No diversification

Pros and Cons of ETFs

Pros	Cons
▸ Tool for implementing asset allocation strategies	▸ Brokerage costs may vary
▸ Passive diversification	▸ Liquidity varies across funds
▸ Transparency of price	▸ Relatively new with limited track record
▸ Tax efficiency	▸ Limited selection in certain categories
▸ Potential cost advantages	
▸ Protection against cash drag	

Remember, your investments can increase or decline, so your account will also increase or decline depending upon the performance of the investments you've made.

Mutual funds can be a combination of several companies' stocks, or several companies' bonds. Some mutual funds are a combination of stocks and bonds. Mutual funds are quite popular because investors are not picking just one company and risking their entire "bet" on the performance of this single investment. By investing in a mutual fund composed of several companies' stocks or bonds, the weak performance of a single company in the group could be offset by the more productive performance of another.

Mutual funds are also usually grouped by whether they are small companies, medium-size companies, or large companies, and known as small cap, midcap, and large cap companies. There are also mutual funds that are classified by types of assets such as growth, blend, value, domestic, international, etc. In addition, mutual funds may be grouped by the type of industry they're in, such as the technology sector, or the health sector, or the "green" sector, etc. Actually, there are thousands of mutual funds worldwide from which to choose! Of course, your 401(k) plan will not have this many choices for you, but will be limited to a select number that your plan sponsor has approved for your company's plan. If your company's plan is a good one, your investment options will provide you with a sufficiently wide range of opportunity to grow the funds in your account.

There is a strong degree of risk in all investments, and there are no guarantees, so seeking the advice of an investment professional is very wise and could be the best choice for you. Not every investment professional is as experienced or capable as you might like, and selecting an investment advisor who can customize your portfolio to effectively and efficiently reach your financial goals is a key factor to the success you hope to enjoy during retirement. We'll look more closely at this in Chapter 6, Working with My Personal Investment Advisor.

Rollovers

You may already know what a rollover is, but just in case, a rollover is when you transfer funds from one tax-free retirement plan to another, such as moving your 401(k) funds into an IRA, or your IRA funds into a 401(k) plan, etc. In essence, you are "rolling it" from one retirement program into qualified plan another.

The figure below shows which retirement plan rollovers are available.

Figure 28: 401(k) Rollover Matrix.

401(k) Rollover Matrix		401(k)	403(b)	457(b)	IRA	SEP IRA	SIMPLE IRA	Roth IRA	Designated Roth Account	Qualified Plan
						Going To				
Roll From	401(k)	Yes	Yes	Yes	Yes	Yes	No	Yes	Yes	Yes
	403(b)	Yes	Yes	Yes	Yes	Yes	No	Yes	Yes	Yes
	457(b)	Yes	Yes	Yes	Yes	Yes	No	Yes	Yes	Yes
	IRA	Yes	Yes	Yes	Yes	Yes	No	Yes	No	Yes
	SEP IRA	Yes	Yes	Yes	Yes	Yes	No	Yes	No	Yes
	SIMPLE IRA	Yes	Yes	Yes	Yes	Yes	Yes	Yes	No	No
	Roth IRA	No	No	No	No	No	No	Yes	No	Yes
	Designated Roth Account	No	No	No	No	No	No	Yes	Yes	Yes
	Qualified Plan	Yes	Yes	Yes	Yes	Yes	No	Yes	Yes	Yes

When you do a rollover correctly, your money will be safely stashed in the new plan and you will have no taxes or penalties. If you do it wrong, you may wind up paying some tax, and a penalty, and also lose the opportunity for this money to grow tax-free. Not a good idea. The key is knowing what the rules are and then following them closely.

Moving your money from one plan to another can be simple; the rules are generally very clear and you can always seek professional help. Where it gets tricky is that sometimes there are a number of choices to make; we'll look at those choices now.

There are only a few good reasons why you might consider rolling over your 401(k). You may have left your original employer and now you want to move your 401(k) funds over to your new employer's 401(k) plan.

Should you choose to rollover your 401(k) funds, there are only two rollover options:

1. Regular rollover: This type of rollover means the trustee of your funds will send you a check for the amount being rolled over, but 20% of these funds will be withheld to make sure the other 80% is deposited properly in a tax-advantaged retirement plan. You'll have 60 days to transfer the money, and only under rare circumstances will you be allowed to take more than 60 days. If you don't get the money transferred within the 60 days, you will also be assessed a 10% penalty if you are not yet 59 ½ years old. As for the 20% that was withheld, the money will be unavailable to you until after you file your annual income taxes...which means you've just helped the U.S. government by providing an interest-free loan!

2. Direct rollover: We think this is the smarter choice. With a direct rollover, also known as a "trustee-to-trustee" transfer, you will not receive a check payable to you, and the funds are transferred directly from your existing account to the new account with no danger of temptation, taxation, or penalization! It's possible you might be given a check which you are to give to your fund's new trustee, but in this

case you are simply the errand boy; you will not be able to cash the check.

When authorizing your funds for a direct rollover, the administrator of your company's 401(k) plan will provide you with a form which identifies how much money you want to transfer and where it's going. Once the form is processed, the funds follow relatively soon, usually in no more than about two weeks and possibly faster.

Some dollars cannot rollover. If you've borrowed money from your 401(k) account and these monies have not been paid back, they will be a "deemed distribution", meaning this money will be regarded as a payment to you. As you know, that means the money now becomes taxable, will not be available for continued tax-free growth, and there may be a 10% penalty as well.

Leaving Your Employer: If the balance in your account is more than $1,000 but less than $5,000 and you don't direct the plan administrator, your employer must either leave the money in your account, or could rollover the funds into an IRA of your employer's choosing, in your name. If your balance is under $1,000 and you don't direct the plan administrator, the funds will probably be cashed out and distributed to you. Your company's plan will dictate what happens.

Rollover Destinations: Most 401(k) plans allow you to rollover the funds in your former employer's 401(k) plan to the new 401(k) plan. Be sure to check eligibility requirements because you don't want to get into a hassle by authorizing a trustee-to-trustee transfer prematurely. If your new employer's 401(k) plan is not attractive to you, you can always rollover into an IRA, but be sure to take a close look at other strategies that might be more lucrative for you. One of the key lessons of this book is that "you don't know what you don't know". It is the wise person who consults with an investment and tax professional before taking any action, to make sure the options are clear and the best choice can be made. There are many stories of people who thought they knew what they were doing and have rolled over their funds into an account that was less advantageous for them, resulting in paying more taxes than they would otherwise have had to pay.

<u>Leave the Funds with Your Employer</u>: About one third of all 401(k) plan participants who leave their employers also leave their 401(k) funds with their former employer. Of course, you'll be unable to make new contributions to this particular account, and you won't be able to borrow from it after you go, but your funds and all the investment earnings will continue to be sheltered from taxes.

Again, it's important that you consider the different options that may be available to you. On the one hand, if you're not sure what to do, or your new employer is a start-up company that may not last the test of time, or you prefer the investment choices you have with your former employer, or you have an outstanding loan on your 401(k) and your previous employer's plan allows you to continue making repayments, then you may have good reason to leave the funds where they are, at least for the present. On the other hand, you may decide to rollover your funds because the new employer's 401(k) plan has better investment options, or you want to consolidate your investments under one roof, or your former employer is changing some of your old plan's features. Careful consideration combined with a professional's advice is always the best way to go.

How Safe Is My Money?

The danger is not in criminal activity that assaults your funds and robs you of your money. There are very stringent protocols on how the money transfers from your paycheck into your 401(k) account, and anyone who is discovered tampering with your funds will probably wind up going to jail. However, there are several areas where your 401(k) funds are vulnerable:

1. <u>Divorce</u>: In a divorce, your soon-to-be ex-spouse could request that the court assign part or all of your 401(k) funds to assist with the need

for alimony and child support, plus anything else the court would regard as legally permissible.

2. <u>The IRS</u>: There is no stopping the IRS if you owe the government tax money. Gov-zilla will get your money, one way or the other.

3. <u>The Biggest Risk</u>: The biggest risk to the money in your 401(k) account is you. It's the investment decisions that you make about how to allocate your money within the investment choices available through your employer's plan. In most cases, your company's 401(k) plan probably has about 30 or 40 different choices you can make. The real question is how educated are you in knowing the difference between these investment choices? How much time do you spend reading about and studying the history and the projected growth of these investments? What do you know about the different industry sectors? What cycle is the economy in these days? How much have you read about diversifying your investment funds, and do you know which percentage allocations are the best choice for you, given your current age and your financial situation? Have you bothered to attend the quarterly or annual company meetings with the plan's investment advisor to learn how you might increase your fund's performance? For most people, it's evident they would seriously benefit from the services of an investment professional. Unless you've spent a lot of time reading, learning, and practicing financial investment, you're likely to be too inexperienced to make the best choices.

 Important:
The biggest risk to the money in your 401(k) account is...YOU.

If you're too inexperienced to make the best choices, you really shouldn't make them at all. Would you ask a ballerina to tune your car engine? Would you ask a car mechanic to do a jeté? Well, you might, and maybe they could, but you see the point. Why would you want to risk your money and years of investment potential on making important decisions that could affect several decades of your life... without having the experience to do it right? This is a topic with serious implications, and that's why we've dedicated an entire chapter, Chapter 6, Working with My Personal Investment Advisor, for your consideration and lifelong benefit.

Watch Out for These Signs: Even though we've said that criminal activity may be the least of your worries, it is to your advantage to know some telltale signs. If you're not receiving a periodic statement that shows the contributions being made to your account; if the statement is too far behind in reporting these contributions; if you've requested but never received your company's summary plan description (SPD); if you notice the investments in your account do not match with the investments you've made; there's a big drop in your account's balance; your account is always being corrected for errors...these can be indicators that your funds may be in jeopardy. If you suspect there may be trouble, you should seek the advice of an attorney. You'll be able to speak to a representative, who is a government official, authorized to listen to your concerns and provide guidance.

Summary

This chapter introduced you to the common features of a 401(k). You now know that a 401(k) can be a very strong advantage for your retirement portfolio because in most cases your employer is matching your contribution, joining you in funding your retirement. We've reviewed the key points of borrowing from your 401(k), withdrawing funds, briefly reviewed investment options, considered the details of rollovers, and repeated our point that your money is only as safe as your ability to invest wisely. The next chapter will show you a very strong model for developing your retirement plan.

Chapter 2 Review Questions:

1. In a 401(k) plan, the employer is required to make a dollar for dollar match.

   A. True

   B. False

2. The employee decides how his or her 401(k) dollars are invested from among the fund choices in the plan.

   A. True

   B. False

3. The summary plan description (SPD) explains all the features of a company's 401(k) plan.

   A. True

   B. False

4. A fiduciary is a person with legal responsibility for the 401(k) plan.

   A. True

   B. False

5. It's usually okay to borrow from your 401(k) account.

   A. True

   B. False

6. The IRS has placed an annual limit on the amount of money an employee can contribute to their 401(k).

   A. True

   B. False

7. All investments have risk.

   A. True

   B. False

8. If my company's 401(k) plan allows it, an employee could choose to rollover his or her IRAs into the company's 401(k) account.

   A. True

   B. False

9. If an employee leaves the company, they can leave their 401(k) funds with their former employer, and the funds and all the investment earnings will continue to be sheltered from taxes.

   A. True

   B. False

Answers

1. Answer: B. The employer can choose how much to match. It could be dollar for dollar, or it could be ten cents per dollar... or no match at all. The employer typically decides how much to match based on the economics of the company and how much the company will save in taxes. Providing a powerful benefit to the employees is also part of the decision.

2. Answer: A. Each employee can choose the fund or funds for their 401(k) contributions from those that are available in the plan. An important part of this decision is knowing your investment goals and your tolerance for risk. Be sure to read the information on the Required Rate of Return (RRR) in Chapter 4.

3. Answer: A. The SPD contains all the important information about your company's plan in a condensed form.

4. Answer: A. A fiduciary must always act in the best interests of the clients.

5. Answer: B. Borrowing from a 401(k) account will limit the potential of the account's growth...which limits your retirement funds.

6. Answer: A. The limit is currently $17,500 per year.

7. Answer: A. Even "safe" investments like Treasury bonds have some degree of risk. There is no such thing as a no-risk investment, and every investor should determine their tolerance for risk.

8. Answer: A. It might be a good idea to have your IRA rolled into your 401(k) account where you have the advice and services of a financial advisor.

9. Answer: A. It might be best to leave your investment funds in the 401(k) so you have the advantage of a financial advisor's services.

Chapter 3:
Developing My Retirement Plan

When you have finished reading this chapter, you will:

- Know the three steps of your lifestyle protection plan

- Understand the importance of setting short-term, midterm, and long-term financial goals

- Be familiar with a "financial pyramid", and know how to create one for yourself

- Identify the five taxes that may have an impact on your financial well-being

- Begin thinking about how to assess your risk tolerance

- Know the four legal documents that protect your financial wealth

Having a retirement plan may not be essential to retiring, but it will give you the best chance of having a decent retirement. Do you remember the last vacation you took? One of the things you probably did was pull out a map, and maybe consult the Internet about some of the important details of your trip. Well, just as you wouldn't get into your car and take a 3,000-mile road trip without a map and some idea of where you were going, neither should you assume that the money you'll need in retirement will be there in 10, 20, or 30 years without making some plans now on how you expect to have enough.

Money is quite a magical thing. If you're careful with your money, and save a reasonable amount of it, the time value of steadily adding to your savings will multiply what you have many times over. Yes, you could win the lottery and have millions of dollars to do whatever you please. If that happens, you'll still need to know how to prepare financially for your retirement. The news repeatedly tells the stories of people who had fortunes and then squandered them.

In this chapter we're going to discuss some key elements for building your financial strength, and show you ways you can plan to protect your lifestyle throughout your life and into retirement. Much of what you're about to read is common knowledge, but many people, perhaps you, have not considered the tools and information that follows; too often, financial education has not been available through our parents or schools. Even if you are familiar with the following material, we believe you'll discover some new gems to consider that may make a big difference in the way you can prepare now for improving your relationship with money and providing what you'll need later in life.

The three steps of your lifestyle protection planning:
We offer three steps for you to consider in designing a plan which will serve your current lifestyle, and help you preserve this lifestyle when you reach retirement. The three steps are setting short-term, midterm, and long-term financial goals; understanding your financial pyramid and developing it; and then setting a pattern of allocating resources toward your goals that results in your financial success.

Set Your Goals

Very rarely can significant gains be realized without first setting goals. There are shelves and shelves of books on this topic because the value of doing so is so clearly recognized. We're not going to spend any time talking about their importance, and will assume that you already realize their worth. Instead, we're going to jump right into discussing the three types of financial goals.

Note:
Here is a clear explanation of the kinds of goals you can set for your financial well-being.

Short-term goals: Short-term financial goals are important because life sometimes presents unexpected surprises. Having a few thousand dollars set aside and easily available for an emergency is a smart thing to do. Having some handy cash will limit the headaches and stress you may already be suffering during a period of uncertainty.

In case there is a medical emergency or the sudden need to see the dentist...or perhaps something happened to your home like the refrigerator giving out, or there is flooding in the basement...or maybe all of a sudden your car has to go into the shop...these are all circumstances that are difficult to handle if you don't have a rainy day fund designed for an unexpected emergency. When a difficult situation appears, you can't keep it on the back burner; the situation needs to be resolved right away, so having some money set aside will protect you from having to use a credit card and incurring outrageous interest, or having to ask a relative or friend to bail you out. You need an emergency fund for life's stressful moments, which are bound to happen!

The first thing to do is to figure out how much money to set aside in your emergency fund. Start by making a list of the potential costs that might suddenly appear. You probably have insurance for your car, but you might have to have enough money set aside to cover your deductible, so find out what that dollar amount is and calculate it into the total. You also probably have medical insurance, but there might be an annual deductible that first has to be paid; determine what that amount is and add that into the total. What does it cost when your child needs to see the dentist? Make a guesstimate and add that to the total. If you own your own home, think about which appliances might suddenly need to be repaired or replaced; maybe it's the lawnmower, or an aging tree might need to be taken down; consider the cost and add that into your total.

You should also think about setting aside six months of income so just in case you or your spouse/partner should lose their job, or their work hours are cut back, you have the resources to get through the hard times until a new source of income can be established. If you haven't done so already, you should create a monthly budget and write down all the expenses you typically have every month such as mortgage or rent, utilities, food, and transportation. Take a close look at what your monthly expenses are, and then consider which of them are essential and which you could cut back if your income was reduced. Multiply this dollar number by the six months of cushion you should build, and add it to the total.

 Important:
Short-term goals are for saving money for emergencies, and six months of income in case you lose your job.

Now that you know what your short-term savings goal should be, you should begin setting aside money each month until your short-term goal is reached. These contingency funds should be kept in a safe and stable investment option that provides you immediate access. You can park this money in a savings account at your local bank, but you might also consider saving the money in a money market fund offered by your bank because you may earn a little higher interest than you would in just a savings account.

You can also include such things as paying off a specific debt, or replacing an appliance you know will soon require your attention as an emergency expense.

Short-term goals could also include something fun, like maybe a nice vacation, or a new wardrobe. Once your emergency fund is established, you can then consider other expenditures that allow you to enjoy the spice of life.

If you plan your short-term savings' goals wisely and execute your plan, you will be more capable of overcoming any financial hurdles or emergencies that present themselves, and you may also be able to sleep better at night knowing you have all the immediate bases covered.

Midterm goals: Midterm financial goals are goals you establish for 3 – 5 years down the road. Examples of midterm goals are saving up enough money to replace a car, pay off your debts, or complete coursework for a degree or certificate.

When setting your midterm goals, it's best that you keep your goals realistic and flexible. If your goals are set too high, frustration could keep you from reaching them. It's not that hard to save money for such things as an annual vacation or a new bedroom set, but when the price for more costly things gets higher and the amount of time it takes to get them is pushed further away, it can require real dedication to your purpose in order to remain disciplined and on your savings path.

If one of your midterm goals is to save enough money for a down payment on a home, or you want to set aside the funds you'll need for your daughter's wedding, or you decide to create a savings fund for your child's college education, you'll have to have the discipline to save a certain amount of money every month. A very wise rule that's common knowledge is when you're in a savings program and you receive your paycheck, the first person you pay is yourself. What this means, of course, is that you pay into your savings plan just as if your savings plan is a monthly bill. Like paying your rent, or paying your utilities, you also pay your savings plan every month with a deposit. The reasoning here is that, for most people, saving money is an option, not a requirement. And so, typically, there is never any money to save because the money that could have been used for savings was spent on a variety of miscellaneous temptations and nonessential purchases.

Important:

Midterm goals are for funds you'll need in the next 3-5 years.

This is why it's so important to establish a monthly budget and stay within it. You'll be surprised at how you spend your money monthly when you keep a financial log to record every penny you spend during that month. When the month is over, and you see that you spent $75 at Starbucks, $150 for cell phone service, $25 on birthday and anniversary cards, and $200 on fast food lunches, you'll see that by taming or eliminating certain habits you'll have enough money to achieve an important financial goal if you are deliberate and consistent.

Since midterm goals require a longer time to achieve, and since you won't need this money immediately as you would for an emergency, these funds can be invested differently. You should always check with your financial advisor, a topic which will be discussed further in Chapter 6, but generally speaking, your midterm savings might be placed in a growth mutual fund where your funds are relatively safe and have the opportunity to grow until it's time to use the money.

Long-term goals: Long-term financial goals are goals that may take more than five years to achieve. Substantial long-term goals are such things as saving and investing enough money for a comfortable retirement, and paying off all your debts, including your mortgage. This will be the focus of the next chapter, Chapter 4.

 Important:

Long-term goals are for financial needs that are further than five years away, such as saving for retirement and to pay off your mortgage.

Whether or not you can achieve your financial goals depends on how much you save, how long you save and invest the funds, how much time you have remaining before retirement, and thoughtfully deciding on the kind of lifestyle you want to have in retirement.

One of the best ways to meet important long-term goals is by funding your retirement account with your employer's 401(k). By the way, if your employer does not have a 401(k) plan, consider giving him or her this book and asking them to consider establishing a company 401(k) so the company will save money otherwise spent for taxes, the owner and top executives can increase their retirement savings with pretax dollars, and the company's employees will also benefit with a very powerful retirement savings plan.

On top of that, not only will you have a financial program that builds everybody's retirement account, but also, because everyone's taxable income is also reduced, there will be an additional tax savings there as well.

Something we haven't discussed yet, but which will be coming soon, is that a general rule of thumb for families is they should try to save at least 10% of their monthly gross income for retirement; single people should allocate an even larger percentage of their monthly gross income. That's because, when you're young, even though there are a zillion exciting things to on which to spend your money, the day will come when your priorities will change and you'll want to have a home, maybe raise a family, and prepare for the funds you'll need in the last third of your life.

Evaluate Your Financial Pyramid

A convenient way to look at your financial situation and understand how to plan for your financial future is to consider your finances in the shape of a pyramid, as shown below. As you can see, there are three sections to your financial pyramid.

Figure 29: Personal Financial Pyramid.

Goals		
Short Term	*Mid Term*	*Long Term*
Emergency Fund Prepare Wills & Trust Evaluate Life Insurance Needs	Wealth Accumulation Pay College Expenses Start a Business	Retirement Sell Business Leave an Estate

Taxes

Higher Risk

Play Porfolio

Core Portfolio

Moderate Risk

Mid Term   Long Term

Short

Lower Risk

Risk Tolerance

| Cash Flow
Budget
Daily Living
Needs | Emergency
Fund
4-6 Months
Liquidity | Insurance
Medical &
LTC
Life |

Legal
Documents

The pyramid's base: The base of the pyramid is composed of all the essentials you need for your daily life. All of these items are the necessary costs of basic necessities, with one or two exceptions.

Cash Flow: Cash flow is the money you need for all your living expenses. These are for the items in your monthly budget and to take care of all your daily living needs. This includes such things as the roof over your head, food in the fridge, gas in the car or money for the bus, and utilities.

Add to this some of the extras such as household supplies, clothing, cell phones and entertainment...which might be nonessential, but you allow yourself some of these "splurges". Frankly, a little discretionary spending, if it's contained and sensible, is probably a good thing because it keeps a smile on your face. Too much, however, and the dollars you could be using for more important purposes are being squandered. Remember, every dollar at 10% becomes eight in 21 years, and because of inflation, every dollar today may only buy a third tomorrow of what it buys today.

Emergency Fund: Also in this segment of the pyramid is your emergency fund, discussed a few pages back. If you have an emergency fund from which you can draw when the urgency arises, you won't have to dip into your investments to rescue you.

Key:

Protecting your wealth is as important as creating it. There are different kinds of insurance, and you should meet with a financial advisor who can show you how insurance can protect your finances.

Remember, you don't know what you don't know. Speaking to a professional can mean the difference between always struggling...or having financial protection.

Insurance Planning: This is another important factor because it is effective in protecting your economic health. Unexpected medical attention is partly or completely covered with medical insurance, protecting you and your family from an unwelcome surprise that could consume a great deal of your savings. The same is true for life insurance because in the event of a catastrophe, the life insurance policy will provide your survivors with the funds they'll need to pick up the pieces of their lives.

Some people may not think so, but disability insurance is also an insurance you should consider having as part of your insurance shield. Most people may be eligible for workers' compensation, but it probably won't be a lot of money nor sufficient to handle your monthly costs while you're unable to work. If something were to happen to you that prevents you from working, and you wind up in rehabilitation for six months or a year, you and your family will need sufficient revenue to sustain yourselves until you can return to work. The price of the insurance is a lot less costly than doing without income for a sustained period of time.

Another important insurance to consider is long-term care (LTC) insurance. We all know that sooner or later, unless we die prematurely, as age takes over we're going to need support of a certain kind in our elder years. You've probably seen it happen, or heard about it from others, that long-term care facilities and retirement homes can be very costly and will sometimes consume the elder's entire estate. One way to protect against this debacle is by looking into LTC insurance and purchasing an appropriate policy at an early age. Money is a powerful resource, and having a good idea of what lies ahead enables you to look at the future with steady eyes, steady nerves, and make informed decisions.

These are the elements that compose the base of the pyramid: budgeted cash flow to serve your daily living needs; an emergency fund to whether unexpected events; and several types of insurance to protect you and your family from catastrophe and from the inevitable.

The pyramid's core: The next section of the pyramid is focused on helping you build your wealth and is composed of three types of investment portfolios.

Short-term Investment Portfolios: Investing in a short-term portfolio is best when you are saving money for a short-term need, such as your annual vacation, to replace an aging appliance, or some other short-term need for which you are preparing. Otherwise, short-term investing is generally considered either risky, or a misuse of these funds' potential.

Midterm Investment Portfolios: Similarly, midterm investments are for those expenditures you foresee are 3 – 5 years away. This would include your child's college fund, your daughter's wedding, and perhaps the purchase of a replacement car. Investments of this type should be in conservative funds so you can be reasonably assured the money will be there when you need it.

Long-term Investment Portfolios: Your long-term investments are meant to secure your financial future at the far end of the horizon. The more time you have, the more risk you can absorb. We'll discuss the topic of risk in the next chapter, because it is a very important concept to understand when you are making rational investment choices. Suffice it to say for now, the money you put into your long term investments should remain there so you can benefit from the anticipated increase of your funds over time. Time is an ally, and it can truly make your Golden Years golden.

The pyramid's top: The top of the pyramid is reserved only for higher risk, higher return investments, which are investments that have a magnified element of risk; this means these funds may or may not provide the investment returns you seek, and for that reason they are at the top of the pyramid and are employed only when your basic and core investment needs are well-satisfied.

Taxes: Taxes are a necessary evil no matter where you are in building your pyramid. In some circumstances, such as in your 401(k), your taxes can be deferred until many years later when you withdraw these funds and use them. Even so, tax planning is a top to bottom issue.

There are five taxes that are likely to have an impact on your financial well-being in varying degrees. The first one is your income tax; every year, citizens are required to submit their income tax form and pay the government for the benefits of living and working in the United States. The second tax is a tax that may affect your beneficiaries; should you leave an estate of a certain size, there may be an estate tax. There is also a gift tax; this tax is levied when you have sufficient funds and choose to make a substantial gift to your family members or friends. Then there is a generation transfer skipping tax; this is a tax on property that is transferred in a will or trust from a grandparent to a grandchild or great-grandchild. The fifth tax is the excise tax; these are the sales taxes you normally pay when purchasing goods and services such as gasoline for your car, non-food items for your home, etc.

The point of all this is that you should be aware, as is likely already the case, that taxes and money go together. Therefore, it's important you plan as well as you can to legally limit your taxation. When means are provided so you can save more of your hard-earned money, it is in your own best interests to accept the opportunity! Remember, your retirement may last three decades or longer, and you may need every penny that's available, especially in the final years of your life when you may not be able to work at a job anymore.

A significant gem of wisdom is to conserve your funds and pay less in taxes. This is why it is so important you receive advice from a competent financial professional. And, this is why we ask you to consider working with your own personal investment advisor in Chapter 6.

So, even though taxes are a necessary evil, there may be ways to limit their impact on your financial health and wealth so you have more money for your lifestyle and retirement savings.

Risk tolerance: Risk tolerance means the amount of risk that is acceptable for your investments given your personally unique situation.

When we talk about risk, what we mean is that there are no guarantees when you are investing your money. Every investment carries a certain amount of risk based on the nature of the investment. For example, if you are investing your money in the stock of only one company, your risk is very high; should the company falter, the value of your stock may decline, or if the company goes out of business, you could lose your entire investment. You purchased the stock because you believed the stock would increase in value and thus the money you invested would grow. Yet, your decision could backfire and you would wind up losing all your money. You took the risk, or the chance, that the stock purchase would increase your money. If, however, you had purchased a government bond from the United States government, your investment would be very secure, but there would still be risk that your invested money could decline.

Important:

All investments have risk. Risk can be controlled, and a financial advisor will show you how to invest and increase your money while protecting it.

When we think about tolerance, we are referring to your particular circumstances and your ability and willingness to suffer investment losses through the risks you are taking. As an example, if you are in your 20s and you have four decades before you'll reach retirement, your ability to overcome investment risk is stronger than a person who is two years from retirement and relying on these funds. Risk tolerance is different for everyone, and is based on their individual financial circumstances.

Getting back to the personal financial pyramid on the previous page, you'll notice that risk tolerance is labeled on the right side of the triangle. At the bottom of the pyramid, which is the source of your daily living needs and emergency fund, there is a very low risk tolerance because these are monies that must be close at hand. You need to have these monies available immediately, and cannot tolerate risking these funds.

The core portfolio in the middle of the pyramid, which contains your short-term, midterm, and long-term investment portfolios, can tolerate varying degrees of moderate risk because these portfolios have specific time frames for their use. The amount of moderate risk can only be defined based on a person's unique circumstances, such as how much time they have before they'll need these different accounts.

The top of the pyramid, which consists of your high risk, high reward investment portfolio, is where the highest risk is assigned. Your tolerance for discretionary investing can be considered only after all the other segments of your financial pyramid have been built.

Legal documents: As was noted above when we discussed the value of insurance planning as a way to preserve your financial value, so also can certain legal documents have a major impact with protecting your financial wealth.

Will: Everyone should have a will so there will be no complications with transferring your financial wealth to others. If you don't have a will, your beneficiaries may have to wait an undue period of time to receive your estate's funds, which could be tied up in probate as the court sorts out all the details of your estate.

Power of Attorney: Another important legal document is the power of attorney; this authorizes a person, named by you, to act on your behalf, should you become disabled in some manner that affects your ability to manage your assets. The power of attorney can be revoked at any time, assuming you are legally competent to make decisions. If you become incompetent, the power of attorney terminates.

Durable Power of Attorney: A possibly better legal document is the durable power of attorney; the word "durable" means that the power of attorney remains in effect until officially revoked, despite your incapacity to care for your assets. By having a power of attorney or a durable power of attorney, your financial assets can be managed and protected when you are unable to do so.

Physicians' Directives: Another important feature to your estate planning is communicating your choices about healthcare in the event you become incapable of making your own choices. There are three different directives you should consider: the living will, the durable power of attorney for healthcare, and the health care power of attorney. Conducting some research on the Internet will give you a good starting point for understanding and then incorporating them into your financial planning.

Allocate Resources Toward Your Goals

At the beginning of this chapter, we discussed the importance of setting the three different levels of financial goals. After your goals have been determined, the next step is to analyze your financial house and decide how much money you can save each month, and annually. Once you know how much money you have available to set aside for achieving your financial goals, the next step is to allocate where to place this money.

Because your daily living needs and your emergency fund are primary, the best decision might be to direct your monthly savings into the emergency fund, providing you with the reassurance that you are able to meet unexpected financial burdens.

Or, depending on your circumstances, it could be a good idea to fund each of your short-term, midterm, and long-term goals with a third of the money you can set aside for savings. Once the short-term savings goal has been achieved, it could be a good idea to then allocate your monthly savings amount to your midterm and long-term goals on a 50-50 basis. By doing so, you can meet your midterm goals while the money placed in the long term investment portfolio has additional time to grow.

Once the midterm investment portfolio is completely funded, then 100% of your monthly savings can be allocated to your long-term investment portfolio. Then, once the long-term portfolio goal has been achieved, money can be allocated to your discretionary investment portfolio. The idea is that your savings feed your investments in a priority fashion based on the financial goals you originally set.

Should something unfortunate occur that requires your immediate financial attention, money can be drawn from your emergency fund. If more money is needed, your short-term portfolio can be drained. Then, if still more resources are needed, the midterm portfolio could then be used. The money in your long-term investment portfolio should be the last to go because you want to keep these funds invested as long as possible. In a sense, we are protecting ourselves from ourselves because the long-term investments, most of which are likely to be in your 401(k) or other tax-deferred accounts, will create painful taxes and penalties if you need to dip into those accounts.

By allocating your financial resources according to a plan, your goals can be steadily realized. Equally important, any withdrawals you'd need to make are designed to cause the least disruption to your goals as possible.

Summary

When developing your retirement plan, the first step is setting a series of goals that support your expectations for retirement. Once your goals are set, your personal financial pyramid can be designed to accommodate your daily living needs, which includes a six-month emergency fund; your core portfolio of short-term, midterm, and long-term investments; and eventually provide funding for a high risk discretionary investment portfolio. In addition, you'll want to be aware that every transaction could create a taxable event. We also considered risk and established that everyone has their own unique degree of tolerance that's based on their personal circumstances; furthermore, several necessary insurances and legal documents were mentioned to protect your financial health. Finally, there was also a brief discussion about the rationale used for allocating financial resources to achieve your retirement plan's goals.

Your retirement plan should become an essential feature of regular interest to you throughout the year. No one but you and your family will have more than a passing interest in your retirement preparations, so it's incredibly important that you establish your retirement plan as soon as you can, begin making allocations right away, and seek professional advice at least annually about the progress you're making toward achieving your goals. With some forethought and determination, you can build your retirement account and live comfortably in the last third of your life.

In the next chapter we're going to look at the Big Picture and explain the steps for calculating how much money you're going to need when you retire.

 # Chapter 3 Review Questions:

1. Short-term financial goals focus on having money for the unexpected.

   A. True

   B. False

2. Midterm financial goals are for such things as a down payment on a home, or saving for your child's wedding.

   A. True

   B. False

3. Long-term financial goals focus on saving and investing for a comfortable retirement.

   A. True

   B. False

4. A good rule of thumb for a married couple is to save at least 10% of your monthly gross income for retirement.

   A. True

   B. False

5. Every investment has a certain amount of risk.

    A. True

    B. False

 ## Answers

1. Answer: A. Short-term goals are for protecting yourself with emergency funds, and in case you need six months of income, should you lose your job.

2. Answer: A. Midterm goals are for events that may occur in the next 3 – 5 years, such as buying a car, paying for a wedding, or a child's college expenses.

3. Answer: A. Long-term goals are for such things as saving and investing enough money for a comfortable retirement, and paying off all your debts, including your mortgage.

4. Answer: A. Single people should allocate even more of their gross monthly income while they have the opportunity…before starting a family with all the associated costs of children, a house, etc.

5. Answer: A. The degree of risk depends on the nature of the investment.

Chapter 4:
The Big Picture ... How Much
Do I Need When I Retire?

When you have finished reading this chapter, you will:

- Know how to find out how much money you need when you retire

- Understand the importance of the Required Rate of Return (RRR)

- Realize the value of time when saving money

- Explain the difference between a capital consumption model and a capital conservation model

- Realize the effect of inflation on savings and its erosion of purchasing power

- Value the purpose of rebalancing your portfolio every few years

The burning question, to which everybody wants the answer, is "How much money do I need when I retire?" To answer this question sensibly, there are several variables that need to be defined and understood.

It seems that everybody wants to retire because they look forward to not having to go to work, and instead having the time to do the things that bring personal satisfaction. For some people, it's finally having time to enjoy your hobbies, or your grandchildren, or to take enjoyable trips to different parts of the globe, or maybe just sit out in your backyard and watch the grass grow. Now is a good time to consider what your retirement dreams mean to you, because once you know what you want to do in the last third of your life, besides staying healthy, you can then begin to calculate the true number of dollars you'll need to fund the lifestyle you are now imagining.

Before we get into the details that will show you how a financial plan is designed to accumulate the retirement dollars you'll need, there is a very important concept you need to know because it is likely to change your thinking about how money is created, and subsequently, how your retirement fund planning will be structured.

It's one thing to aimlessly throw your money into various investment accounts, praying you'll get lucky and your investments will grow into a vast fortune, or even half of a vast fortune. This is unrealistic; the dartboard approach is a foolish way to expect that the money you'll need will be available when you want to retire. There is, however, a more mathematical approach which will more precisely provide you with the answer you seek.

The Required Rate of Return (RRR)

This is a gem of information for you, and the essential key to your success. The required rate of return is the cornerstone of your personal financial analysis. Once you understand the value of this idea, and once you know the percentage of return that will achieve your financial goals, the entire map of your journey becomes clear. The required rate of return is vital to understanding the potential of your retirement future. Are you ready? Here we go!

You already know what a "rate of return" is; when you put money in your bank's savings account, you know that if the money sits there for a full year, it will grow by an established percentage rate. The rate could be 2% or 3%; years ago, banks were offering 4% and 5%. Certificates of deposit are another example of financial investments that offer a rate of return. Different rates of return are available depending on the amount of money you put into the CD account, and for the length of time, or term, you select. $1,000 in a 12-month CD will earn a smaller rate of return than $1,000 in a five-year CD. A rate of return is the amount of interest your account is earning based on the amount of money and the term.

Definition:

The Required Rate of Return (RRR): The minimum annual percentage an investment must earn annually to achieve the investment's goal for growth. The RRR is different for different investments, and for different people.

The required rate of return is the return required to make your financial plan's goals a reality, and it is presented as an annual percentage rate. The required rate of return is unique for each investor because each investor's individual expectations for their portfolio are different. This book cannot tell you what your RRR should be because your unique circumstances will require a customized answer based on your personal financial factors. As we've mentioned before, some of these factors are your age and the number of years until retirement, the amount of money you can set aside annually for retirement investments, your life expectancy, other financial resources you may have, and the kind of lifestyle you would like to afford when you retire...which may or may not be possible depending on your own particular circumstances. Very shortly, Linda Nelson's financial situation will be reviewed to show how her financial advisor determined her required rate of return to help her achieve her retirement goals, as an example of how you might do the same.

Again, we reiterate the value of seeking professional advice, which we cover in Chapter 6. The fees for this service will be reasonable, and are likely to provide the information you'll need to guide you with investing wisely, earning the maximum growth you can safely achieve, and possibly have your retirement fund ready when you are.

The Four Steps of the RRR Process: The first step is to come to a conclusion about how much money you'll want to spend every year in retirement until the end of your life. Many people think that when they reach retirement, they won't need as much money every year, but this doesn't seem to be true in real life. Most people are used to a certain lifestyle, or a certain amount of expenditures, and are unwilling to cut back on their spending habits. Therefore, you should probably accept that you'll want to fund your retirement years at 100% of the cost of how you're living now.

The figure below illustrates the process of determining the required rate of return (RRR) based on each person's unique financial circumstances. This is the process our fictitious person, Linda Nelson, followed.

Figure 30: Required Rate of Return.

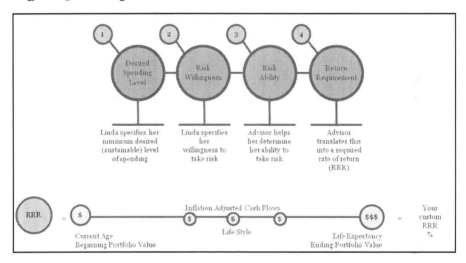

Yes, you or your financial advisor will have to adjust your cash flows for inflation, taxes, fees and expenses, and all the other drags that may affect your true spending power, but your financial advisor will understand this and know how to make the appropriate calculations.

The second step in determining your RRR is understanding investment risk, and being willing to assume some risk. As we've mentioned before, every investment has a specific degree of risk. Some people are willing to accept more risk in their investments because they have more time to recover from a loss, or they are using discretionary funds which have been allocated for high risk investments. Other people have a very low tolerance for risk and are more interested in preserving their wealth than unduly increasing it.

Some people may have waited too long to get serious about investing for retirement and have to accept an uncomfortable risk to make up for lost time, or be willing to lower their retirement lifestyle expectations. Everyone is different, and each person or family can choose the best course for them...once they know the true value of their current financial situation, the projected value of your financial resources in time, and the level of lifestyle they wish to live in the future.

Key:

Once you know your required rate of return (RRR), you will be able to track your portfolio's progress from year-to-year, and very clearly know if you are on course for achieving the goals you set for your retirement.

Remember, you can always adjust your RRR. It's a good idea to meet once every year or two with your financial advisor to review your progress toward achieving your retirement goals. Time is on your side, so occasionally checking on your progress when there is time to spare provides the flexibility for making changes while you still have years ahead of you.

The RRR's third step is to consult with a financial advisor to determine your ability to take risk. The lifestyle you want to live in retirement might not be available to you, given your resources, spending desires, and your tolerance for risk; and yet, the retirement lifestyle you desire may very well be available to you, which can be determined and hopefully confirmed through consultation with a financial advisor. In general, the following provides you with a higher ability to accept risk:

- A larger investment portfolio

- A long time horizon

- A large fixed income

- A low level of desired spending

Of course, the opposite of these four factors would indicate a lower ability to accept risk.

The final step in the RRR process is for the planner to reverse-engineer your required rate of return using information gathered from the first three steps, and your initial portfolio value.

The purpose for determining your RRR is to know the percentage of return that is required (required rate of return) to grow your retirement funds in the time remaining until retirement so the amount of money you have stated you want available to you in retirement will be accessible in the year you need it, and for every year throughout the remaining years of your life.

Linda Nelson's Case Study

Let's meet Linda Nelson. Linda is an employee at Pacific Specialty Lighting Supply, Inc., a company owned by her supervisor, Michael Kendall. Linda has worked for Michael for the past few years, and was one of his first employees. As the company grew, so has Linda's responsibilities and paycheck. In fact, they have a strong employer-employee relationship, and Michael and Mary, his wife, are fond of Linda. Linda enjoys her work, likes her fellow employees, has a good annual income that will continue to increase, and Linda has decided she will probably continue to work for Michael until retirement.

Michael is grateful to Linda and his other employees for making his company a success, and because he cares about these people, Michael decided to start a company 401(k) plan to reward and retain his staff, as well as because it was a great retirement program for himself and Mary, too.

Over the past few years, as her salary increased, Linda has carefully built her personal financial pyramid. She now has a healthy 9-month emergency fund to carry her through most unexpected difficulties, has satisfied several short-term and midterm goals like protecting herself with disability insurance, placing a down payment on a cozy home in a good neighborhood, and upgrading a few key home improvements. Now Linda is financially prepared to seriously devote her attention to saving and investing for her retirement, so it was fortuitous that Michael decided to sponsor a company 401(k) plan. Actually, it was a combination of several things...Michael's financial consultant recommended it as a way the company could save taxes and build the company's value...and Linda had been doing some reading about retirement planning, and brought up the subject of a 401(k) plan at the same time as Michael's advisor!

 ## Important:

Linda knows what kind of lifestyle she wants to have when she reaches retirement. A home, some money for travel and to support a few hobbies, being able to pay her bills, purchase a rental investment to add to her income...

Do you know exactly what your retirement goals are? If not, it's wise to do some serious thinking now so you can begin planning and investing as soon as possible...and have the money later for the purposes you've set today.

Seeing what was coming, Linda met with her personal financial advisor; after some discussion, the following was clarified:

- Linda wanted her retirement funds to provide an annual income of $50,000 every year for the last 30 years of her life

- Linda was 30 years from retirement

- Linda currently had $25,000 in an IRA

- Linda could set aside an additional $17,500 every year ($1,458 per month) through her contributions and her employer's matching contribution

Linda's financial advisor considered the information she had provided, and identified all the financially important assumptions in a chart that looked like this:

Figure 31: Linda Nelson's Required Rate of Return Assumptions.

General Assumptions		
	Participant	
Retirement Age	60	
Years Until Retirement	30	
Life Expectancy	90	
Portfolio Assumptions		**%**
401(k) Account Balance	$25,000	100.00%
Avg Mgt Fee		0.00%
Avg Turnover		0.00%
Tax rate at distribution		25.00%

Income Assumptions						
Participant			Start	End	Tax	%
Source	Dollar Amount	Inflation %	Year	Year	Rate	Taxable
Social Security	$18,000	2.00%	37	61	25.00%	85.00%

Other Cash Flow Assumptions						
			Start	End	Tax	%
Source	Dollar Amount	Inflation %	Year	Year	Rate	Taxable
Retirement	$50,000	2.00%	31	61		
401(k) Savings	$17,500		1	30		
Rental Income	$6,000	2.00%	31	61	25.00%	100.00%

Figure 32: Linda Nelson's Required Rate of Return.

Required Return 6.01%

Participant Age	Fixed Income Participant	Retirement Expenses	401(k) Savings	Rental Income	Taxes	Total Tax Adj Flows	Beginning Value	Cash Flows	Ending Balance
30			$17,500			$17,500	$25,000	$17,500	$45,054
31			$17,500			$17,500	$45,054	$17,500	$66,314
32			$17,500			$17,500	$66,314	$17,500	$88,852
33			$17,500			$17,500	$88,852	$17,500	$112,744
34			$17,500			$17,500	$112,744	$17,500	$138,072
35			$17,500			$17,500	$138,072	$17,500	$164,922
36			$17,500			$17,500	$164,922	$17,500	$193,387
37			$17,500			$17,500	$193,387	$17,500	$223,562
38			$17,500			$17,500	$223,562	$17,500	$255,550
39			$17,500			$17,500	$255,550	$17,500	$289,462
40			$17,500			$17,500	$289,462	$17,500	$325,411
41			$17,500			$17,500	$325,411	$17,500	$363,521
42			$17,500			$17,500	$363,521	$17,500	$403,922
43			$17,500			$17,500	$403,922	$17,500	$446,751
44			$17,500			$17,500	$446,751	$17,500	$492,154
45			$17,500			$17,500	$492,154	$17,500	$540,286
46			$17,500			$17,500	$540,286	$17,500	$591,311
47			$17,500			$17,500	$591,311	$17,500	$645,403
48			$17,500			$17,500	$645,403	$17,500	$702,746
49			$17,500			$17,500	$702,746	$17,500	$763,535
50			$17,500			$17,500	$763,535	$17,500	$827,978
51			$17,500			$17,500	$827,978	$17,500	$896,294
52			$17,500			$17,500	$896,294	$17,500	$968,716
53			$17,500			$17,500	$968,716	$17,500	$1,045,492
54			$17,500			$17,500	$1,045,492	$17,500	$1,126,881
55			$17,500			$17,500	$1,126,881	$17,500	$1,213,163
56			$17,500			$17,500	$1,213,163	$17,500	$1,304,630
57			$17,500			$17,500	$1,304,630	$17,500	$1,401,595
58			$17,500			$17,500	$1,401,595	$17,500	$1,504,387
59			$17,500			$17,500	$1,504,387	$17,500	$1,613,358
60		-$92,379		$11,086	-$2,771	-$112,087	$1,613,358	-$112,087	$1,591,503
61		-$94,227		$11,307	-$2,827	-$114,329	$1,591,503	-$114,329	$1,565,957
62		-$96,112		$11,533	-$2,883	-$116,615	$1,565,957	-$116,615	$1,536,453
63		-$98,034		$11,764	-$2,941	-$118,948	$1,536,453	-$118,948	$1,502,702
64		-$99,994		$11,999	-$3,000	-$121,327	$1,502,702	-$121,327	$1,464,401
65		-$101,994		$12,239	-$3,060	-$123,753	$1,464,401	-$123,753	$1,421,226
66	$37,452	-$104,034		$12,484	-$11,080	-$86,903	$1,421,226	-$86,903	$1,414,520
67	$38,201	-$106,115		$12,734	-$11,301	-$88,641	$1,414,520	-$88,641	$1,405,569
68	$38,965	-$108,237		$12,988	-$11,527	-$90,414	$1,405,569	-$90,414	$1,394,200
69	$39,745	-$110,402		$13,248	-$11,758	-$92,222	$1,394,200	-$92,222	$1,380,231
70	$40,540	-$112,610		$13,513	-$11,993	-$94,067	$1,380,231	-$94,067	$1,363,467
71	$41,350	-$114,862		$13,783	-$12,233	-$95,948	$1,363,467	-$95,948	$1,343,701
72	$42,177	-$117,159		$14,059	-$12,477	-$97,867	$1,343,701	-$97,867	$1,320,713
73	$43,021	-$119,503		$14,340	-$12,727	-$99,825	$1,320,713	-$99,825	$1,294,268
74	$43,881	-$121,893		$14,627	-$12,982	-$101,821	$1,294,268	-$101,821	$1,264,117
75	$44,759	-$124,331		$14,920	-$13,241	-$103,857	$1,264,117	-$103,857	$1,229,996
76	$45,654	-$126,817		$15,218	-$13,506	-$105,935	$1,229,996	-$105,935	$1,191,621
77	$46,567	-$129,354		$15,522	-$13,776	-$108,053	$1,191,621	-$108,053	$1,148,694
78	$47,499	-$131,941		$15,833	-$14,052	-$110,214	$1,148,694	-$110,214	$1,100,896
79	$48,449	-$134,579		$16,150	-$14,333	-$112,419	$1,100,896	-$112,419	$1,047,889
80	$49,418	-$137,271		$16,473	-$14,619	-$114,667	$1,047,889	-$114,667	$989,312
81	$50,406	-$140,016		$16,802	-$14,912	-$116,960	$989,312	-$116,960	$924,783
82	$51,414	-$142,817		$17,138	-$15,210	-$119,300	$924,783	-$119,300	$853,895
83	$52,442	-$145,673		$17,481	-$15,514	-$121,686	$853,895	-$121,686	$776,218
84	$53,491	-$148,587		$17,830	-$15,824	-$124,119	$776,218	-$124,119	$691,292
85	$54,561	-$151,558		$18,187	-$16,141	-$126,602	$691,292	-$126,602	$598,631
86	$55,652	-$154,589		$18,551	-$16,464	-$129,134	$598,631	-$129,134	$497,716
87	$56,765	-$157,681		$18,922	-$16,793	-$131,716	$497,716	-$131,716	$387,997
88	$57,901	-$160,835		$19,300	-$17,129	-$134,351	$387,997	-$134,351	$268,891
89	$59,059	-$164,052		$19,686	-$17,471	-$137,038	$268,891	-$137,038	$139,778
90	$60,240	-$167,333		$20,080	-$17,821	-$139,778	$139,778	-$139,778	$0

Let's review this chart closely to understand the importance of the various factors, and to provide insight about how your financial advisor will calculate the appropriate RRR for your personal circumstances. At the top of the chart there are four sections that define this chart's financial assumptions. Here is an explanation for each of these elements.

General Assumptions: At the top left of the chart are three general assumptions. Linda wants to retire when she is 60 years old; she has 30 years until retirement; and she expects to live until she is 90. (The life expectancy for women in the United States in 2013, as calculated by the World Health Organization, is 82.2 years.)

Portfolio Assumptions: Four items, as follows:

1. "401(k) Account Balance: $25,000; 100%." Linda was able to set aside $25,000 in a tax-deferred IRA account. The company plan at Pacific Specialty Lighting Supply, Inc., where Linda works, allows the addition of IRA rollovers, and Linda decided to move her IRA funds into her new 401(k) account.

She believed this would simplify her financial picture and she also wanted to take advantage of the access to professional financial advice provided by her company's plan. This way, all her retirement funds could be managed from one location, and under the guidance of a professional.

2. "Avg Mgt Fee: 0.00%." Another portfolio assumption is that there are not now nor ever will be any management fees. Linda's company plan favors its employees and has determined that all fees will be paid by the company plan.

3. "Avg Turnover: 0.00%". In addition, there'll be no investment turnover that generates taxes. Since a 401(k) is a tax-deferred vehicle, taxation is not an issue until money is withdrawn, and Linda's RRR chart assumes that Linda will not make any withdrawals until retirement.

4. "Tax rate at distribution: 25.00%". When Linda does retire, her financial advisor calculated that she will be in the 25% tax bracket. Therefore, when Linda retires at age 60 and decides to live on her retirement account, all the monies that are annually withdrawn from her 401(k) retirement account will be taxed at 25%.

Income Assumptions: "Social Security: $18,000; 2.00% Inflation %; Start Year 37; End Year 61; Tax Rate 25.00%; Taxable 85.00%."

In this segment of the spreadsheet, Linda's Social Security is listed and analyzed. The amount of Social Security Linda will receive annually is estimated to be $18,000. This amount will increase by an estimated 2% per year due to inflation. Linda's Social Security will not begin until Year 37, which is when Linda turns 66 years old. Her Social Security income will end in Year 61 at the age of 90, when it is assumed that Linda has died. The tax rate on her Social Security income will be 25%. The amount of her Social Security income that will be taxable is estimated to be 85%; this is because Social Security is seldom taxed at 100%, and Linda's financial advisor has assumed a reasonable percentage.

Other Cash Flow Assumptions: Three items, as follows:

1. "Retirement: -$50,000; 2.00% Inflation %; Start Year 31; End Year 61."

Here, Linda has stated that she wants $50,000 a year when she is in retirement. The amount of money she'll need each year in retirement will increase by 2%, which is the estimated inflation rate. Linda will start receiving funding from her retirement account in Start Year 31, when she is 60 years old. The last year Linda will receive funds from her retirement account is Year 61, when she turns 90 years old, presumed to be her final year.

2. "401(k) Savings: $17,500; Start Year 1; End Year 30."

Linda will annually invest $17,500, starting in Year 1 when Linda is 30 years old. Linda's End Year is Year 30 which is at the end of her 59th year, the last year she can contribute to her 401(k) savings before turning 60 years old. The Inflation % and the Tax Rate are not applicable because this is money going into the 401(k) account.

3. "Rental Income: $6,000; 2.00% Inflation %; Start Year 31; End Year 61; Tax Rate 25.00%; Taxable 100.00%."

Linda has been thinking she would like to acquire additional income when she's retired, so her plan is to purchase property that provides rental income. Her financial advisor has estimated that Linda will be able to afford property that will bring in $500 a month, which is $6,000 per year in net rental income before tax in today's dollars. The rental income will increase by an inflation rate of 2% each year so that in her first year of retirement, the net rental income before tax would have grown to $11,086. The plan is that Linda will purchase the property in Start Year 31 when Linda is 60 years old, the year she retires. The rental income will terminate in End Year 61 when Linda is 90 years old, the final year of her life. Her rental income will be taxed at a 25% rate because that's the estimated tax rate for her annual estimated income in retirement. 100% of her rental income is taxable.

These four sets of assumptions are the basis for the columns of numbers in the chart. Now let's see how these assumptions appear numerically.

Participant Age: This column begins when Linda is 30 years old and ends when Linda is 90 years old, the year she is deceased.

Fixed Income Participant: The fixed income Linda is receiving is her Social Security income. It starts when Linda is 66 years old and she is receiving $37,452 in her first year as a Social Security recipient. Notice that at the top of the chart the Social Security income assumption was $18,000 and yet, now, when she is 66 years old, she is receiving $37,452. This is because the $18,000 noted in the Income Assumption section at the top of the chart is the value of dollars measured in today's dollars; the $37,452 when Linda is 66 years old is the value of dollars measured 36 years in the future, appreciated by the annual inflation rate of 2% over the course of 36 years. As you can see, Linda receives a larger amount each year during her retirement which is the continuing increase by 2% inflation.

Retirement Expenses: The money in this column begins when Linda is age 60, which is the first year of her retirement. We stated above that Linda wants to live on $50,000 per year in today's dollars. However, over the course of the next 30 years, inflation will require a higher amount of dollars, as measured by dollars 30 years from now, in order to maintain the $50,000 per year lifestyle she envisions. Actually, based on the assumptions, a $50,000 per year lifestyle today will cost $92,379 in 30 years. The reason the figures in this column are negative numbers is because this is the dollar amount being withdrawn each year from her retirement funds to provide the $50,000 per year lifestyle Linda has planned. As you can see at the bottom of this column, today's $50,000 per year lifestyle will cost more than triple the amount 60 years from now. This should be an eye-opener for you, to help you realize how important it is to begin your retirement savings as soon as possible, and with as much as you can reasonably afford to set aside each year.

401(k) Savings: Each year Julie has faithfully added $17,500 to her 401(k) retirement account. Linda's financial advisor based this number on the maximum dollars allowed annually by 401(k) regulations. This adds up to more than half a million dollars; these dollar amounts could increase if the 401(k) regulations are adjusted by the U.S. government. Also, it is assumed that Linda is not making any withdrawals from her 401(k) retirement account.

Rental Income: When Linda finally purchases the rental income property and begins receiving rent when she is 60 years old, the annual income she'll receive from rent will be $11,086. These dollars are inflation-adjusted from the $6,000 originally calculated in today's dollars. Linda will receive rental income until her 90th year.

Taxes: The taxes shown in the tax column are the taxes Linda will pay on her rental income; in her first year as a landlord, she'll pay $2,771. As you recall from the assumptions section, Linda is in the 25% tax bracket and 100% of her rental income is taxable. Since Linda is receiving $11,086 in rent each year, she'll pay $2,771 in taxes, which is 25%. As for her 401(k) contributions, they are in a tax-deferred account, so there is no taxation until Linda withdraws these monies.

Total Tax Adj (Adjusted)Flows: This column's purpose is to show the cash flow of money into her retirement account from Linda's age 30 to age 59, and the cash flow of money out of Linda's retirement account from age 60 to 90.

The effect of taxes: Please take a close look at the chart when Linda is 60 years old. You'll notice that Linda's retirement expenses for this year are -$92,379. As we said above, this is a negative number because this money is being withdrawn from her account to provide money to live on in Linda's first year of retirement. Moving across to the rental income column, we also see that Linda is expected to receive $11,086, of which $2,771 will be paid out in taxes.

However, in the next column, "Total Tax Adj Flows", you'll see a -$112,087 figure. This number represents the actual net dollars being withdrawn from Linda's retirement account so she can afford the $92,379 of living expenses. The reason there's just about a $20,000 difference is because in order for Linda to have $92,379 to live on, she must also pay taxes. Since Linda has calculated a lifestyle based on $50,000 in today's dollars, in 30 years she'll need to withdraw $112,087 to afford both her living expenses and the taxes she has to pay in her first year of retirement.

Once again, this should provide new incentive to start saving right away so the value of time can work with you, and not against you.

Note:

What is your required rate of return (RRR)? Your RRR is based on achieving the amount of money you'll need in retirement for your desired and reasonable retirement lifestyle. Meet with a financial advisor who can calculate your RRR and guide you with making the investments that will help you achieve your RRR and retirement goals.

Linda's required rate of return (RRR): At the beginning of this chapter we explained that the required rate of return (RRR) was an essential concept in understanding how to create a meaningful and effective plan for building your retirement funds. The RRR identifies the growth by which your retirement funds must annually increase to reach your retirement goals.

<u>Required Return 6.01%</u>: Linda's required rate of return is 6.01%, and is based on these factors:

- The amount of time she has left until retirement (30 years)

- The amount of additional pretax monies she can annually contribute to her 401(k) in the next 30 years ($17,500)

- The amount of pretax monies she can rollover into her 401(k) ($25,000)

- The amount of rental income she'll annually receive in today's dollars once she is retired at age 60 ($6,000)

- The projected amount of taxes she'll pay on her rental income and her retirement fund withdrawals once she is retired at age 60 (25%)

- The lifestyle Linda stated she wanted in retirement ($50,000 annually in today's dollars)

Linda's financial advisor calculated all these factors and concluded that Linda's pretax savings account, which is her 401(k), would need to achieve an average growth rate of at least 6.01% every year for the next 30 years in order for Linda to have the amount of money she would need to live the lifestyle she desires.

6.01% annual growth is reasonable to achieve, assuming Linda has good advice and follows a sensible plan. Many people are hesitant to seek the advice of a professional and often wind up chasing hot stocks or hot trends and completely miss the boat, rather than following a plan for steady growth. When your car has engine trouble, most people find a mechanic. When you need medical attention, most people visit the doctor. It's the same thing with your investments; it's wise to seek the expert advice of a professional. The money you need in retirement may be within your grasp...if only you will accept that you don't know what you don't know and need to find out so you can have the security of a decent lifestyle when you reach retirement age.

A detail requiring consideration is that Linda needs an RRR of 6.01%, and this is an annual and average rate of growth. Linda's financial advisor knows that in some years Linda's account will achieve less than 6.01%, and in other years Linda's portfolio will grow by more than 6.01%. The 6.01% needed every year is an average over the course of the 30 years Linda has remaining until retirement. Overall, by the end of the 30 years of investment time, Linda's portfolio must have achieved at least a 6.01% growth rate.

Another detail to consider is that even though the entire portfolio of funds in Linda's retirement account must together achieve an annual and average RRR of 6.01%, Linda and her financial advisor both know that some funds in her account will perform better than others. We'll discuss this further in the next chapter, but for now it's important to recognize that Linda's portfolio consists of 10 or 20 or more individual investments, some of which will perform well, or not well. It's the combined performance and growth of Linda's selected funds that must average 6.01% annually and over the course of the 30 years until Linda's retirement.

Linda is single at age 30; she's dating and may find a husband in the next year or two; if she does, Linda will need a new RRR drawn up that reflects her and her husband's combined financial circumstances. However, since Linda is single now, she realizes the value of planning now as a single person. Linda also knows her RRR analysis should be performed every few years to make sure Linda is on track to meet her goals.

Planning for your retirement is best served within the context of a rational structure. Yes, of course, you can't plan for everything...

we all know that. A flaming asteroid could change our lives as much as winning a $40 million lottery. However, the tools needed for projecting future income are available, and the professional advice you need to take advantage of these tools is also available!

Beginning Value Column: On the right side of the chart is the section labeled "Required Return 6.01%", and there are three columns. The first column, labeled "Beginning Value", illustrates the projected year by year increase at 6.01% over the next 30 years until Linda's retirement at age 60. The column begins with $25,000 because this is the amount of money in Linda's IRA, which she rolled over into her company's 401(k) account. By the time Linda has retired at age 60 she has $1,613,358. This is the high point of her retirement monies because at age 60 she will begin to withdraw money from her retirement fund for her living expenses.

It's interesting to note that putting away $17,500 every year for 30 years grew to become more than triple the total of her annual contributions. This is the value of investing money over the long term.

$$\$17,500 \text{ x } 30 \text{ years} = \$525,000$$

Because of the power of growth at her 6.01% RRR, steady contributions, taking advantage of pretax dollars, investing the maximum allowed by law, refraining from loans and withdrawals, and three decades of time, Linda's money grew to $1,613,358.

Cash Flows Column: This column shows the flow of money into the account from age 30 to age 59; each year Linda adds $17,500 to her 401(k) account. At age 60, the column shows the flow of her resources out of the 401(k). Please remember that Linda has chosen a lifestyle based on $50,000 per year in today's dollars; however, to live in the future on the value of today's dollars, at age 60, which is 30 years from now, she'll need $92,379 plus the $11,086 in rental income, less the taxes she'll have to pay on her rental income and her withdrawals from the 401(k) which will then be taxable. In the first year of her retirement, Linda will need to withdraw $112,087 from her retirement funds. Thereafter, the amount Linda needs to withdraw increases every year until her projected death at age 90. The reason she needs to withdraw an increasing amount each year is because of the continuing inflation, estimated to be 2% annually.

Ending Balance Column: The last column illustrates her retirement account's annual ending balance. The account keeps increasing every year until her retirement at age 60, after which it begins to decrease as Linda makes withdrawals for her retirement living expenses. You'll notice that Linda runs out of money at age 90, which is the projected age of her death.

The Ending Balance column also shows the addition of the annual 6.01% increases:

$$\$25,000 + \$17,500 = \$42,500 \times 6.01\% = \$45,054.$$

Capital consumption model: When developing a retirement plan, an initial consideration is determining which of two models to use. There is the capital consumption model, and the capital preservation model. The capital consumption model consumes all the individual's assets, reducing the estate to $0. The capital preservation model is designed to preserve the individual's resources so an estate can be left to heirs. Due to Linda's circumstances, Linda was unable to preserve her estate, and will consume all her financial resources during her 30 years of retirement. The good news is that in the last third of her life, based on all the preceding assumptions, Linda will have enough resources to live the lifestyle she chose.

Definition:

Capital Consumption Model: A retirement plan that uses up all the money in the person's estate; no funds are available for the heirs.

Capital Preservation Model: A retirement plan that uses up only the interest of a person's estate; funds are available for the heirs.

<u>The Elephant in the Room</u>: Yes, if Linda lives longer than 90 years, she will outlive her money, and if Linda dies before she reaches 90 years old, she will leave an undetermined estate for her heirs. Remember that 30 years is a long time, and Linda's retirement plan can always be adjusted based on new information and changing circumstances. If Linda's health continues to be excellent, and there is reason to believe she may live longer than 90, Linda and her financial advisor can develop an alternative plan which might include owning an additional rental property for increased annual income; or perhaps Linda might consider moving to a geographic location where living expenses are less; or the decision might be made that the RRR needs to be recalculated to accept more risk, or secure more safety.

The key thought here is that it is wise to have a financial plan that's based on standard investment wisdom. Having a realistic plan is absolutely better than no plan at all, and thereafter, modifying the plan based on new information is an efficient process.

Linda was very satisfied, and relieved, with the information her advisor had developed. She believed her retirement planning was realistic, and would secure the future she desired.

The Effect of Inflation

It's important to also look a bit more closely at the effect of inflation. It's not uncommon to hear newscasters mentioning that inflation is up or down, that this year it's 3% or 2%, or it's projected to be 4%... These percentage numbers are typically measured by the Consumer Price Index, or CPI, part of a government program that produces data every month showing changes in the cost of representative items paid by urban consumers. The price changes indicate the direction and the amount of monthly inflation. The calculations usually exclude energy, which is usually one of the biggest costs people have, aside from food and housing. Sometimes the government manipulates the factors that compose the inflation rate to make themselves look good, but typically there is a CPI number everybody accepts as realistic.

Everybody knows that whatever you're spending your money on today will most likely be more expensive in the future because of inflation; the question is how much higher will it be? Nobody knows, but we need to assume a reasonable rate to calculate this risk, and build it into the RRR calculation. The inflation rate has been as high as 18% in 1914, and as low as -10.5% in 1921; the actual percentages may differ depending on the source, but this gives you an idea of the range. Even so, despite this wide 28% difference, the average U.S. inflation rate for the last hundred years is close to 3%. Therefore, a 3% inflation rate would be a sensible factor to use when calculating the amount of money you'll need in retirement.

However, it's not really as simple as that. As with anything, the deeper you look into something, the more is revealed. The CPI is based on the criteria used by the government, but you're not the government. You are a real live flesh-and-blood person who does buy food, and does consume energy, yet these commodities are not considered in the government's reporting. You also pay a mortgage or rent, and probably have a whole number of expenditures that are unique to you and your lifestyle. For example, college costs have increased a lot more than 3%; medical care for seniors has also increased much more than 3%. Certain items can increase dramatically, so while we can generally understand the steady increase in the cost of items, some of these commodities or products and services that you use may actually increase their costs more rapidly.

On the other hand, some items may not increase at all. For example, for those people paying a mortgage, the mortgage is typically a hefty 30% of the monthly expenditures...but it's a fixed expense, so inflation does not impact their budget for this item. If you're making car payments, the same idea is true; the monthly payments are fixed at a set price and inflation does not influence these expenditures.

Ideally, the best way to account for inflation is by category, and to base those calculations on the categories that are specific to your lifestyle or anticipated lifestyle. Your inflation rate could either be much higher or much lower than the inflation rate calculated in the CPI. Not only will this be a significant calculation to do before your retirement, but it will also be very effective when you are in retirement. Building a retirement budget specific to the particular goods and services you purchase in your retirement years, and the effect of inflation on those goods and services, will more thoroughly define your circumstances and allow you to better improve your budgetary thinking and planning. This is how the inflation rate can be better understood, and planning can be much more purposeful and meaningful with this further level of examination.

Here are two figures about the impact of inflation on dollars over time. The first figure graphically illustrates how different inflation percentages erode the value of money over a 39-year period. The second figure is a numeric representation of the same destructive effect.

Figure 33: The Graphic View of the Erosion of Money.

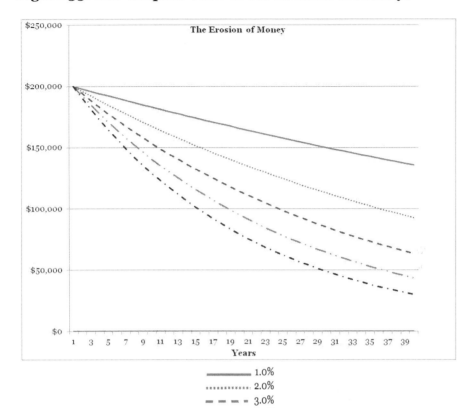

Figure 34: The Numeric View of the Erosion of Money.

Year	Value Today		$200,000		
	1.00%	2.00%	3.00%	4.00%	5.00%
	Future Purchasing Power	Future Purchasing Power	Future Purchasing Power	Future Purchasing Power	Future Purchasing Power
0	$200,000	$200,000	$200,000	$200,000	$200,000
5	$190,293	$181,146	$172,522	$164,385	$156,705
10	$181,057	$164,070	$148,819	$135,113	$122,783
15	$172,270	$148,603	$128,372	$111,053	$96,203
20	$163,909	$134,594	$110,735	$91,277	$75,378
25	$155,954	$121,906	$95,521	$75,023	$59,061
30	$148,385	$110,414	$82,397	$61,664	$46,275
35	$141,183	$100,006	$71,077	$50,683	$36,258
39	$135,674	$92,390	$63,151	$43,324	$29,830

As you can see, the erosion of the dollar's value is extreme, and because of this risk to the value of your money, a sensible and effective plan for building and preserving your retirement funds is absolutely necessary.

Important:

You should consider rebalancing your portfolio periodically so you can maintain your RRR. Most people neglect to do this and place their retirement future in jeopardy. Putting your portfolio on autopilot may result in a diminished retirement fund. Stay interested! It's your retirement!

Rebalancing the portfolio: Occasionally your financial advisor may suggest that your 401(k) portfolio needs to be rebalanced. What this means is that the original plan for building your retirement funds is not being met by the assets originally selected and currently in your 401(k) account. The financial investments in your account are not achieving the annual required rate of return (RRR), for whatever reason, and some investments will need to be exchanged for others that are believed will be capable of achieving your account's RRR. Perhaps small-cap funds are growing too slowly, but mid-cap funds are anticipated to perform quite well as the economy adjusts through its cycles; maybe your international funds have seen their day for the time being, and now it makes sense to decrease the percentage of their presence in favor of large-cap funds, or some other investment sector that will help you achieve your RRR. Here are two examples of what diversified portfolios might look like; the percentages of each category are adjusted from time to time based on the planning underlying your RRR.

Figure 35: Two Examples of a Diversified Portfolio.

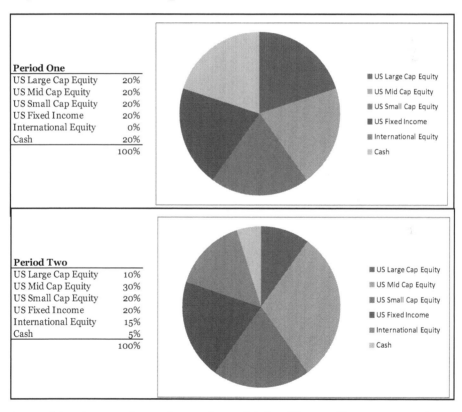

Period One	
US Large Cap Equity	20%
US Mid Cap Equity	20%
US Small Cap Equity	20%
US Fixed Income	20%
International Equity	0%
Cash	20%
	100%

- US Large Cap Equity
- US Mid Cap Equity
- US Small Cap Equity
- US Fixed Income
- International Equity
- Cash

Period Two	
US Large Cap Equity	10%
US Mid Cap Equity	30%
US Small Cap Equity	20%
US Fixed Income	20%
International Equity	15%
Cash	5%
	100%

- US Large Cap Equity
- US Mid Cap Equity
- US Small Cap Equity
- US Fixed Income
- International Equity
- Cash

Something interesting to know, but which will not affect your 401(k) account, is that when a taxable portfolio is rebalanced, a taxable event is triggered. When funds are sold, taxes on gains must be reported and paid as part of your annual income tax, depending on your year's financial activity. The reason rebalancing your 401(k) account does not create a taxable event is because the funds in your 401(k) are tax-deferred until you withdraw the money. If, however, you possessed taxable investment accounts, the gains would be eligible for taxation. While no one enjoys paying taxes, it's better to rebalance your portfolio and be eligible for those taxes than allow your portfolio to drift farther away from the targeted allocation mix, which will increase your risk and make your portfolio less efficient, and cause you to lose the advantage of time working in your favor. You never want to let the tax tail wag the tax dog. You always want to choose the best overall economic decision; so while taxes are important and must be considered, if it's in your best interests to rebalance your portfolio and protect the long term achievement of your investments, then rebalancing and paying the tax is the wisest decision. In general, it's empirically proven that rebalancing periodically and paying a little bit of tax along the way is the prudent thing to do because in the end your portfolio performs better and you make more money. It's like pruning a tree; you'll lose some fruit in the short-term, but the tree will be healthier and you'll grow much more fruit later.

The good news is that rebalancing your 401(k) portfolio will keep your plan on track and could result in improved performance, and there is no tax penalty. Of course, we know you might be thinking, and wisely so, that it's best to have your investment professional help you with rebalancing the portfolio because he or she spends all day, every week, each month, and the entire year working with investments and doing this type of work, and your advisor could be essential to your long-term success.

Summary

Because individual financial needs are different for each person, this chapter could not answer the question of how much money you would need when you retire. Personal circumstances and future lifestyle projections are unique, so the only way to identify the amount of retirement funds you will need depends on various factors and the result of those calculations. However, this chapter revealed those factors and explained how the calculations are conducted. Most important is understanding the value of determining your required rate of return (RRR), because this clears away the fog of uncertainty, allowing you to precisely know the growth rate target of your investments year after year, which is instrumental to following your path to a financially fulfilling retirement.

 ## Chapter 4 Review Questions:

1. The Required Rate of Return (RRR) is the annual rate of growth your portfolio must maintain so you can reach your financial goals.

    A. True

    B. False

2. Annual inflation averages about 5% a year.

    A. True

    B. False

3. Inflation can affect your mortgage payments and your car payments.

    A. True

    B. False

4. The funds in your 401(k) account do not create a taxable event.

    A. True

    B. False

Answers

1. Answer: A. The RRR is your guidepost, pinpointing the annual growth necessary to fund the goals of your retirement years.

2. Answer: B. Annual inflation averages about 2% – 3% per year.

3. Answer: B. Your mortgage payments and car payments are fixed, so they are not going to change as the inflation rate rises or falls. Inflation fluctuation has already been calculated into your payments.

4. Answer: A. This is because your 401(k) funds are tax-deferred until you withdraw the money; that's when the withdrawn funds are taxed.

Chapter 5:
Insights to Wealth

When you have finished reading this chapter, you will:

- Value the importance of attending the free financial training your company's 401(k) plan provides

- Realize the financial effect of time by saving money sooner, not later

- Possess insight on how much to save every month

- Understand how your financial advisor calculates the amount of money you'll need in retirement

- Recognize the importance of understanding your company's 401(k) rules

- Know why it may be a good choice to rollover your 401(k) funds into an IRA at retirement

- Appreciate the benefits of developing your own Investment Policy Statement (IPS)

- Consider your portfolio's diversification and how best to invest your funds within your company's 401(k) plan

- Be able to explain the difference between compounding, and negative compounding.

- Know why a stable portfolio with a steady rate of growth is better than a volatile portfolio with aggressive growth

The truth is, and you know this already, no one is going to care more about your money than you are. This is why it's so important to take good care of your future by being a good steward now. Finances may not be your thing, but our advice is you begin to change your thinking and start paying attention to the various pathways for increasing your wealth. The day will come when you'll wish you had, and so we fervently hope that that day is today. It's not hard, it doesn't take a whole lot of time, but it does require you take your financial future seriously and begin now to sow the seeds which will lead to an abundant harvest 10, 20, or 30 years from now.

This book provides quite a few gems of information which, when you follow the advice, will help you make good decisions with happy results. You won't need a BA in finance to secure a comfortable retirement; we recommend, however, that you take advantage of the training your company's 401(k) plan provides, attend the quarterly meetings conducted by the financial advisor to learn what you can about the economic updates and your account's performance in relation to the economy, and schedule the free one-on-one consultations with your company's 401(k) advisor when the opportunity permits so you can enjoy further insights about how your personal account is performing and gain from suggestions for improving the results.

What we believe you'll find is once you take an interest in building your retirement fund, and once the vocabulary and general idea of how the markets work and how money is accumulated becomes familiar, you'll be more attuned to financial information, improving your understanding of how to strengthen your fund's growth. If you ignore it, it may grow in spite of you...but if you ignore it, the opportunity to further increase your growth and comfort in retirement might very well be a casualty of your ignore-ance. It won't hurt to pick up a Money magazine once in a while, and it will definitely be to your advantage to browse the financial section of your local bookstore now and again. Once you really start taking interest, you might consider signing up for an enewsletter from a financial advisor, or starting an investment club at work or among your friends. These are all ways to make your financial future more than just a bothersome task, because by taking action and spending a little time learning about money and investing is truly the best way for protecting your future. The future is coming, and someday it will be here; there are millions of people who will be filled with regrets, but you have had the foresight to see the future, prepare for the future, and enjoy the future you built.

Key:

Educating yourself about your company's 401(k) plan and your investment account will help you learn how to secure your financial future. Always go to your company's education workshops, and also ask if you can meet privately with your company's financial advisor about your portfolio.

Use the information in this book to ask questions that will help you develop and achieve your financial goals!

Generally, your company's 401(k) financial advisor will conduct an employee meeting every three months or so to update all the important news that's relevant to the company's 401(k) plan, and will then be available for one-on-one sessions with employees to help them individually. Sadly, most advisors report they have sat in an empty room more times than they can count. People won't come... They don't think they have enough funds in their account, so they don't care. Actually, they usually do have enough money to make it worth their time, and they should use this excellent free opportunity to meet with an expert advisor, gain the information they need, and improve the potential for a better life. It's your money. It's your life. People tend to think, "Well, I don't know... I'm not a sophisticated investor... I don't know any of this stuff..." Well, exactly! That's why you have a retirement plan and an advisor! Take advantage of these free benefits, participate, expand your knowledge, learn what you can so you put your best resource, Time, to work for you today. As with most good things in life, you get out what you put in.

Save...Sooner or Later, but Save!

If you've heard this once, you've heard this 1,000 times. It's no surprise that this same message appears in this book a few times as well. The reason is simple: it's true!

One of the key messages of this book is that you have a very powerful ally on your side, and it's Time. Time can be your enemy, they say, but when it comes to investing, Time is your best friend. In the next few pages we're going to show you an amazing example that will convince you to start saving as soon as possible...today...now. There is a saying you probably have heard: "Numbers never lie". What these three words mean is that mathematical calculations are invariably true. Just like 2+2 = 4 is acknowledged as an unwavering truth, the use of formulas and calculations are always accurate in their application.

The example that follows is a simple mathematical excursion to demonstrate the value of saving as early as possible. Though it's never too late to start saving and investing for the future, it's always best to save early so the value of Time can be as fully harnessed and utilized as possible.

We're going to revisit our friend, Linda Nelson, and be a fly on the wall during one of her one-on-one sessions with the company's advisor. When Linda met with the company advisor, their conversation began casually as Linda explained that she was thinking about whether or not to go on an expensive vacation cruise with her girlfriends. Linda was considering reducing her monthly 401(k) contributions for six or eight months and saving that money to pay for her trip to the Caribbean. It had also crossed Linda's mind to maintain her current level of contributions and instead set aside money from the remainder of her paychecks for a shorter and less expensive vacation, maybe to Mexico. The company advisor pulled out a chart, and shared it with Linda. Here is the chart he showed her as he explained its contents:

Figure 36: Early Saver/Late Saver Assumptions.

Early Saver		Late Saver	
Current Age	30	Current Age	40
Years to Save	10	Years to Save	20
Retirement Age	60	Retirement Age	60
Savings	$17,500	Savings	$17,168
Rate of Return	5.00%	Rate of Return	5.00%

Figure 37: Early Saver/Late Saver Dollars.

		Early Saver			Late Saver		
Year	Age	Beginning Balance	Annual Contribution	Year-End Balance	Beginning Balance	Annual Contribution	Year-End Balance
1	30	0	$17,500	$18,375	0	$0	$0
2	31	$18,375	$17,500	$37,669	$0	$0	$0
3	32	$37,669	$17,500	$57,927	$0	$0	$0
4	33	$57,927	$17,500	$79,199	$0	$0	$0
5	34	$79,199	$17,500	$101,533	$0	$0	$0
6	35	$101,533	$17,500	$124,985	$0	$0	$0
7	36	$124,985	$17,500	$149,609	$0	$0	$0
8	37	$149,609	$17,500	$175,465	$0	$0	$0
9	38	$175,465	$17,500	$202,613	$0	$0	$0
10	39	$202,613	$17,500	$231,119	$0	$0	$0
11	40	$231,119	$0	$242,675	$0	$17,168	$18,026
12	41	$242,675	$0	$254,808	$18,026	$17,168	$36,954
13	42	$254,808	$0	$267,549	$36,954	$17,168	$56,828
14	43	$267,549	$0	$280,926	$56,828	$17,168	$77,696
15	44	$280,926	$0	$294,973	$77,696	$17,168	$99,607
16	45	$294,973	$0	$309,721	$99,607	$17,168	$122,614
17	46	$309,721	$0	$325,207	$122,614	$17,168	$146,771
18	47	$325,207	$0	$341,468	$146,771	$17,168	$172,136
19	48	$341,468	$0	$358,541	$172,136	$17,168	$198,769
20	49	$358,541	$0	$376,468	$198,769	$17,168	$226,734
21	50	$376,468	$0	$395,292	$226,734	$17,168	$256,097
22	51	$395,292	$0	$415,056	$256,097	$17,168	$286,928
23	52	$415,056	$0	$435,809	$286,928	$17,168	$319,301
24	53	$435,809	$0	$457,599	$319,301	$17,168	$353,292
25	54	$457,599	$0	$480,479	$353,292	$17,168	$388,983
26	55	$480,479	$0	$504,503	$388,983	$17,168	$426,458
27	56	$504,503	$0	$529,728	$426,458	$17,168	$465,808
28	57	$529,728	$0	$556,215	$465,808	$17,168	$507,124
29	58	$556,215	$0	$584,026	$507,124	$17,168	$550,507
30	59	$584,026	$0	$613,227	$550,507	$17,168	$596,059
31	60	$613,227	$0	$643,888	$596,059	$17,168	$643,888

Total Invested $175,000   Total Invested $360,527

Difference $185,527

Let's take a look at the numbers. At the bottom of the chart, you'll notice that the Year-End Balance for both the early saver and the late saver is exactly the same; they both have an ending balance of $643,888. What you will also notice is the total amount of money the two savers invested. The early saver invested a total of $175,000 during the 10 years this person saved; after the 10th year, the early saver did not add one penny more of annual contributions; the early saver's account grew only by the 5% rate of return. In other words, this person invested $175,000 over the course of a 10-year period which then magnified by an additional $468,888 over the next 20 years... only through the interest this account was earning.

It's a different story for the late saver. This person did not invest early, choosing instead to begin investing exactly when the early saver stopped investing. It took the late saver 20 years and $185,527 more than the early saver to earn the same amount of money the early saver achieved in one-third the contribution time with less than half the contributions. ($360,527 - $175,000 = $185,527.) Using this example, and stating this in another way: If you save later, you'll have to save twice as much money for twice as long.

This is the value of Time.

Is this a gem of knowledge? You bet it is! The early saver now has more than half a million dollars by saving and investing for only 10 years, and putting the money to work at 5% interest per year during the 30 years shown by the chart. The late saver had to make more financial sacrifices ($185, 527) over a longer period of time to achieve the same results as the early saver. As you can see, it's never too late to start saving and investing, but it's better to start sooner rather than later.

When Linda Nelson saw this chart, her mouth fell open, she took a quick breath, the light bulb went on, and Linda decided right then and there on the trip to Mexico.

How much should I save? This is a very important question, and it's the question that only you can answer. The amount of contributions you should invest every paycheck depends on your realistic expectations for how you will spend your retirement years. It's probably normal to think that one can never have enough money, especially when you're earning years are behind you and you'll have to live on your savings, investments, and the government benefits you've earned. The biggest fear that older people have is the fear of outliving their money. Being the recipient of welfare, or having to ask family for support, is distasteful to most people. The best way to know how much money to save is by very clearly knowing your retirement goals. Do you expect to live in your own home? Do you expect to have money for travel? Do you want to own and operate a business? Before there can be an answer to how much money you should save, the first consideration is deciding what you want to do and have when you retire.

Reverse Engineering the RRR: Your financial advisor can help you figure out how much money you'll need in order to retire at the lifestyle you wish...but not until you've figured out how you want to live in retirement. The way the advisor does this, simplistically explained, is by placing an annual dollar amount on the components of your intended retirement. Then, once he or she knows how much money you need to live each year in the retirement lifestyle you've chosen, calculations will derive the amount of dollars you'll need to set aside in the years remaining until retirement. The following figure explains this process:

Figure 38: How Much Should I Save?

Assumptions:	
Savings Goal	$1,000,000
Years to Save	30
Rate of Return	7.00%
Current Balance	$0
Requried Annual Savings	**$10,586**

Figure 39: Required Annual Savings to Accumulate $1,000,000.

		Required Annual Savings to Accumulate $1,000,000							
					Rate of Return				
		0.00%	2.00%	4.00%	5.00%	6.00%	7.00%	8.00%	10.00%
	5	$200,000	$192,158	$184,627	$180,975	$177,396	$173,891	$170,456	$163,797
	10	$100,000	$91,327	$83,291	$79,505	$75,868	$72,378	$69,029	$62,745
Years	15	$66,667	$57,825	$49,941	$46,342	$42,963	$39,795	$36,830	$31,474
of	20	$50,000	$41,157	$33,582	$30,243	$27,185	$24,393	$21,852	$17,460
Savings	25	$40,000	$31,220	$24,012	$20,952	$18,227	$15,811	$13,679	$10,168
	30	$33,333	$24,650	$17,830	$15,051	$12,649	$10,586	$8,827	$6,079
	35	$28,571	$20,002	$13,577	$11,072	$8,974	$7,234	$5,803	$3,690
	40	$25,000	$16,556	$10,523	$8,278	$6,462	$5,009	$3,860	$2,259

So, for example, reading the chart above, if you want to accumulate $1,000,000 and you have 30 years to do this, if your account can earn 7% a year (RRR of 7%), you'll need to set aside exactly $10,586 per year, or an average of $882 per month. Being a millionaire now seems do-able, doesn't it?

In Linda Nelson's case, she wanted to own a small apartment with a guest bedroom in a warm and sunny part of the country. Linda also wanted enough money to afford one annual vacation to either Europe or the South Pacific. She also anticipated she would marry, have children and then grandchildren, and so she wanted enough money to be able to visit her family, send occasional gifts, and even help with the college funds. Beyond that, Linda was very satisfied with just paying her bills, enjoying her hobbies, going out occasionally for dinner or movies, the theater, tending the garden, and taking classes at her community college to learn about the various things that intrigued her. For Linda, this was a wonderful way to spend her retirement, and this is true for most people as well. Now we are able to ask the question, "How much should I save?" and have a reasonable expectation for a sensible answer.

Once you're able to identify how you want to spend your years in retirement, your financial advisor can calculate the cost of your future lifestyle and then work backwards to recommend a strategy and investment plan to achieve your monetary goals. While there is never any guarantee that your investment plan will achieve or exceed your goals, you've increased your chances of being successful when you set a plan based on sound professional advice, follow it, and adjust it when appropriate.

The required rate of return (RRR): This is a gem of knowledge we discussed in Chapter 4, and we'll review it again now. The required rate of return is the minimum annual percentage an investment must earn to achieve the investment's goal for growth. The RRR is different for different investments, and for different people.

Figure 40: Required Rate of Return.

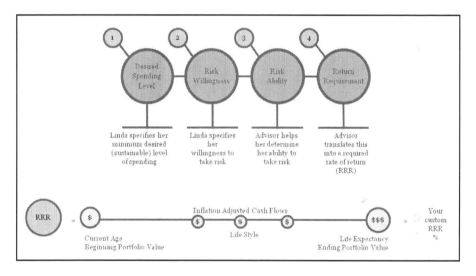

Here's the example we used in our case study for Linda Nelson: Linda's 401(k) account needs an RRR of 6.01% every year for 30 years so she can achieve the total amount of retirement money she wants to have when she retires. We all know that in some years her 401(k) account will average a higher performance than 6.01%, and we also recognize there will be those years when her 401(k) account earns less than a 6.01% annual return. However, over the course of the 30 years of investment time that Linda has, her 401(k) account must average 6.01% return. If it does, then Linda will have the amount of money that was determined she would need.

 Important:

Your portfolio may contain a variety of funds. Your return is based on the combined performance of this group of funds. Some funds may be conservative and some funds may be aggressive, but together they create a reasonable expectation that you will annually earn your required rate of return.

Remember, it's important to review your portfolio periodically. It might be necessary to rebalance your portfolio so you can continue to achieve your RRR.

We can go a step further. Linda's 401(k) account is composed of several different investments. She has a large-cap fund, a mid-cap fund, a small-cap fund, a bond fund, and a money market fund. Linda also has an aggressive investment fund. With the advice of her company's 401(k) financial advisor, Linda has been allocating a percentage of her monthly contributions to each of these different funds, all of which are within her 401(k) account. Overall, these five funds must together achieve an annual required rate of return (RRR) of 6.01%. This doesn't mean that each one must separately achieve the 6.01% RRR, but together they must all average 6.01% RRR.

Continuing with our example, and assuming that each fund had an equal amount of dollars, in one year the large-cap fund earned a 9% return, the mid-cap fund earned a 7% return, the small-cap fund earned a 4% return, the bond fund earned a 2% return, and the money market fund earned 1%. Linda's aggressive fund, however, earned a whopping 14% return during this same year. Altogether, the average of these six funds' RRR for this year was 6.17%, which exceeded Linda's required rate of return (RRR) of 6.01%. It was a good year for Linda... which is good because there will be those years when Linda's 401(k) will perform less than her RRR. As you can see in the tables below, the combination of Linda's 401(k) assets, together with the outside account's aggressive fund, achieved a return of 6.17%.

Figure 41: Linda Nelson's 1-Year Asset Portfolio Return of 6.17%.

401(k) Asset Class	Asset Weight	Expected Return	Contribution to Portfolio
Aggressive Fund	16.66%	14.00%	2.33%
Large Cap Fund	16.66%	9.00%	1.50%
Mid-Cap Fund	16.66%	7.00%	1.17%
Small Cap Fund	16.66%	4.00%	0.67%
Bond Fund	16.66%	2.00%	0.33%
Money Market Fund	16.66%	1.00%	0.17%
	100%	**Expected Return**	**6.17%**

We strongly recommend you meet with your financial advisor to determine your RRR because it is an essential tool in calculating your overall savings and investment goals, and your annual performance to stay on target to reach those goals. Remember, too, that your 401(k) may not be your only retirement funding source. If you have IRAs, or a pension plan, or other investment instruments to consider, your RRR should be calculated based upon the analysis of all these investments working together.

Understand Your Plan Options

The best way to play a card game is by knowing the rules. You can't win at Monopoly if you don't know how to read the property cards or build hotels and houses. Think of your company's 401(k) plan as an exciting new way to make money. All of a sudden, there is this new game in town, and you're allowed to play it. The game's rules are structured in your favor, and the odds are excellent you can be a winner. However, before you can play this game well, and to your advantage, you have to know what the rules are. Make sense?

Plan eligibility requirements: The first thing to do is to find out when you can play the game. Every company establishes its own requirements for being eligible; before you can enroll in your company's 401(k) plan, you have to know what the eligibility requirements are.

Age: Some companies set the eligibility age of plan participants at 18 years old; in some instances, 401(k) eligibility may not be available until an employee reaches 21. If you are a young employee, you should ask your plan administrator for this information.

Months of Service: Many 401(k) plans restrict employee participation if an employee is working part-time, or has not worked a specific number of hours per week, or has not been with the company long enough to merit inclusion in the plan. Find out if you are eligible based on your work history with the company.

Plan entry date: This is the date when you can begin as a plan participant. New employees may need to wait three months, or longer. Part-time employees may need to wait until they've worked 30 consecutive days, etc.

Types of contributions allowed: A variety of contributions may be permitted by your company's 401(k) plan. Here is a simple list explaining each:

Pretax Employee Deferrals: This is the most common contribution; these are the dollars that you are voluntarily contributing to your 401(k) account before your paycheck is taxed.

After-Tax Roth Employee Deferrals: In some instances, a company's 401(k) plan may permit the addition of Roth deferrals, which are voluntary employee contributions made to the 401(k) account after these dollars have been taxed.

<u>Employer Matching</u>: Many employers want to encourage their employees to fund their retirement, so an employer may choose to match the employees' contributions with a percentage contribution such as 2% or 3% of the contribution made by the employees.

<u>Non-elective Profit Sharing</u>: Some companies have a profit sharing plan, and every qualified employee receives a share in the company's profits. Of those companies with a profit sharing plan, those monies may be assigned to the 401(k) accounts of the eligible employees.

<u>Rollovers From Other Qualified Plans or IRAs</u>: It's common for companies to allow rollovers from an assortment of other qualified plans or IRAs into the company's 401(k) plan. An advantage is that these funds will be managed by a professional advisor and are consolidated in one place, instead of being scattered among several investment categories. A disadvantage may be that your company's 401(k) plan has limitations that restrict the variety of investment opportunities. You'll need to discuss whether a rollover from another qualified plan or an IRA is the best choice for you.

<u>Accessing Your Money</u>: Another important feature of your company's 401(k) plan is whether or not you can access your money in case you need it, before you retire. Gaining access to your 401(k) funds is usually possible, but not easy. The reason for this is that your retirement fund has been set up for a purpose...which is to give you the best opportunity for a comfortable retirement. If you take out a loan, or withdraw the money permanently, you are defeating the purpose. Even so, your employer recognizes that there may be times when one of life's major emergencies could appear, and you may have no alternative except to borrow or withdraw your 401(k) funds. This is why we recommend you very thoroughly build the base of your personal financial pyramid and have a well-funded emergency fund.

<u>In-service Withdrawals</u>: Find out what the rules are for withdrawing your money in case you have a serious need. It's quite likely that your company's plan will place severe restrictions on your ability to access

this money; remember that if you make a withdrawal, you will have to pay a 10% penalty, which is a lot.

Hardship Distributions: A hardship distribution is defined as being an "immediate and heavy financial need". Some examples of an immediate and heavy financial need are medical care expenses, funds needed for the purchase of a principal residence, tuition and specific educational fees, payments to avoid eviction or foreclosure of a primary residence, funeral expenses, and certain costs for the repair of damage to a principal residence. Again, there will be penalties and taxation on the monies withdrawn, so not only will you diminish your account's growth, but you will also lose money due to costly fees and penalties.

Upon Retirement: This is the most appropriate reason to access your retirement funds, of course. This is a significant event, and will require your careful attention so the funds you've saved and invested all these years are distributed to you in the most financially sensible way. Make sure you meet with your company's 401(k) financial advisor to guarantee your monies are carefully handled.

Rollover Your 401(k) to an IRA at Retirement

As your retirement approaches, it's important to begin thinking about making the right choice for you and your retirement funds. If you want to, it's perfectly okay to stay with your company plan, but you should also carefully consider whether it might be an even better choice for you to rollover your 401(k) funds into an IRA.

Figure 42: 401(k) Rollover Matrix.

Figure 42: 401(k) Rollover Matrix.

401(k) Rollover Matrix (Roll Over From)	Going To								
	401(k)	403(b)	457(b)	IRA	SEP IRA	SIMPLE IRA	Roth IRA	Designated Roth Account	Qualified Plan
401(k)	Yes	Yes	Yes	Yes	Yes	No	Yes	Yes	Yes
403(b)	Yes	Yes	Yes	Yes	Yes	No	Yes	Yes	Yes
457(b)	Yes	Yes	Yes	Yes	Yes	No	Yes	Yes	Yes
IRA	Yes	Yes	Yes	Yes	Yes	No	Yes	No	Yes
SEP IRA	Yes	Yes	Yes	Yes	Yes	No	Yes	No	Yes
SIMPLE IRA	Yes	Yes	Yes	Yes	Yes	Yes	Yes	No	No
Roth IRA	No	No	No	No	No	No	Yes	No	Yes
Designated Roth Account	No	No	No	No	No	No	Yes	Yes	Yes
Qualified Plan	Yes	Yes	Yes	Yes	Yes	No	Yes	Yes	Yes

There are, of course, pros and cons to rolling over your funds. Most of the time it's a good idea to rollover your funds because typically you'll have a lot more control and flexibility. The company's 401(k) plan document was written with rules about when you can take your money out, and how you can take your money out, and when you die there are rules about how your beneficiaries can get the money out, so your 401(k) funds are subject to all the rules and regulations of the company's plan, which may or may not be bad...but they may not be what you would like. Additionally, most of the time 401(k) plans have a limited investment world from which to choose, containing only a short list of several portfolio models and a few funds which are available to you. This is why when you rollover your monies, you typically have more planning flexibility, more investment flexibility and more estate planning flexibility. You won't have to get permission from your plan for anything you care to do; you can just go and do it the way you want to do it, and this immediacy and flexibility is highly regarded by many. That's why most retiring employees will roll those monies over into an IRA.

Remember that your company's financial advisor may be a fiduciary, and if so, this means he or she must always act in your best interests. That's great! The nature of this relationship also limits, to some degree, what your fiduciary advisor can advise. The fiduciary advisor may be conflicted, and this is because he or she has a fiduciary responsibility to you when you are a participant of your company's 401(k) plan, and recommending you rollover your funds into an account managed by the advisor may appear self-serving and could jeopardize the advisor's reputation and threaten his or her professional credentials. However, your advisor might suggest you move your account, now that you are retiring, in order to lower your expenses while still maintaining the same investments and degree of service. This is to your benefit, and your advisor is clearly upholding his or her fiduciary responsibility. So, if you like working with your advisor and want to continue your working relationship with him or her, you should be the first one to introduce the discussion.

There are several considerations when deciding to rollover your 401(k):

1. Roth or Traditional: Is it better to rollover to a Roth IRA or a traditional IRA? If you rollover to a Roth IRA, you will incur taxes, but not if you rollover to a traditional IRA. You may have a good reason for doing either.

2. Indirect Rollover: If you choose to receive the rollover with the intention of placing the funds in a new IRA by yourself, this is called an "indirect" rollover. The custodian will temporarily withhold 20% of the funds as required by law. You'll have 60 days to reinvest the funds you received in a new retirement account...or the payout will be regarded as a distribution and taxable.

3. No Fee Advertising Claims: Be wary. Ads sometimes suggest there are no fees to rollover the funds...but there may be hidden expenses. Be diligent!

4. Biased Interests: Always ask the person offering to handle your rollover how they will benefit from opening the new account.

5. Services and Options: Companies offer different benefits and choices. Decide what is best for you and then seek the company that provides those services for a reasonable price.

6. Fees and Expenses: Fees and expenses come out of your account and decrease your returns, so always be mindful of your costs. If you have a choice, shop around.

7. Ask Questions: Discuss services, fees, expenses, and tax implications with your advisor. This is your money. Take the time to understand the information you receive; if you don't understand something, keep asking questions...or say no.

8. Company Stock: If your 401(k) portfolio includes company stock, there may be tax issues if you choose to rollover. For example, you may be able to take advantage of lower capital gains by doing an in-kind transfer, which could save you from paying significant taxes. Find out first so you can avoid being surprised.

Take a Total Portfolio Perspective to Investing

It's also very important to view your financial savings and investments as a whole and not broken into separate pieces acting independently of each other. When viewed as a whole, your planning and your outcomes can be more secure and deliberate. Think of this as though you were the quarterback of a football team. As the leader of the team, you don't think of your tackles and guards independently from your wide receivers and running backs. Rather, you think of all these important but different units working together to achieve the main outcome, which is scoring a goal. As an investor, you may also have a variety of different investments, all serving a purpose; some of your investments may be like a guard, providing security, while others are aggressive like a wide receiver running 40 yards downfield. Together, your investments serve the purpose of moving your nest egg's football downfield and across the goal line, earning the cheers of a stadium full of delirious fans.

Setting the course: You can't get where you're going if you don't know where you want to go. In order to move your football team downfield, you have to have a game plan which describes your financial goals, and how you plan to achieve them. The best way to measure your success is by comparing your progress to key benchmarks that mark your step-by-step progress toward the goal line. Just like the quarterback can mark his progress with 10-yard markings, so also can you read the map of your financial accomplishments.

<u>The Personal Investment Policy Statement (IPS)</u>: Another important gem is to develop your own IPS. The IPS is an effective tool for guiding your investment strategies. Just like a football coach has a playbook detailing a variety of strategies to move the ball downfield, your IPS describes key concepts intended to help you achieve your retirement goals. For example, your IPS will:

- State your investment goal and the year you expect to achieve it, including factoring in the erosion of dollars through inflation

- State the current value of your assets and document your asset allocations

- Project the required rate of return (RRR) needed to achieve your goals

- Identify the criteria for making investments, such as investing only in no-load funds, or investing in funds whose managers have been with the fund for at least five years

- Indicate the frequency with which you check on your portfolio, and the criteria you will use to evaluate whether or not you're on track to meet your goals

- Identify your tolerance for risk to safeguard you from overexposure and potential loss

Your financial advisor will work with you to develop your IPS so it is effective in serving your main goal...financial independence during retirement.

The efficient frontier: This is an important term to know. It sounds kind of catchy, doesn't it? Like something you'd hear in a sci-fi movie. The efficient frontier actually refers to an investment portfolio that contains a mix of assets that provide expected rates of return with the lowest possible risk...thus it's efficient because it achieves a desired outcome on the "frontier" of your edge for risk and return.

In the chart below, you'll see the dynamics between risk and the expected rate of return. In this particular example, an investment portfolio, earning a 7% return with a 9.0 risk value, was improved or made more efficient by finding a way to increase the return while maintaining the current risk. This portfolio is now efficient because it did not increase the risk, yet now earns a healthier return.

Figure 43: The Efficient Frontier.

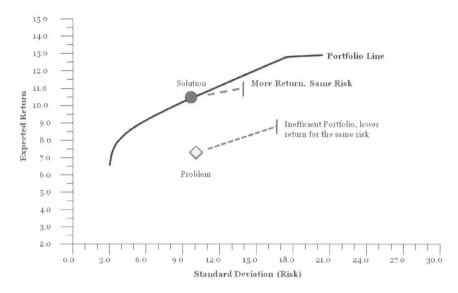

Expected Return: This is one of the two elements of the efficient frontier, establishing the rate of return you expect to earn on your investments. Everyone's expected return is different based on their own unique set of circumstances. For one person, their expected return would be 7%, but for somebody else to return might need to be 5%. Once the expected return is known, you and your advisor can decide which investments would be most efficient to achieve the results you want.

Expected Risk: This is the second of the two elements of the efficient frontier, identifying the level of risk contained within each investment you choose. Investors know that every investment has a certain amount of risk; there is no such thing as a guarantee when you invest your money. Actually, the only guarantee is the guarantee that your money is at risk. However, when it comes to investing, investors are willing to take a risk in order to increase their wealth. The degree of risk you are willing to accept must be rational and reasonable, or you should not be investing. This is why it's so important to know what you're doing when it comes to investing, because your money is subject to loss. And yet, if you didn't invest, you would lose your money anyway because inflation is constantly eroding the value of your dollars. So you're in a kind of Catch-22. You're damned if you do and damned if you don't. This is why you need to know what you're doing, which is a good reason for obtaining the advice of a professional investment advisor who will guide you with making wise decisions based on your specific set of circumstances.

Diversification: You've heard the proverb "Don't put all your eggs in one basket". If the basket falls, you could lose all your eggs. It's the same thing with putting your nest egg all in one investment; if anything bad happens to that investment, you could be a very sad farmer. Diversifying your assets in a well thought-out spread of investments will decrease your risk, and may also increase your growth. A sensible selection of investments would include investments of different types so that when one asset class is growing slowly, another asset class in your portfolio is growing steadily. As you probably know, the market moves through cycles, so it's usually a wise investor who has investments in a variety of asset classes; as the market moves through its phases, your portfolio continues to grow, and at the required rate of return (RRR) that is specific to your retirement goals.

Another highly important aspect of diversification is calculating the correlation coefficient. This is a fancy pair of words, which you'll soon understand.

Most people know they have to diversify their assets among different types of investments and different sectors within those investments to limit market risk. This should not be an arbitrary task, but rather a carefully calculated process.

The essence of proper diversification is the function of three factors:

1. The expected return

2. The expected risk

3. The correlation of how the assets work together

Once these three factors are known, asset allocations can then be made, resulting in the diversification of your resources.

The correlation coefficient ensures that the assets in your portfolio are working together to increase your potential for growth while limiting your potential for risk.

Again, here is another excellent example of how you would significantly benefit from the services of a financial advisor.

Continuing on the topic of diversification, Figure 44 provides an example of diversification among types of asset classes:

Figure 44: Diversification of Asset Classes.

Asset Class	%
Stocks	60%
Bonds	25%
Cash	15%
Total	**100%**

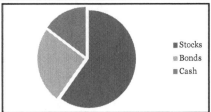

Not only could a portfolio be diversified by asset classes as shown above, but the asset classes themselves can also be diversified as shown on the next page.

Figure 45: Diversified Allocations Within Asset Classes.

Allocation With Asset Class		
Stocks (Equities)		
Large Cap Growth	6.0%	
Small Cap Growth	6.0%	
Mid Cap Growth	6.0%	
International	6.0%	
Large Cap Value	18.0%	
Mid Cap Value	18.0%	
Total		**60%**
Bonds (Debt)		
Mortgage-backed	6.25%	
U.S Govt.	6.25%	
Corporate	6.25%	
Municipal	6.25%	
Total		**25%**
Cash		**15%**
Total Portfolio:		**100%**

Furthermore, a portfolio can also be diversified by a variety of different types of stocks and bonds, and combinations of both as well, as shown below.

Figure 46: Example of Different Types of Investment Funds.

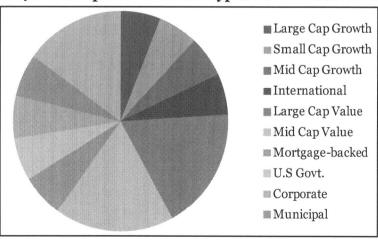

While you want to limit your risk and accelerate your growth, you must also give careful consideration to the percentage of the money you assign to each of these investments. For example, if you have five different asset classes, should you put 20% of your money in each of them; or maybe 60% in the large-cap fund, and 10% in each of the others? What is the best apportionment for your money, given the current market cycle, and your ability to accept risk? Again, seeking the advice of a financial expert can be instrumental with improving your safety and your performance.

How to invest inside the plan: If you are currently a plan participant in your company's 401(k) plan, you have several different choices about how to invest your money within the plan. Not all plans offer all these choices, but here is a rundown of the choices you may have available to you:

Follow Your Advisor's Model: Your company's financial advisor may have created several different portfolio models that are customized for the different demographics of employees at your company. One portfolio may be for younger people, and it has a more aggressive bias because young people have more time for investment, and can take more risk. Another portfolio may be designed for older people, and because they have less time to invest and require more security for their money, this is a conservative collection of investments that is composed mostly of balanced funds and conservative funds. Look closely at the different portfolio models that are available to you, and engage the advisor in a discussion about which one is right for you. The good thing about having a model available is that it's been created by a financial expert whose primary obligation is fiduciary, meaning that he or she must provide an investment model based on prudence. This means that your risk as an investor has been limited; this also means that its performance may also be limited. All in all, portfolio models may be the best choice for you because the portfolio has been deliberately created with clear expectations for performance.

Figure 47:   Advisor's Models and Target Date Models.

<u>Advisor's Models</u>

Conservative

Moderate Conservative

Moderate

Moderate Aggressive

Aggressive

<u>Target Date Models</u>

Retirement 2015

Retirement 2020

Retirement 2025

Retirement 2030

Retirement 2050

<u>Target Date Funds</u>: A "target date" fund is a fund designed for a person expecting to retire at a specific year in the future; the fund is based on a mix of asset classes which become more and more conservative, and thus less risky, the closer the target date to retirement approaches. This type of investment provides convenience, and the inherent recommendation of the investment experts who created it. It is still a good idea to examine the investments included in this fund, and also find out how this fund's investments adjust over time.

<u>Build Your Own Asset Allocation Model</u>: This may not be your best choice if you have limited experience in selecting investments, but it is an option for you. Truth be told, there are a lot of do-it-yourselfers who follow the AAII (American Association of Independent Investors) model, and other investors have their own idea of how they want to invest; they may want to do 60% stock and 40% bonds, or they may have preconceptions and only want to invest in green companies, etc. Sometimes an investor has an advisor who is not the company's

financial advisor and they prefer to take investment advice from the professional they know. In other situations, the company's plan may be so big that there really isn't going to be any good custom-oriented advice, so having an investor who can understand the participant's preferences, and who is willing to rebalance the participant's investments and allocations might be the best choice for some investors.

Figure 48: Asset Classes for Selection by Participant.

Asset Class For Participant Selection
Commodities
Emerging Market Bond
Emerging Market Equities
Global Bond
High Yield Bond
Intermediate Bond
International Bond
International Equity
Large Cap
Mid Cap
Real Estate
Short-Term Bond
Small/Mid Cap
TIPS

It's also a legitimate idea that your company's financial advisor can help you with the tax deferred funds in your 401(k) account, while your familiar advisor can help you with the funds that are not in your 401(k) account. In this case, it might be helpful if both advisors knew about your other investments so they have a perspective of your Big Picture and won't be full of anxiety thinking your investments are unbalanced. Yes, advisors worry about these things because, remember, they have a fiduciary responsibility to advise you in a prudent manner, so when they see an imbalance with the funds you are investing under their guidance, it is their responsibility to warn you. Letting each advisor know they are only seeing a portion of your financial iceberg will settle the professional anxiety they have for you.

<u>Select Individual Funds by Matching Your Investment Objectives with the Objectives of the Funds</u>: Another investment tact you can employ is reading the prospectus of each fund in the company's plan to learn about the individual fund's investment objectives. Then, once you have determined the investment objectives for each of the funds, you can select those funds with the same investment objectives you have. The investment choices in your company's plan will probably include stock funds, bond funds, money market funds, and other types of funds like real estate investment funds. Each of these funds must declare its investment objective, which helps you select the funds that

Figure 49: Mutual Fund Menu.

```
            Mutual Fund Menu

      Fund 1

      Fund 2

      Fund 3

      Fund 4

      ETC.....
```

Your advisor will provide a menu of choices, and you can pick any fund you want, or a little of each.

How to invest outside the plan: If you have investments which are not included in your 401(k) account, you should be educating yourself about how best to invest these resources. Again, consulting a financial advisor could be a very smart move for you.

A financial advisor can help you with a wide variety of services that can help you put your financial house in order. Figure 50 shows the many different ways a professional financial advisor can strengthen your personal finances with guiding your investment decisions, limiting your taxes, protecting your exposure to risk, and planning the structure and disposition of your estate. Consulting with a financial advisor can significantly improve your financial well-being.

Figure 50: Financial Planning.

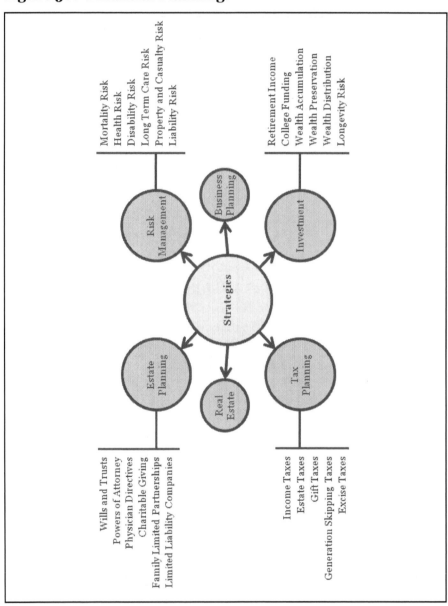

<u>Multiple Strategy Approach</u>: Since you are now thinking about your investments from a total portfolio perspective, knowing about a multiple strategy approach could be insightful for you and provide you with another way of thinking about your investments.

1.   Alpha strategies: An alpha strategy chooses funds which are designed to provide returns that exceed the benchmark, or the average, performance of investments of a similar type. For example, if the technology sector funds are achieving an average 9% return, the alpha strategy would study technology funds and select those that might return 10% or higher. Of course, there is additional risk in doing this. An Alpha strategy is also known as "active investing", in which an investor picks stocks that are believed will outperform the index.

2.   Beta strategies: A beta strategy selects funds that are likely to have returns which are similar to the benchmark for funds in that sector. This strategy prefers growth with limited risk. A beta strategy is also known as "passive investing", in which an investor purchases stocks that represent the performance of the index.

3.   Conservative strategies: The conservative strategy is more concerned with safety and the preservation of the principal than with growth. This strategy is best for people who will soon need to have these funds available.

Staying on course: Of course, once you set sail and invest your money in selected funds, it's quite likely that over time the investments you selected may underperform, or the content of the portfolio has shifted. Our best advice here is that you should review your investments' performance every three months to make sure the decisions you made are having the results you intended.

<u>Rebalancing</u>: You might have to rebalance, or adjust, your investment portfolio if an imbalance diminishes the possibility of your achieving your goals.

1.   Adjusting your portfolio goals: As you grow older, you may find

that your investment goals are changing, and you now prefer security more than growth. Or, perhaps you've done very well, and can afford to allocate a portion of your investments to more aggressive growth because you can now accept more risk. Reviewing the investment goals in your Investment Philosophy Statement (IPS) once a year is a great idea.

2.   Adjusting for market conditions: There will also be times when you may need to rebalance your portfolio because of the changing market conditions. If the economy goes through a long, slow decline, or the economy suddenly heats up and inflation increases, your portfolio may no longer be in balance with the market conditions and your investment goals. Being a smart investor means periodically studying your investments' performance in respect to the financial changes occurring in the global and national economy.

Your Social Security Benefits

Though this book is about the value of having a 401(k), a few words should be said about your Social Security benefits. For many Americans, Social Security is the primary source of income in their elder years. It is our hope that you will fund your retirement with a healthy 401(k) which will support a lifestyle you enjoy, but if you start late or can only contribute limited dollars to your 401(k), Social Security will be an additional source of income.

The two most asked questions about Social Security are:

"How much money will I receive?" and "When is the best time for me to start receiving my benefits?"

How Much?

The amount of money you receive from Social Security is based on the number of years you contributed to the Social Security program, and the dollar amounts you contributed each year. Of course, there are exceptions. Even if a spouse has never worked and never contributed to Social Security, the spouse is still eligible to receive funds based on the earnings of the other spouse. As you probably know, Social Security also provides funds for people with specific disabilities, and funds other programs to help people in need.

When?

As for the best time to begin receiving your benefits, it's an individual choice based on each person's unique circumstances. In some cases, the taxpayer may need to claim benefits as early as possible due to a serious illness or injury, a job loss, or slender savings. Other taxpayers may choose to wait to receive their benefits because they have the luxury of sufficient resources and can afford to delay until after they have turned 70, and thus receive larger monthly payments.

To receive Social Security benefits, you must be at least 62. There is no value in delaying your benefits after the age of 70, so within this nine-year range, you have three choices:

You can take early retirement between the ages of 62 and full retirement

- You can take full retirement at your full retirement age

- You can choose a delayed retirement, which is the period between full retirement age to age 70

- It's important to know that your full retirement age is based on the year you were born:

- If you were born between 1943 and 1954, your full retirement age is 66.

- If you were born between 1955 and 1959, your full retirement age is 66 and several months, depending on your birth year.

- If you were born in 1960 or thereafter, your full retirement age is 67.

Once you're eligible, you can begin receiving your Social Security benefits, but you should know that your monthly benefits will be less the earlier you start taking your benefits. Every year you delay, your monthly benefits increase.

> The first taxpayer to receive a check from Social Security was Ernest Ackerman of Cleveland, Ohio. A retired motorman, he received a lump-sum payment of 17 cents in January 1937. Mr. Ackerman retired one day after paying five cents into the Social Security program.

Many Details, Many Choices

Again, it's a matter of what is best for your personal financial situation. We believe it would be wise to consult with a financial advisor who will consider your overall financial goals and circumstances with you, calculate your various options, and then help you make the best decision.

There are a lot of important details to the Social Security program, so it's important that you speak with someone who has experience with the variety of choices and situations that affect this program. For example, when a worker chooses to start their benefits before their full retirement age, benefits are permanently reduced. The percent of reduction can be as high as 30%. This is a significant loss of potential income, especially at a time when you may need as much income as possible.

On the other hand, delaying your retirement benefits are likely to result in larger benefits. Every month you delay your benefits beyond full retirement age, your benefits increase by two thirds of 1%, or 8% per year. This could mean an increase in your benefits of up to as much as 32%.

Everybody's personal circumstances are different, of course, so there truly is no right way to make such an important decision without careful review and consideration, and a financial advisor who can calculate your benefits with a variety of scenarios pertinent to your unique situation will help you make the best choice.

Married Workers

If you're married, a financial advisor can help by examining your options for maximizing your Social Security benefits. Married couples have more alternatives than single taxpayers, and this advantage could result in more income.

Your financial advisor could counsel you to "file and suspend", for example. In this scenario, the higher earner files for benefits, and then, upon approval, suspends the benefits claim immediately. This allows the other spouse, who must be 62, to file a spousal benefits claim, even if he or she never worked or contributed to Social Security. The higher earner can keep working while the spouse collects benefits, adding to their monthly income. At age 70 or sooner, the higher earner now receives greater monthly benefits because payment was deferred.

Another strategy is known as "restricted application" or "free spousal benefits". In this example, both spouses continue working, and the higher earner claims spousal benefits as the spouse of the lower earner. Later, the higher earner can claim his or her own benefits, which will now be even greater because payments were deferred.

Divorced Workers

There is also a strategy for divorced workers. In this case, an ex-spouse waits until full retirement age and then claims a spousal benefit. The ex-spouse can receive 50% of the other spouse's benefit without the divorced spouse ever knowing. Then, when the ex-spouse is 70 years old, he or she can claim their own benefits, which are now greater because payments have been deferred.

Once again you can see the wisdom in speaking with a financial advisor who can review these options with you... Remember: you don't know what you don't know, so it's important that you speak with an experienced and knowledgeable advisor.

> Ida May Fuller from Vermont was the first person to ever receive a monthly Social Security check. Retiring at 65 as a legal secretary, the first monthly check ever issued was for $22.54. Ms. Fuller lived until 100, and in the 35 years of her retirement, she received more than $22,000.

Your financial advisor will look at your entire financial picture, which may include future income from your 401(k), other investments you may have, IRAs, real estate property you may own, a pension, your Social Security benefits, and the financial details relating to your spouse's retirement income.

To completely understand the variety of choices that may be available to you, we can recommend no better decision than meeting with an advisor who understands your financial and retirement goals and guides you with the decisions that will help you achieve the security and peace of mind you desire and deserve.

Careful thought and wise consultation is your best choice!

Be Smart!

Remember how we started this chapter: no one is going to care about your money as much as you are. It's all well and good to have a financial advisor who has created an investment model for you, and it's also really great if you have your own financial advisor guiding you on the investments that are not in your company's 401(k) plan. But where the rubber really meets the road is when you take the time to learn the basics about investment, and then expand your knowledge so you can make decisions that are sensible and realistic in light of your own unique circumstances. Here are a few more gems for you to consider.

 Note:

Chasing a hot investment is like a dog chasing its tail...no good can come of it.

Don't chase the hot investment, trend, or fad: You've heard the story about the person who invested in a new company and the value of the stock shot through the roof just a few weeks later. Could it happen to you? It might, it might not. The odds of this happening are slim to none. Most mathematicians privately giggle that the lottery is for people who are bad at math; yes, someone wins the lottery, but how recently have you won the lottery? The main point here is that chasing the trends is just that; by the time you get on board, the money has been made and you'll be buying an investment that is already overpriced. Then, when the value drops, you'll lose the value of your stock. The best way to grow your investment dollars is by having a plan based on steady growth over a long period of time. If you want to spend some mad money, take your family out for double banana splits, but don't throw your money away on investments that promise explosions and deliver fizzles.

Here is another very important concept to understand. In fact, this next segment is actually a gold nugget. It will make a huge difference in your thinking, in your investment planning, in your investment outcomes, and in the quality of life you can have in retirement.

Most people have heard of compounding, but hardly anyone has heard of negative compounding. Compounding, of course, is the continual growth of money based on an ever-expanding sum consisting of the initial principal and the ongoing accumulation of interest. Negative compounding is the concept that what goes down has to go up even more to break-even, to get back to the original sum.

Here's an example: if you have $100,000 and you lose 10%, your
account is reduced to $90,000. Most people think that if they earn
10% the next year, they're back to where they started. However, that's
not the case because 10% of $90,000 is $9,000; that would bring your
account to $99,000, which is $1,000 less than where they started.
Therefore, to break-even, you require not a 10% return, but an 11.1%
return.

Another analogy is a 4.0 student. If you are a 4.0 student and you
receive a B in one class, mathematically you can never be a 4.0
student again. You might be a 3.9 student or something like that, but
you'll never again be in 4.0 student. This is a very powerful concept
to understand because what it teaches is the value of not chasing a
return...but rather, preventing a loss. Part of the wisdom of making
money is preventing losses.

You can visually see this concept in the table below:

Figure 51: Negative Compounding.

	Period One	Period Two
Beginning Value	$100,000	$90,000
Return	-10%	+10%
Ending Value	$90,000	$99,000

Break-Even 11.1%

Now that you understand this concept, we will take a look at the next
chart. The next chart shows the losses of an account with a beginning
value of $100,000. The different percentage losses in the second
column result in the new ending value in the third column. The fourth
column shows you the percentage needed just to break-even, and the
last column shows how many years it would take to break-even based
on the different percentage losses this account suffered.

This chart assumes that the market is averaging a 7% increase. Using
the table below, you can see that if you lost 50% of your $100,000,

your account was reduced to $50,000. You would need 100% to break-even. If you could earn 7% return on your remaining $50,000, it would take you 10.24 years to have your original $100,000 back again.

So, if you're in retirement, the last thing you want to see happen is that you retire, lose money, and then wait 10.24 years to get your money back. If this happened to you, it would mean you would probably have to go back to work.

Using the same chart below, if your account suffered a 10% loss and was reduced to $90,000, you would need a break-even return of 11.1%, and it would take you 1.56 years to break-even. Another example is when the S&P 500 was down approximately 40% in 2008; anyone who was caught in that downturn needed 66.67% to break-even, and at 7% return it would take them 7.55 years...just to break-even.

As the chart above explains, when your investments depreciate, you have to earn an even higher rate of return to restore what was lost. The example above shows a loss of 10% requiring a rate of 11.1% to regain the original value.

Here are a few other examples to give you a chill:

Figure 52: Break-Even Scenarios.

Beginning Value	Percentage Loss	Ending Value	Percent to Break-Even	Years to Break-Even (Assumes 7% Annual Return)
$100,000	-5%	$95,000	5.26%	0.76
$100,000	-10%	$90,000	11.11%	1.56
$100,000	-15%	$85,000	17.64%	2.40
$100,000	-20%	$80,000	25%	3.30
$100,000	-30%	$70,000	42.86%	5.27
$100,000	-40%	$60,000	66.67%	7.55
$100,000	-50%	$50,000	100%	10.24

Now that you can see the damage caused to an account that suffers losses, let's take a look at the next chart. The graph lines show two portfolios, both managed by the same advisor. One portfolio is stable and its growth is 10% +10% +10% +10% +10%. Obviously, its five-year average return is 10%. The other portfolio is volatile, and its growth is 10% +10% +10% +10% +10%; its five-year average return is also 10%, even though it's up 20%, down 40%, up 50%, down 30%, and up 50%.

Both portfolios have averaged 10% over a five-year period, so if your advisor asks you if you would like the portfolio with the 10% average return, or the portfolio with the 10% average return, you might be inclined to say, "I don't care! They both averaged 10%...", and yet we can see the effect that negative compounding has had on the performance of the volatile portfolio. The stable portfolio resulted in almost $48,000 more than the volatile portfolio...$161,000 versus $113,000...and yet both averaged 10% over a five-year period. The lesson should be clear: it's better to take the path of least volatility. It's not the return that is the most significant factor; it's also about avoiding losses. The goal here is to prevent negative compounding and to retain as much of your principal as possible to benefit from the effect of compounding.

Figure 53: Growth of a Dollar.

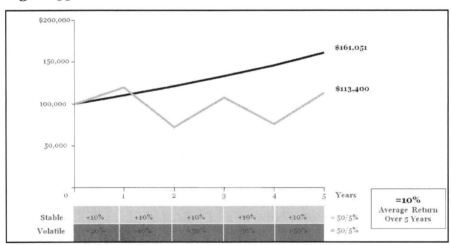

This example is based on an initial investment of $100,000; earnings are compounded annually. The results assume no taxes, fees or other investment costs. This hypothetical example is for illustrative purposes only and is not the actual performance of any mutual fund.

It would be wise to change a contemporary misunderstanding among investors that proclaims the ability of youth to accept aggressive investment risk. "Hey! You're 25 years old; you've got 40 years until retirement; just go out and be as aggressive as you can!" The first part is true; a young person does have a lot of time ahead of them, but is it wise to subject your account to the destructiveness of volatility?

The goal is to have the highest amount of money at retirement, not achieve the highest return. Why would a person want to subject their account to volatility and push for a high return when it's wiser to be conservative and achieve a higher ending balance? Though it's true that a young person has plenty of time ahead of them, and they have the benefit of the long view, the attitude that it's okay to lose money because they have plenty of time to earn it back is incorrect thinking. It's irrational for anyone to go backwards for 10 or 15 years just to break-even. There is no point to taking a step forward, taking two steps back, taking a half step forward, taking one step back, taking three steps forward, taking one step back... As an investor, you always want to be moving forward, and to keep moving forward, and to keep increasing your financial wealth, it's imperative to manage the downside volatility and not chase the upside return. Your best choice is to find an advisor who is expert at managing the volatility and spends more time focusing on that task than on chasing a return; when you follow this mathematically proven strategy, you can actually earn more money with a lower return! This attitude is not intuitive; it's counterintuitive and it takes some education to understand it. Now you have the benefit of seeing this financial truth revealed. This is an absolutely key point for retirement savings, and the preceding three charts are proof. This is a Gold Nugget.

Oh, yes. There's only one case when the opposite is true, and that's if the markets only go straight up. If the markets only go straight up and there is no volatility, the highest return will win. But if there's any volatility, and there always is, you can't simply look just at the return. A good advisor understands this and looks at the dynamic interrelationship between risk and return, not just risk, and not just return. They must be evaluated together.

This is not just a two-cent opinion...it's a $1,000,000 idea.

Put money into your plan; don't take it out: The whole idea of having a 401(k) retirement plan is to build your wealth. If you borrow your money with a loan, you're limiting the growth of the money you'll need in your future. This is why we've explained how important it is to build an emergency fund that can carry you through most financial emergencies. Sometimes life will throw you a fastball, and you have no choice but to borrow against your future. This is why the 401(k) plan makes it so difficult for you to borrow...if you can find a way to pay for your emergency in a different way, you can prevent having an emergency later when you are retired.

Do not over-invest in your company's stock: Many employees have a tendency to want to over-purchase their company's stock. This is usually because they believe they have an insider's view about the future of the company, or they have a lot of faith in their employer and believe the company's stock is a strong investment. This is not always the case. Remember that you want to always have a balanced approach to your financial decisions. This is why we recommend the diversification of your investments, and apportioning your asset allocations according to a carefully thought-out plan protecting you from undue risk. Remember the efficient frontier? The efficient frontier is a strategy for investing your funds based on the most growth with the least risk according to your unique circumstances. Over-investing in your company's stock may not be a good fit for your total portfolio, and there are occasions when the healthy appearance of a company disguises a serious illness.

Stay educated: The best way to take care of your money is by spending some time now and then reading about investing, maybe buying a subscription to Money magazine, take a class at your community college, or browse the shelves at your local bookstore. Certainly, you should attend your company's 401(k) quarterly meetings and schedule one-on-one conferences with your plan's advisor even if you don't know what to talk about; you can be sure your advisor will have some things to share! It's only by being engaged and interested in learning about investing that you'll be truly protected and more capable of building the resources you'll need for the decades of time when you're no longer working.

Summary

This chapter provided a number of important gems about investing. We provided a very pointed example illustrating how time is your ally, and while it's never too late to start saving and investing, saving early is a better choice than saving late. We also discussed how much money you'll need for retirement, and explored the concept of the required rate of return (RRR). Next, we explained the importance of knowing your 401(k) plan's "rules of the game" so you can play and win. Then we considered the value of rolling over your 401(k) account into an IRA when you retire so you can have more flexibility with your investment choices and less rigidity outside the plan's rules and limitations. The chapter concluded with some insightful advice about being a smart investor to increase your advantage and your opportunity for building a secure and comfortable future.

 Chapter 5 Review Questions:

1. Reverse engineering is when your financial advisor first calculates the cost of your future lifestyle and then works backwards to recommend a strategy and investment plan to achieve your monetary goals.

   A. True

   B. False

2. The required rate of return (RRR) is the minimum annual percentage an investment portfolio must earn to achieve the portfolio's goal for growth.

    A. True

    B. False

3. The RRR is different for different investments, and for different people.

    A. True

    B. False

4. The RRR is achieved by the combined rate of return of all the funds in the portfolio.

    A. True

    B. False

5. Your company's financial advisor may be a fiduciary, and if so, this means he or she must always act in your best interests.

    A. True

    B. False

6. Diversifying your assets in a well thought-out spread of investments will decrease your risk, and may also increase your growth.

    A. True

    B. False

7. Chasing a hot investment, trend, or fad is not a good idea because:

   A. You'll be buying an investment that is already overpriced.

   B. Too much attention has caused the price to rise beyond its true value.

   C. It's likely that the original investors are now selling to make their profit.

   D. Probably all of the above.

8. An important part of making money is preventing losses.

   A. True

   B. False

9. A good advisor understands the dynamic interrelationship between risk and return, not just risk, and not just return. They must be evaluated together.

   A. True

   B. False

10. A good rule is not to over-invest in your company's stock; a balanced portfolio of investments is a wise choice.

   A. True

   B. False

Answers

1. Answer: A. The key to reverse engineering is deciding your financial goals for your retirement years. Once your goals are known, they can then be priced, and that allows your advisor to reverse engineer a strategy for you to follow.

2. Answer: A. In some years, you will exceed your RRR, and in other years your investments will fall short; knowing your RRR tells you if you are on track with saving the funds you'll need to achieve your retirement lifestyle.

3. Answer: A. Everyone's RRR is unique to their retirement lifestyle goals, the time they have until retirement, and their tolerance for risk.

4. Answer: A. Your financial advisor can recommend funds whose combined annual expected performance has the likelihood of achieving your required rate of return.

5. Answer: A. A fiduciary must always act in the best interests of the plan participants. Your company's 401(k) plan may have several people in the role of fiduciary.

6. Answer: A. A combination of investments can result in secure growth. If one fund does poorly, another may offset the poor performance with exemplary performance.

7. Answer: D.

8. Answer: A. When you prevent excessive loss, you have more funds available when the market turns. Your advisor can help you select your funds carefully and according to an investment plan that can secure your funds from excessive loss.

9. Answer: A. Most investments' value fluctuates, and increase and decrease in value over time; an investment's potential for return must be considered with its potential for risk.

10. Answer: A. Most employees tend to favor their company's stock because the company is familiar, but a balanced portfolio is more likely to provide more returns with less risk over time.

Chapter 6:
Working with My Personal Investment Advisor

When you have finished reading this chapter, you will:

- Consider the advantages of having your personal investment advisor

- Know the importance of the six steps of financial planning

- Be able to explain the three phases of a person's financial life, and the characteristics of each

Building your financial resources to have a comfortable and secure retirement is a worthy goal. Longevity has been increasing and it is not uncommon for a person to live into their 80s and even their 90s. It's often a person's greatest fear, because the idea of outliving your savings, being at an advanced age, and relying on your relatives and the government is typically an unpleasant idea.

Your company's 401(k) plan is benefitting from the services of an investment professional with responsibility for educating the employees in the plan, and providing investment advice which serves the best interests of the plan's participants. This expert is available to you, both within the services provided by the plan, as well as outside the plan, should you also wish to hire him or her for more precise personal assistance. In this chapter we're going to consider the value of working with an investment advisor and provide insight on how this business relationship might unfold.

Do I Need One?

You might, and you might not. As we've said before, it's always best to suit the tool to the job. You don't need a bazooka to kill a fly. The facts and circumstances of your individual situation are the best indicators to dictate the level of financial planning and service you need. There are brilliant financial planners who can razzle-dazzle and help their clients with complicated retirement investment portfolios, and there are young financial planners just starting out in their career with good credentials and some experience who are the best choice for uncomplicated retirement counseling. There is no need to hire a starship captain when a competent lieutenant will do.

A financial advisor can provide the information and guidance you'll need so you can develop a competent plan designed to help you reach your retirement goals.

As you can see from the figure below, we've identified six steps that serve in any scenario that involves planning, in this case we are referring to financial planning. The tasks and sequence make good sense. The key, of course, is first knowing and prioritizing your goals because unless you know where you're going, you may never get there; this has been a key tenet of this book.

Figure 54: The Six Steps of Financial Planning.

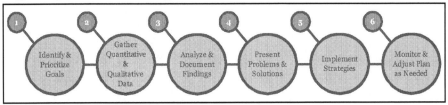

Building Your Lifestyle Protection Plan: We'd like to present a concept that we hope you'll find valuable. Please consider this information thoughtfully and with prudence because it forms the core of your financial prosperity. It may not seem so now, but the day is rapidly approaching when your work life will be over and your retirement life will begin. There is no better time than now, today, to decide on how you want to spend your retirement years; this is an old violin we've played before, but now we want you to see this graphically. Take a look at the next figure:

Figure 55: Lifestyle Protection Planning.

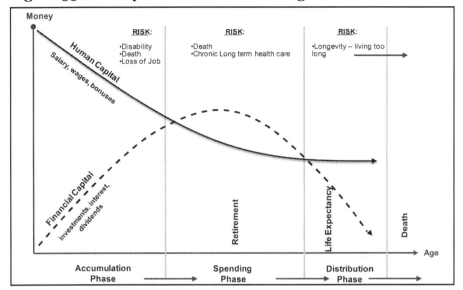

Please study this figure; there are a number of interesting elements to consider. During the first phase, the Accumulation Phase, we know that a young person has mostly human capital, and not very much financial capital. When a young person's work life begins and they have their first job, or start their lifelong career, their financial capital begins to build through the diligence of making investments, compounding interest, etc. Over the course of time there are salary increases, and new opportunities also provide additional financial resources; financial capital increases over time when care and forethought are employed. In the Spending Phase, life tends to be a busy and committed time. This is when most people start a family, have children, buy a house, usually need a car to get around, and want to acquire nice things. In the Distribution Phase, the length of time is diminishing; eventually both life and financial resources prove finite.

As we're sure you understand, the visual representation of the Lifestyle Protection Planning chart clearly indicates the best time to set your goals, implement your investment strategies, monitor and adjust your financial plan, and do everything you can so you are ready for the years which are waiting for you on the other side of your work life. As much as you can increase your portfolio size, it would be wise to do so, so you have no remorse about the insufficiency of your preparedness when your Golden Years are here.

Important:

How important is it that you have enough money in retirement? Isn't it worth it, then, to hire the services of a financial advisor who can check that your investment plan will achieve the results you want and need?

You take your car in for a periodic checkup. You see a doctor and a dentist for periodic maintenance and care. Consider how important it is to also see a financial advisor.

Once the basic goals of your financial planning pyramid have been achieved, it's time to move up a level and into your investment portfolios. You'll remember we had three steps: the first step is to set your financial goals so you know the amount of money you need to achieve; the second step was to determine your short-term, midterm, and long-term investment goals; and the final step was to allocate your resources so each of your investment needs are satisfied. If you've already funded your short-term investment goals, and have also accomplished your midterm goals, then now it's time to allocate your funds and fulfill your long-term goals capacity. If this is exactly where you are, having satisfied all your other financial requirements along the way, and are now beginning to contribute to your long-term investments, then for the time being, just continue funding your 401(k); you won't need much financial advice until you have allocated enough funds in your retirement account. Until the account has grown to a decent magnitude, there isn't much a financial planner can do.

Yes, of course, this is a good time to educate yourself about retirement saving, and about the funds and portfolio models available in your company's 401(k) plan. This is the best choice for your current age and retirement planning situation. Attend the quarterly workshops, read the periodic newsletter about your 401(k) plan, and make a list of questions about the things you don't understand so you can have them answered when the company's financial advisor meets with plan participants one-on-one every three months or so. This is the time to educate yourself about the 401(k) plan so that when your account reaches sufficient size, you can engage the advisor with a mature understanding.

If you have too little money in your 401(k) account, there is not a lot your financial planner can do, but by steadily adding funds to your account, the time will come when consulting a financial advisor will make more sense, and will actually become a necessity. Having a financial planner who can study your unique circumstances and calculate your required rate of return (RRR) will be a significant moment in time.

Even though it may take a few years for your 401(k) account to have enough substance that merits serious financial planning, it's always a good time to consult with a financial advisor when you have a complex situation in your life. When you're faced with a variety of life events that are more complex and you need good answers, that's the time to see an expert because the chances are excellent that you don't know what you don't know; you should never be hesitant to seek professional financial expertise because spending some money to acquire an experienced opinion and service is always much better than taking a chance and making the wrong decision, or a decision that's only second-rate. If you don't know how to fly an airplane, you'd be better off as a passenger; if you don't know how to remodel the kitchen, it's a good idea to hire a contractor. The other part of this is that you don't need to hire a brain surgeon if you don't need brain surgery; you can always find a financial advisor within a reasonable price range who will be happy to guide you with wholesome financial advice.

Here is a list of some of the more complicated life situations:
- Getting married and starting a family

- Buying a home or property

- Changing jobs or surviving unemployment

- Saving for college or managing college expenses

- Starting a business or planning for a business exit

- Getting divorced or suffering the death of a spouse

- Planning for retirement, nearing retirement, or retiring

- Caring for an aging parent or receiving an inheritance/windfall

- Planning for long-term care

- Leaving an estate

These are examples of life-events which might suggest a good occasion to benefit from the advice of a professional trained for guiding you.

Your Advisor's Obligations

Your plan's advisor may actually not have any obligations to you or the plan because they may not be a fiduciary of the plan. A fiduciary is a person who is trusted with someone else's property, and not all 401(k) financial advisors serve in the role of fiduciary. Your plan's advisor might be a salesman, or may not be a certified financial planner or a registered investment advisor RIA, and/or an accredited investment fiduciary (AIF). Obviously, before you seek the advice of your company plan's advisor, assure yourself that they are qualified to serve in your best interests as a fiduciary. An advisor who is a salesperson is representing his company's investment products, and has no obligation to you as a plan participant. You can expect the salesperson to steer you toward purchasing his company's investment products. There's nothing wrong with this, except you would probably prefer having an unbiased opinion when it comes to making investment decisions for your retirement account.

When you select a fiduciary investment advisor, this professional has a fiduciary responsibility to act in the best interests of the plan's participants. The plan, the plan participants, and the participants' beneficiaries are the clients, and their interests always come first. The bottom line is you should always find out if the plan's advisor is a fiduciary of the plan, because if so, you'll know the advisor's primary obligations are to you.

What to Expect

The service you can expect from your plan's advisor will vary depending on the advisor. If the advisor is not certified, or not particularly knowledgeable or experienced, you should expect service that is less customized and offers less advanced financial planning; it's likely that this type of advisor will offer a more generic education about retirement planning. In some cases, if your plan's advisor is being provided through the 401(k) custodian, such as a mutual fund family, you should realize that the information you'll be receiving is specific to the custodians' investment products. Perhaps the 401(k) plan is sponsored by an insurance company; in this case, the plan's advisor is an insurance expert, and this doesn't make the advisor an investment expert. You probably should not expect very advanced planning from an individual that isn't fully trained. If, however, your plan's advisor is from an independent financial planning company without obligation to the type of custodian companies noted above, the advice you'll receive is likely to be more impartial. Therefore, you should expect the service level that's commensurate to the type of advisor associated with your company's 401(k) plan.

Advisor Services Provided by the Plan

The services that will be available to you will be those that have been decided by your employer. Your employer is the plan sponsor and is the reason for the 401(k) plan being available. When the 401(k) plan was being created, your employer and the investment advisor discussed the variety of services the financial advisor could provide, and your employer negotiated and chose the ones that are in your plan now.

Generally, aside from setting up the plan and selecting the investment funds that are available in your plan, the services which the investment advisor can provide will be educational. The frequency and the depth of these educational opportunities have already been defined by your employer. Some employers want the financial advisor to provide meetings for plan participants once every three months, or quarterly, and have asked the advisor to present an economic update, an investment market update, and a fund performance update. Some employers also require the advisor to meet one-on-one with every participant to review their individual statement and discuss any element of the 401(k) plan about which the participant has questions. In some instances, the advisor has special advisory abilities, and can counsel participants about realty services, for example, or perhaps the advisor specializes in insurances, or business planning. Advice of this type might also be included in the services made available through your plan's sponsor. On the other hand, some employers don't want their employees disrupted, so these services may be very restricted, limited to once a year instead of quarterly. Whatever it is that's provided, using this service to your benefit is recommended.

Your investment advisor's company may offer realty services to their 401(k) clients at a discount, so plan participants have this additional advisory benefit if the sponsor has approved it. They may also provide budgeting services, and RRR calculations for customized and personalized planning as well. In some cases, these additional advisory services are priced into the company's plan, and there is no fee to the plan participants.

Advisor Services Outside the Plan

Of course, these services can also be provided outside of the company's 401(k) plan, whether or not an individual is part of the company's plan. If an employee would like to hire an advisor to develop their personal RRR, this would be accommodated. Your plan sponsor doesn't want to pay for everything related to your retirement needs, so some investment advice may have to come out of pocket. In Linda Nelson's case study in Chapter 5, her employer, Michael Kendall, was willing to pay for a lot of his employees' advisory services, but just not everything for everybody, which is quite understandable. However, should Linda decide that even though she is somewhat informed but would like a deeper understanding about how she can more thoroughly plan for her retirement's future, she can always hire a professional advisor to do a customized and personalized RRR on a regular basis, perhaps once every year, or once every three years, providing more insight to the important investment decisions she needs to make.

 ## Key:

Ask your company's 401(k) financial advisor if he or she would be able to work with you outside the 401(k) plan. You can also select a financial advisor by looking on the Internet.

Tell the advisor why you want to meet and ask what the fee will be. You're likely to be pleasantly surprised; if not, find a financial advisor whose fees fit your budget.

Another very important task your financial advisor can perform for you is creating your own investment policy statement (IPS). The reason this might be desirable for you is because the 401(k) might be only one of your assets. If you also have a brokerage account, IRAs, investment properties, a pension plan, or any other financial assets, an investment policy statement which oversees and coordinates all these investments could provide improved performance and increased risk control.

The cost for having your personal IPS developed could be a nominal fee of about $500, or, depending upon the number, variety, and complexity of your investments, the price could be several thousand dollars. Remember, the goal here is to match the tool for the task. As with every service you receive, it always makes good sense to first acquire a written engagement proposal before hiring any consultant. Read the proposal carefully, ask whatever questions you need to ask, add or eliminate anything as appropriate, and negotiate the price if you wish.

Paying Your Advisor

Continuing this discussion, some services are included in your company's 401(k) plan, and there may be services you require that are not.

Inside the plan: Find out which services are offered in your 401(k) plan. As mentioned above, the services will depend on what your employer has decided to include. Every plan is different, so there might be some wonderful benefits available to you. Also, find out which of these services are completely paid for by the plan, and which ones may require you to pay part or all of the fees for that particular service. Do not make any assumptions! You should only make your decision when you know the facts.

Outside the plan: Some employers want the investment advisor to work very closely with their employees, and some tell the advisor not to speak to the participants except at the annual meeting. Your plan's advisor may have additional products to offer you, such as specific financial advising services; some employers encourage the advisor to speak to their employees about them, and other employers instruct the advisor not to do so.

There are also times when a handful of smart and interested employees are eager to take advantage of the services which are only available outside the plan, and they hire the advisor to help them with their personal financial plan and its management. Of course, when the advisor is hired outside the plan, the employee becomes a new client to whom the advisor has a fiduciary responsibility. The advisor is able to do a lot more for this new client then can be done for them in the 401(k) plan when meetings are restricted to once a quarter or once a year.

Remember, too, that the financial advisor is now establishing a strong one-on-one relationship with his or her new client, and over the years the advisor will thoroughly know the client's investments, both within the 401(k) as well as outside the 401(k), and become familiar with their personal financial situation. Once the client reaches retirement age and is no longer working for the company, which is a significant financial event, the same services can continue. The advisor can now provide financial advice and account management services on rolling over the 401(k) funds to other investment opportunities that may not have been available in your former company's 401(k) plan.

For example, the investment funds in your former company's 401(k) plan were selected based on what the plan sponsor, or your employer, felt was appropriate given the demographics of the employees working in the company. This selection may have been restrictive because the plan sponsor had a fiduciary responsibility to assure the government and the employees that the investments selected for the plan were in the best interests of all plan participants. Now that you are no longer a part of the plan, it may be that a variety of other investment types are now available, and some of these may be especially beneficial for you and for the growth or safety of your retirement funds.

By the way, the term "rollover" and "rolling over" refer to moving money from one account to another account...in essence, rolling it from one to the other. In a rollover, money in a tax-deferred account must be rolled over to another tax-deferred account within a limited time period to prevent taxation. If tax-deferred monies were rolled over to a taxable account, the tax and penalties would be expensive.

The fees for the various services your advisor provides will depend, once again, on the types of services you choose, and also the type of advisor you hire. Again, there is a wide range of investment professionals with a wide range of experience and qualifications. Some will be more costly than others, so you'll need to do some inquiries; it might be a good idea to start with your company's financial advisor, as this person may be able to refer you to an associate who is appropriate for your needs and your wallet. Also, the fees will depend on how your advisor chooses to do business, because some advisors operate a fee-only business, while others charge a commission on your investments' performance. There is no harm in asking around until you find the right advisor, and always request a written engagement proposal so the services and the price are quoted before any work is done.

Your advisor's hands may be tied... There is also something important you should know about the working relationship with your advisor. If the advisor is a fiduciary of the company's plan, the advisor has to be extremely careful not to give the appearance of guiding you into a business relationship for work that can only be done outside the plan. You can see why, of course. As a fiduciary, the advisor has to have the best interests of the plan's participants as the primary focus, and cannot appear to be taking advantage of this special fiduciary relationship. Even though the advisor may know you would very clearly benefit from hiring him or her to work on your personal financial tasks, the advisor is wise to not suggest this, and may be hoping you will bring this up on your own accord. The reason is that the advisor needs to maintain some distance since he or she will benefit monetarily from these services, and this may be viewed by regulatory agencies as self-serving and, therefore, a biased and illegal action.

Note:

When you want to hire your company's 401(k) plan advisor for personal services, you must be the first one to start the discussion.

Here is an example of this dilemma. Linda Nelson has been with Pacific Specialty Lighting Supply, Inc. for 30 years, and her retirement is just around the corner. The plan's advisor has managed Linda's 401(k) account all this time, and completely understands the value of Linda's assets, as well as also helping her develop her investment policy statement (IPS), her retirement budget, and even provided realty advice on securing the rental property she'll need to augment her retirement income. Now that Linda is about to leave the company, the advisor knows that Linda will benefit from continued financial advice, especially during this huge financial adjustment period. Linda's 401(k) account has been annually charged 50 basis points in fees, which is a typical cost for a participant in a company plan that's about the size of the company employing Linda. A basis point is one-hundredth of 1%, so Linda's annual fee for the advisor's services is ½% of her account's annual performance. This fee was generously paid by Linda's employer.

Now that Linda is ready to retire, should Linda decide to retain the services of her advisor outside the company's 401(k) plan as a private client with a single account, Linda will be charged 100 basis points, or a full 1%. There is an argument in the investment industry that inviting a client like Linda to rollover her funds into the advisor's continuing care constitutes a violation of the advisor's fiduciary responsibility. Linda can leave her 401(k) funds in the company's plan even though she is no longer an employee and continue to receive the benefits of the advisor's management services. The management services offered through the company may or may not be the best decision for Linda, so the advisor has to be very careful about what he or she says, and cannot tell Linda to automatically roll it over because the suggestion will appear questionable.

Most investment planners who offer to rollover the funds have the best intentions and are not disregarding their fiduciary responsibilities. In fact, most planners will say that doing an individual investment plan is costly to their time, and the fees they receive do not sufficiently compensate them; if you're receiving more services than are offered in the plan, the higher fee may be justified. On the other hand, most planners will also confirm that the services their new client receives with a 1% fee is much different than the service they were receiving when they were in the company plan paying a half percent.

Ultimately, the suggestion by the advisor to roll the funds out of the plan and into the advisor's more complete management is probably totally justified, but this is still an ERISA fiduciary issue that makes advisors nervous and uncertain about whether or not to recommend that the investor do a rollover; of course, nothing precludes the investor from finding their own advisor, but then the familiarity with the investor's funds and history is lost, and the client will need to establish a new relationship with someone who is unfamiliar, and which will take time.

You can see that this is a tender situation, and now, knowing about this, you can choose to invite your company's financial advisor to be your personal advisor after you retire, if this will benefit you. When you're the one who makes this request, the fiduciary obligations are no longer questionable.

It's also possible that your investment fees may diminish. If an investor has a large amount of assets outside the 401(k) plan, the total amount of their investments might be a factor in reducing the cost of the investment fees. In this sense, the client would save money by "buying" in bulk.

Key:

It's best to hire fee-only independent financial advisors. A fee-only advisor will only earn the fee, not a percentage of your invested monies. Also, an independent advisor who is not associated with any investment fund will not have a bias for steering you toward his or her company's products.

A fee-only independent advisor is the best choice because the advisor has only your best interests in mind.

It is recommended that you work with fee-only independent advisors so the potential bias for encouraging you to buy products that enhance the advisor's commissions is eliminated. Hire an advisor who doesn't represent a specific investment company. From this type of advisor's position, it's not necessarily about the fee; it's more about doing what's right and best for the client. However, on the other hand, when an advisor earns their fees on commission and has no stake in your portfolio's growth, there is little incentive to serve you.

Summary

It might be a good idea to hire the services of a professional advisor to manage some of your personal financial tasks. Some of these tasks, like overseeing all your financial assets and fine tuning their performance as the economic cycles and performance cycles wax and wane could be a distinct advantage in increasing your accounts' return and limiting your exposure to risk. On the other hand, if your financial resources are slight, it's probably the wiser choice to not incur expenses until your assets have reached sufficient size to merit expert management. Your advisor may or may not have your best interests in mind if he or she is not your fiduciary, so always confirm the nature of your relationship to avoid making decisions based on biased recommendations. In addition, always request a written engagement proposal, or a price quote for itemized services, so you can clearly know what tasks your advisor will perform, and what the cost will be. The proposal should state how you will pay the fees and expenses, whether through a billable invoice, or as a percentage of the funds' performance.

Finally, remember that advisors would like to retain you as a client after you reach retirement and can move your 401(k) monies to other investment opportunities, and they need to be careful so they don't violate their fiduciary responsibilities nor appear self-surviving. If you like the work your company's advisor has done for you in the past, it could be a great advantage to invite a financial expert who already knows about your financial history and goals, and the personal details of your life as they relate to your financial future, to speak with this professional advisor and friend, and ask to continue the good work and familiar relationship you have both worked to establish over the years.

Chapter 6 Review Questions:

1. The service you can expect to receive from your company's 401(k) plan advisor will vary, depending on the advisor.

    A.　True

    B.　False

2. It's likely that the best service your company's 401(k) plan advisor will provide is educational.

    A.　True

    B.　False

3. If you wish, you can always hire a financial advisor who is not associated with your company's 401(k) plan.

    A.　True

    B.　False

4. The term "rollover" and "rolling over" refer to moving money from one account to another account

    A.　True

    B.　False

5. If your company's 401(k) plan advisor is a fiduciary, the advisor cannot guide you into a business relationship outside the plan when you retire.

    A. True

    B. False

6. When you hire an advisor to work with you outside your company's 401(k) plan, it's usually a good idea to work with a fee-only independent advisor.

    A. True

    B. False

Answers

1. Answer: A. When your company's owner, the plan sponsor, decided to start a 401(k), a financial advisor was hired to provide certain services that may be different from the services other advisors may offer.

2. Answer: A. The more you understand how your 401(k) investments can work for you, the more likely you will be able to achieve your financial goals.

3. Answer: A. There may be services you want that are not provided by your company's 401(k) plan, so you can acquire these services with another financial advisor, if you wish. Fees are usually nominal, and an initial consultation is typically complementary; the advisor should give you a price quote for whatever work you'd like the advisor to do.

4. Answer: A. In a rollover, money in a tax-deferred account must be rolled over to another tax-deferred account within a limited time period to prevent taxation. If tax-deferred monies were rolled over to a taxable account, the tax and penalties would be expensive.

5. Answer: A. Answer: A. When a financial advisor is a fiduciary of your company's 401(k) plan, the advisor must be very careful not to violate the obligations that come with this role. The advisor must always act in your best financial interest.

6. Answer: A. It is recommended that you work with fee-only independent advisors so the potential bias for encouraging you to buy products that enhance the advisor's commissions is eliminated.

Chapter 7:
Interview Insight...
The Top 10 Questions You Want to Ask

When you have finished reading this chapter, you will:

- Understand how to find out how much money you should contribute monthly to your 401(k) account

- Realize how to decide on the best allocation of your monthly contributions in your company's 401(k) plan

- Know how to determine if your company's 401(k) plan is still a good investment even if your employer does not provide matching funds

- Be able to compare the benefits of a regular Roth IRA with your company's 401(k)

- Value meeting with your company's 401(k) plan advisor as often as your plan allows

We've gathered 10 of the most common questions asked by plan participants, and believe you'll find many of your questions answered here!

1. I have no idea how much money I should be contributing monthly to my 401(k) account; how do I figure that out?

The first step is to carefully and thoroughly consider your current financial circumstances. We discussed the concept of your personal financial pyramid in Chapter 3. Please look at Figure 29. As you remember, before you can begin making contributions to your retirement account, you should have sufficient cash flow for your daily needs and sufficient funds set aside for any emergencies that may suddenly appear. In addition, you should seriously think about purchasing certain types of insurance which are appropriate for your current life situation. Once these basic financial considerations are addressed, only then should you begin thinking about setting aside funds from your paycheck and building your retirement account.

The second step is to consider the lifestyle you can reasonably expect to have when you reach retirement age. Most people want to have a home with the mortgage paid, sufficient income to pay all the usual bills, and some extra money for hobbies, some travel, and meeting health care needs beyond what's provided by insurance and the government. This will require some thought and planning so you can determine what you feel is a reasonable annual income for the last 20 or 30 years of your life. Typically, you should probably think about having the same annual income then as you have now. The reason is that even though most people think they will spend less in retirement, they are unable to cut back on their lifestyle, so it's best now to plan on having the same level of income when you retire.

Once you have a good idea of what you will need in retirement, the third step is to meet with a financial advisor who can run some numbers with you. As you are now aware, having read this book, inflation increases every year by about 3%, and you'll need your money invested in funds that will grow at a rate that exceeds the rate of inflation, and also increases your retirement funds over the time remaining before you need this money. You'll want to see an investment advisor because this expert can help you construct a savings and investment plan that will help you achieve your retirement goals. If you do this by yourself, you might be successful or you might not, but this is so important to your financial health and the way you will live in the last third of your life, you should acquire professional guidance for your own sake, and for the sake of your family.

The advisor will work with you to determine your required rate of return (RRR). The RRR is the average percentage your retirement funds should grow annually over the course of time so the money is available when you need it. In the case study in Chapter 5, Linda

Nelson's advisor calculated that 6.01% was Linda's RRR, and by contributing regularly to her 401(k), Linda would have the funds 30 years later. We suggest you also have a similar discussion with your company's 401(k) advisor, or hire your own financial advisor to help you calculate your retirement needs.

Until you know what your financial retirement needs will be, it's really impossible to say what you should be setting aside monthly in your retirement account. However, remember that every dollar that goes into your 401(k) is a tax deferred dollar, and it will grow tax-deferred as well. This is a serious advantage! In addition, if your employer is contributing matching funds to your retirement account every time you do, this might be another great incentive to actively build your 401(k) fund.

This next set of tables is another critical lesson illustrating how a client's investment portfolio might be set-up in a way that allows the client to live throughout their entire retirement just on the interest earned by the account, leaving the principal for his or her heirs. This type of investment plan is called a capital preservation plan, or a sustained withdrawal plan, because the capital in the account is preserved for the beneficiaries.

When you meet with your advisor, a conversation would determine how much income in today's dollars you would like to have in retirement. As indicated in the chart below, Capital Preservation Example, this client wants $50,000 per year in today's dollars during retirement, starting in 31 years. The advisor estimates the inflation rate will be 2%. Therefore, the first year of retirement will require $92,379.44. This will provide the same purchasing power 31 years from now as $50,000 purchases in today's dollars.

Furthermore, if you had a portfolio from which you could draw 3% annually, after fees, taxes, inflation and all the details that need to be considered, your portfolio would have to grow to be $3,079,315 at retirement. In other words, you'll need to have $3 million in order to pull out 3% per year and have $92,000 to spend annually, adjusted for inflation and taxes for the rest of your life, without depleting a penny of the $3 million. So this is your goal; your advisor needs to get your retirement funds to $3 million.

In retirement, if you have $3 million, you're going to have to earn 5.13% a year to preserve the $3 million and not spend down this resource. The 5.13% is the required rate of return (RRR) during your retirement years, which includes the costs of inflation, taxes, and other expenses.

With the goal in mind to grow your portfolio to $3 million in 31 years, your advisor notes that you currently have $25,000 in your 401(k) account. Your advisor has calculated that if your account can earn 8.64% per year for 31 years, you will have to contribute $1,458 a month in order to build your $3 million portfolio. As noted in the chart, if you have $235,861 you could invest now, for 31 years at 8.64% per year, that would also build your portfolio to $3 million. You'll see all these figures in the following chart:

Figure 56: Capital Preservation Example.

Preservation of Capital	
Retirement Income Goal	
Income Goal in today's dollars	$50,000
Inflation Rate	2.00%
Years until retirement	31
Future Income goal at retirement	**$92,379.44**
Retirement Assumptions	
Future Income Goal (net spendable)	$92,379.44
Inflation Rate	2.00%
Sustainable spend down rate	3.00%
Years in Retirement	30
Fees	0.00%
Tax rate on withdrawal	25.00%
Required Portfolio Value at Retirement	
Required Income Goal	$92,379.44
Sustainable spend down rate	3.00%
Portfolio Value	**$3,079,315**
Required Rate of Return (RRR)	
Spend down rate	3.00%
With inflation (apx)	5.06%
With Fees (apx)	5.06%
Actual RRR/IRR	**5.13%**
Required Monthly Savings	
Future Portfolio Value	$3,079,315
Current 401(k) Savings	$25,000
Years of Savings	31
Assumed Real Rate of Return	8.64%
Required Monthly Payment	**$1,458**
Lump sum present value in today's dollars	**$235,861**

This next chart illustrates the savings years. The portfolio started with $25,000; in addition, there are 12 monthly payments of $1,458 into your 401(k) account, which comes to a total of $17,500 annually; and remember there are no fees or taxes in your 401(k). Therefore, during the course of 31 years, with an RRR of 8.64%, your future portfolio value will be $3,079,315.

Figure 57: The Savings Years.

Required Monthly Savings	
Future Portfolio Value	$3,079,315
Current 401(k) Savings	$25,000
Years of Savings	31.00
Assumed Real Rate of Return	8.64%
Required Monthly Payment	$1,458
Annual Payment	$17,500
Lump sum present value in today's dollars	$235,861

This next chart shows the details and confirms that saving $1,458 a month ($17,500) in your 401(k) for 31 years at the indicated rate of return will result in $3,079,315.

Figure 58: $1,458 per month becomes $3 Million.

Year	Beginning Value	Contributions	Fees	Taxes	End Value
1	$25,000	$17,500	$0	$0	$45,454
2	$45,454	$17,500	$0	$0	$67,746
3	$67,746	$17,500	$0	$0	$92,044
4	$92,044	$17,500	$0	$0	$118,526
5	$118,526	$17,500	$0	$0	$147,389
6	$147,389	$17,500	$0	$0	$178,847
7	$178,847	$17,500	$0	$0	$213,134
8	$213,134	$17,500	$0	$0	$250,504
9	$250,504	$17,500	$0	$0	$291,233
10	$291,233	$17,500	$0	$0	$335,626
11	$335,626	$17,500	$0	$0	$384,009
12	$384,009	$17,500	$0	$0	$436,743
13	$436,743	$17,500	$0	$0	$494,219
14	$494,219	$17,500	$0	$0	$556,862
15	$556,862	$17,500	$0	$0	$625,138
16	$625,138	$17,500	$0	$0	$699,553
17	$699,553	$17,500	$0	$0	$780,660
18	$780,660	$17,500	$0	$0	$869,058
19	$869,058	$17,500	$0	$0	$965,406
20	$965,406	$17,500	$0	$0	$1,070,416
21	$1,070,416	$17,500	$0	$0	$1,184,868
22	$1,184,868	$17,500	$0	$0	$1,309,611
23	$1,309,611	$17,500	$0	$0	$1,445,571
24	$1,445,571	$17,500	$0	$0	$1,593,755
25	$1,593,755	$17,500	$0	$0	$1,755,264
26	$1,755,264	$17,500	$0	$0	$1,931,294
27	$1,931,294	$17,500	$0	$0	$2,123,152
28	$2,123,152	$17,500	$0	$0	$2,332,261
29	$2,332,261	$17,500	$0	$0	$2,560,172
30	$2,560,172	$17,500	$0	$0	$2,808,576
31	$2,808,576	$17,500	$0	$0	$3,079,315

The following chart shows the financials of your retirement funds during your assumed total of 30 years in retirement. In Year 1 of your retirement, your beginning value is $3,079,315. In this first year, you needed to spend $92,379, plus $30,793 in taxes, for a total first year payout of $123,173. At the end of your first year, your account's ending value is $3,113,976. The payout of $123,173 represents 3% of your accounts beginning value, after taxes.

This chart also demonstrates that the Actual Spend Down Rate is not linear, that is, it does not remain at 3% throughout the 30 years. It increases to 3.09%, and then 3.12%, etc. By the end, you're having to pull out 5.33% in order to withdraw $167,333 in your 30th and final year of living expenses. This also explains why you needed an RRR of 5.13% (see Figure 56: Capital Preservation Example), because as the retirement years go by, the increase in inflation and taxes must be offset by a higher rate of return so that your spend down rate allows you to maintain your level of spending without consuming your capital.

Then, at the end of the 30th year, which is the assumed year of your demise, you spend $167,333, pay $55,778 in taxes, and there is principal remaining in the amount of $3,079,315...which is exactly the same amount in Year 1 when you started your retirement. Thus, your capital has been preserved as planned, and your heirs will benefit.

Figure 59: The Retirement Years.

Year	Beginning Value	Spending	Fees	Taxes	Principle	Total Payment	End Value	Actual Spend Down Rate
1	$3,079,315	$92,379		$30,793		$123,173	$3,113,976	3.00%
2	$3,113,976	$96,112		$32,037		$128,149	$3,145,439	3.09%
3	$3,145,439	$98,034		$32,678		$130,712	$3,175,950	3.12%
4	$3,175,950	$99,994		$33,331		$133,326	$3,205,412	3.15%
5	$3,205,412	$101,994		$33,998		$135,992	$3,233,717	3.18%
6	$3,233,717	$104,034		$34,678		$138,712	$3,260,753	3.22%
7	$3,260,753	$106,115		$35,372		$141,487	$3,286,401	3.25%
8	$3,286,401	$108,237		$36,079		$144,316	$3,310,533	3.29%
9	$3,310,533	$110,402		$36,801		$147,203	$3,333,016	3.33%
10	$3,333,016	$112,610		$37,537		$150,147	$3,353,708	3.38%
11	$3,353,708	$114,862		$38,287		$153,150	$3,372,457	3.42%
12	$3,372,457	$117,159		$39,053		$156,213	$3,389,104	3.47%
13	$3,389,104	$119,503		$39,834		$159,337	$3,403,480	3.53%
14	$3,403,480	$121,893		$40,631		$162,524	$3,415,406	3.58%
15	$3,415,406	$124,331		$41,444		$165,774	$3,424,693	3.64%
16	$3,424,693	$126,817		$42,272		$169,090	$3,431,141	3.70%
17	$3,431,141	$129,354		$43,118		$172,471	$3,434,537	3.77%
18	$3,434,537	$131,941		$43,980		$175,921	$3,434,658	3.84%
19	$3,434,658	$134,579		$44,860		$179,439	$3,431,267	3.92%
20	$3,431,267	$137,271		$45,757		$183,028	$3,424,113	4.00%
21	$3,424,113	$140,016		$46,672		$186,689	$3,412,932	4.09%
22	$3,412,932	$142,817		$47,606		$190,422	$3,397,444	4.18%
23	$3,397,444	$145,673		$48,558		$194,231	$3,377,353	4.29%
24	$3,377,353	$148,587		$49,529		$198,115	$3,352,349	4.40%
25	$3,352,349	$151,558		$50,519		$202,078	$3,322,100	4.52%
26	$3,322,100	$154,589		$51,530		$206,119	$3,286,260	4.65%
27	$3,286,260	$157,681		$52,560		$210,242	$3,244,459	4.80%
28	$3,244,459	$160,835		$53,612		$214,446	$3,196,312	4.96%
29	$3,196,312	$164,052		$54,684		$218,735	$3,141,408	5.13%
30	$3,141,408	$167,333		$55,778	$3,079,315	$3,302,425	$0	5.33%

This sequence of tables was presented to explain how your advisor would construct a capital preservation plan to help you determine the amount of money you need to set aside monthly, over the course of your working years, so you build sufficient funds to live comfortably through your retirement years while preserving your principal and leaving an estate which benefits your heirs.

If you should decide that you don't need the $3 million at the end of your life, as a gift to your beneficiaries, then your financial advisor would employ a different methodology. This is a discussion you should have with yourself and others whom you care about, so that your intentions are known to your financial advisor who can then work with you to achieve the goals you desire.

2. Of all the choices available in my company's 401(k) plan, what is the right allocation for me? I really don't know what risk category is best.

Your risk category is determined by the financial goals of your retirement plan. As mentioned above, you need to consider your retirement lifestyle and then plan accordingly. Obviously, you don't want to expose yourself to more risk than necessary, but until you determine your RRR, you're not really going to know the best risk tolerance for achieving the retirement monies you'll need.

Once you know your required rate of return (RRR), you'll then be able to make reasonable decisions about which of the investment funds in your company's 401(k) plan are best for you. Various allocation models will have different long term returns they are expecting to achieve. Without some proper planning, your targets are elusive and you're shooting in the dark. The job of a financial planner is to help people understand their options and help them make the appropriate financial decisions that guide them toward their goals.

3. My employer doesn't provide matching funds. Is it better to just save the money in a regular investment account?

If your employer does not provide matching funds, the company's 401(k) plan may still be the best investment for you. A financial planner can discuss your choices after reviewing the full picture of your unique financial circumstances. When you allocate funds into your company's 401(k) plan, you're setting aside tax-deferred money each payroll period.

Having your taxes deferred serves you in two ways. The first benefit is that these salary deferrals are going directly into an investment plan, right from your paycheck, before being taxed; this means more of your dollars are being saved. The second benefit is that you save additional tax dollars because your paycheck is reduced by the amount of money you're allocating to your retirement fund, so you'll pay less income tax.

In addition, a third benefit is that your company may have a 401(k) plan financial advisor who has set up several investment portfolio models from which you can choose, and they are managed by this financial professional; this means you can take advantage of the advice and experience of an investment professional who can discuss your best investment options, potentially helping you grow your retirement fund in a safe and steady manner. A regular investment account may not provide these three benefits which are likely to be available through your company's 401(k) plan.

4. What are the benefits to doing a regular Roth account versus my 401(k)?

With a regular Roth account, you are depositing money that has been taxed; these are post-tax dollars. When the time comes to withdraw these monies, none of the amount, contributions or gains, will be taxed again. The difference is that with a 401(k) account, your pretax dollars are being deposited in your account, and these monies are growing tax-deferred until you withdraw them in retirement. All the monies you withdraw later, both your contributions and gains, will then be taxed at your income tax bracket when you're in retirement, and this is likely to be a lower tax bracket than you're in now, saving even more tax dollars.

As you can see, we are in the position of comparing an apple to an orange. With the Roth, your money is being taxed right away; these are post-tax dollars. With the 401(k), taxation is delayed (deferred) and these are pretax dollars.

What is the advantage of one over the other? Again, your best decision depends on your particular financial circumstances. For some people, paying taxes before the money is placed in the Roth account, and letting the money grow tax-free from that point forward, is the right choice. With the 401(k), a person deposits pretax dollars, the earnings grow tax-deferred until withdrawal in retirement, and because of the decreased paycheck, they save additional income tax. You'd have to ask your financial advisor to calculate and determine which is the better choice for the circumstances of your particular situation.

5. My plan offers a Roth 401(k) and deductible 401(k) option; which one is the wiser choice for me?

It depends on your financial circumstances. In general, if you're older and closer to retirement, the deductible 401(k) account could be the best choice for you because now you are at the highest level of your earning years, and reducing your taxes might be the higher priority and best decision for your financial picture.

If you are in your early 20s, though, your payroll may not be very large, and your taxes are also not very high; in this case the Roth 401(k) might be your best choice. For those people who are between their 20s and late 50s, it's hard to say which choice is best because everybody's financial circumstances are unique, and would need to be considered on a person-by-person basis. Remember, too, that you may also have the option to diversify your retirement fund allocations by splitting your contributions between the Roth 401(k) and the traditional 401(k). Still, making a sensible decision will depend on an analysis of your financial big picture. To some, the need for additional income tax deduction is important (deductible contributions), but for others who don't really need a deduction of their income, the Roth 401k might be fine.

6. I'm young, and I want to use my income for a lot of other things besides funding my retirement. Does it really make much difference if I contribute only a little bit now? I'll increase my contributions later.

We understand the temptation of spending your money on the things you need, and the things you want. Enjoying life is certainly an attractive idea, and spending money on consumer items instead of building a retirement fund is especially appealing for young people with limited salaries.

One of the advantages of being young is you have a great deal of time until you retire, so it's not uncommon to think, with so much time ahead of you, you can make it up later when your salary is a bit bigger. You're thinking that with about 40 years until retirement, there's certainly enough time to get serious later.

Of course, as with most people, as you get older your lifestyle changes and you'll find your expenses increasing. You may decide to get married, have children, and buy a house... All of these wonderful life events are expensive, and you may find that the money you'll need to support this new lifestyle and also begin building your retirement fund is just as difficult to fund as when you were younger.

Now, when you're young, is the perfect time to seriously begin building your retirement fund. It may not be apparent to you yet, but the years flow by very quickly; right now, time, which is your one abundant resource, is exactly the resource you're talking about misusing. It's tough to think about what your life might be like 40 years from now, but the day will come when you'll be living it, and you really don't want to come up short then.

What we're saying is that delaying retirement savings at present is going to create more urgency later when you have other obligations and even less time to build a substantial retirement fund for you and your family. We're not advocating you put aside every spare dollar, but developing the mindset for a steady pattern of saving and investing is quite likely going to bring you a strong degree of satisfaction and comfort in the future. It could be helpful to reread the discussion that Linda Nelson, our fictitious employee, had with her advisor about the choice between an expensive Caribbean cruise or a less luxurious vacation to Mexico. See Chapter 5.

Use the time you have wisely; set aside a reasonable portion of your salary for retirement savings and investment; get into the habit of wise discipline; plan and then take action for the future you know is coming.

7. If the market goes down, should I hold off on my contributions for a while?

No, because when the market goes down, that's a good time to add to your holdings. Think of it as going to a department store sale. When the shirts or dresses or jewelry you like to buy are on sale, do you go to the department store or stay away? Of course! You head right to the store to pick up a few things at a reduced cost that you would normally pay a higher retail price to own. It's the same thing when the market goes down. The investments you are buying at a higher cost are now available to you at a reduced price. Since the investment funds in the 401(k) have been selected by a professional investment advisor and are part of a company 401(k) plan designed to help you grow your retirement wealth while also guarding you against undue risk, you can have confidence that the investment funds in your account are safe. The market goes through its cycles, and sometimes the market is up and sometimes the market is down. When you continue making contributions in a steady and disciplined manner, there will be times when you're paying either more or less for the funds in your account.

There's actually a fancy name for this; it's called dollar cost averaging. Dollar cost averaging is when you buy a fixed dollar amount of an asset on a regular schedule without regard for its current price. Over the course of time, there will be occasions when you pay a higher dollar amount for the asset, and there will be times when you pay a lower dollar amount for the same asset, because the price keeps changing. Since you are not varying the regularity of your purchase, over time there will be an average cost you've spent on buying the asset, and that average price has blended the times when you paid a higher amount with the times you've purchased a bargain.

8. I have no idea if I'm paying any fees or expenses in my 401(k) account. Is there a way to find out?

The best way to find out if you're paying any fees, and how much, is to speak with your plan administrator. All fees and expenses are required by law to be disclosed.

Depending upon your company's 401(k) plan, all the fees and expenses could be paid by your company, or by you and your fellow plan participants, or the fees and expenses could be paid by a combination of both the company and the employees in the plan.

9. Should I just pick my own funds or use the prescribed allocations? What is the benefit?

Unless you're a trained auto mechanic, you probably wouldn't want to hoist your car's engine and change all the belts, or replace the distributor, or tear apart the ignition box. By the same token, how much do you know about selecting investment funds? Do you know the difference between an aggressive portfolio, an emerging market mutual fund, and a commodities hedge fund? It would be unusual if you did.

Your company's 401(k) plan investment advisor was probably selected based on his or her investment experience, training, and credentials. It doesn't mean this person knows everything, but unless you have a serious reason to believe you know more, it would be a very good idea to take advantage of the prescribed allocations.

When the advisor was hired to recommend investment funds for the company plan, part of his or her obligation was to recommend quality investments which are appropriate for the employees in your company. The advisor was also asked to build several portfolio models with different degrees of risk tolerance so plan participants could choose the investment model that best suits their investment purpose. In addition, these model portfolios are actively managed by your company's financial advisor, which means that periodically, usually quarterly, the advisor will study the performance of the funds in that portfolio and determine if the funds are performing as expected, or if the collection of funds needs to be refreshed, with some eliminated and others added. The advantages should be clear; an investment expert has selected specific investment funds and collected them into model portfolios, and manages them to assure they produce the anticipated results. The great thing about this is you now have access to these investment portfolios, and can benefit from the expertise of an investment professional. At your earliest convenience, you should make an appointment to meet with the plan's advisor and discuss the value of this selection for your own particular investment needs.

10. When the investment advisor gives us an update at the quarterly meetings, I have no idea what to ask. How do I determine if I'm doing well?

The best thing to do might be to make an appointment to meet one-on-one with the advisor after the group meeting. During your appointment, ask the advisor for two things. First, ask for a review of your personal investment statement, and have him or her explain anything on the statement you don't understand. Secondly, it would be a very good idea to ask the advisor to provide some reading materials so you can more completely educate yourself on investing for retirement.

Remember, investing successfully for retirement depends on knowing what your goals are and establishing a plan to meet those goals. This should simplify the question of whether or not you're doing well, because you will be able to mark your progress against the goals you've set. For example, assuming you know your retirement goals, and you've established an investment plan, and you're allocating your contributions on schedule, and you know your required rate of return (RRR), you should very clearly be able to know whether or not your personal retirement plan is on target.

Here's an example: You've decided you need an annual income of $50,000, in today's dollars, 30 years from now when you reach retirement. You and your investment advisor have decided you can allocate $17,500 every year toward your 401(k) account. $17,500 is $1,458 every month. You know you can do this because your regular monthly expenses are sufficient to permit you to set this amount aside every month, and you have a nine-month emergency fund for the unexpected, and you've purchased the appropriate insurances to protect the various facets of your life. Your RRR is the same as Linda

Nelson's; at 6.01%, in 30 years, after the steady allocation of tax-deferred dollars into your 401(k), you'll have about $1,500,000 dollars in your retirement fund. You'll know if you're on target to reach your retirement finance goals if your 401(k) investments are annually achieving the RRR of 6.01%.

Remember, in some years your 401(k) funds will perform better than your RRR, and in some years your funds may perform less than your RRR; but if your retirement portfolio averages your RRR's 6.01% growth over a period of years, you are doing well. You'll want to keep an eye on your account's performance, so by annually determining if your portfolio is meeting your RRR, you'll have a meaningful benchmark for knowing the monetary value of its performance and your progress toward meeting your retirement goals.

Summary

We hope you found the answers to some of your most pressing questions. Since you probably have more questions you'd like to ask that are particular to your unique set of circumstances, we recommend you jot them down and speak with your company's financial advisor, and also consider hiring your own financial advisor to review your financial picture and help you start down the path for a secure and comfortable future.

 ## Chapter 7 Review Questions:

1. The best way to figure out how much money you'll need in retirement is to decide what your goals are for retirement.

A. True

B. False

2. It's best to plan for the same annual income in retirement that you have now.

    A. True

    B. False

3. Which of the following two statements about having your taxes deferred is true?

    A.) Salary deferrals are going directly into an investment plan, right from your paycheck, before being taxed; this means more of your dollars are being saved.

    B.) You save additional tax dollars because your paycheck is reduced by the amount of money you're allocating to your retirement fund, so you'll pay less income tax.

    1. A is correct.

    2. B is correct.

    3. Both are correct.

    4. Neither is correct.

4. When the market goes down, you should continue making monthly contributions.

    A. True

    B. False

Answers

1. Answer: A. Without setting goals, you can't really know how much money you'll need in retirement, and you also can't create a plan to save the money you don't know you'll need.

2. Answer: A. Most people think they will spend less in retirement, but are unable to cut back on their lifestyle

3. Answer: 3. You save money by investing tax-deferred dollars, and your income tax is less because your payroll is reduced.

4. Answer: A. When the market goes down, that's a good time to add to your holdings. The investments you were buying at a higher cost are now available at a reduced price.

Chapter 8:
Summary

The second half of this book, Section 3, was dedicated to providing the information that you, as a plan participant, need to know about the value of the 401(k) plan available now, or soon, through your company.

You are, of course, welcome to read the first part of this book because it will give you good insight about why your employer, the plan sponsor, has chosen to establish a new 401(k) plan in your company, and also will help you understand the mechanics of the plan as well.

In Section 3 we've presented the basic details defining a 401(k) and the indications of how you can tell if the plan offered through your company is a good savings and investment choice for you. We suggest that you carefully read your plan's details so you know the features being offered, and how these features may benefit you.

We also went into detail about developing your own retirement plan, which includes setting your financial goals, evaluating your financial pyramid and allocating your resources to accomplish the goals you've set. In Chapter 4 we presented a key concept called the required rate of return (RRR) and introduced you to a fictional character, Linda Nelson, using her story as an example of how you might proceed with ensuring your own financial security in retirement.

We believe there are seven key takeaways which are essential to understand and which will help you make the right choices for your financial future. They are:

1. Become familiar with your company's plan: In order to feel comfortable and informed, ask to read the Investment Policy Statement (IPS). This document summarizes all the features of your company's 401(k) plan. This will give you the overview you need and help you see the benefits of participation.

2. Join the plan if you are eligible: There are a variety of features in 401(k) plans, and the features in your company's plan depend on the choices made by your company's plan sponsor, which is your employer. Some plans have more features than others, but in one sense all 401(k) plans are the same...they are an amazing tool that can help you set aside tax-deferred dollars which can then be invested tax-free, resulting in the continued growth of the financial reserves you'll need in the remaining years of your life...which could be 20 or 30 years. Your employer may be willing to match your monthly contribution with a contribution of company dollars; so not only are you setting aside tax-deferred dollars but you're also receiving and investing company dollars as well. Our point is that the sooner you become a plan participant and can begin your savings plan, the more you're likely to have when you retire.

3. Start saving as soon as possible: We've gone to an extreme degree to point out the value of money and how it grows over time. If you're 10, 20, or 30 years from retirement, time is on your side and the money you set aside now will increase to such an extent, based on your circumstances, that you can enjoy a safe and happy retirement. Start saving at once because every delay reduces your potential for having the money you'll need in your future.

4. Determine your goals: Educating yourself about money and setting your financial goals are in an important step toward achieving financial success. The choice is yours...you can have a safe and secure retirement, or you can choose to enter your retirement years with anxiety and uncertainty. No one will do this for you; as it is for most people, only you can secure your financial future. When you set your goals and make a plan to achieve them, you are more likely to have success than when you're unsure of which direction to go.

5. Stick to your plan: Once you have a plan, which includes your goals, the activities you'll do to achieve those goals, and the timeline of when you expect those activities to be completed, you should review your plan periodically to make sure you're doing what your plan

requires and that your plan is still focused properly on the goals you've identified.

6. Use the required rate of return (RRR) in your planning: The required rate of return is a gem of information for you. Once you determine your goals, either your company's financial advisor or a financial advisor you choose to hire will help you plan for your retirement by calculating the number of dollars you'll need to live in what may be the last third of your life. Knowing your individual RRR and checking periodically to see if you're earning the RRR you require will probably provide many restful nights and the confidence that your plan is achieving its goals...which is your financial security in retirement.

7. Consider hiring your own advisor: Just as you would consult with a mechanic about the noise in your engine, or you'd go to the dentist for a semiannual cleaning and health check, you should also consider the value of periodically consulting with a professional financial expert. Increasing your financial resources and safeguarding those funds is too important to leave to chance. Learn to make money your friend by reading about investments, attending company 401(k) workshops, and being familiar with your own financial plan. The best person to care about your financial well-being...is you.

We sincerely hope you've enjoyed reading this book, and that you found value with some of the financial insights we've provided. If your company does not yet have a 401(k) plan, you might consider giving this book to your employer because he or she may quickly realize the benefits of establishing a new plan for your company. We wish you success, and happiness, and a secure and comfortable retirement lifestyle!

Addendum 1:
Key Terms

3(21) Fiduciary: An investment advisor who only recommends investments; investment decisions remain the responsibility of the plan sponsor (employer).

3(38) Fiduciary: An investment advisor who is appointed in writing by the plan sponsor to manage the plan's investments, and is solely responsible for selecting, monitoring, and replacing investments. The trustee and other fiduciaries have no investment decision responsibilities.

401(k) Plan: The IRS defines a 401(k) plan as a defined contribution plan in which an employee can choose to make contributions from his or her salary, pre or post-tax, as permitted by the plan. The employee selects the investment options they wish from the choices available in the plan. In addition, an employer may elect to make matching contributions and/or a profit sharing contribution. SIMPLE 401(k) and Safe Harbor 401(k) plans have mandatory employer contributions.

408(b)(2): A required form filed annually identifying the plan's service providers and the direct and indirect compensation they receive.

After-tax Dollars: Dollars remaining after taxes have been levied.

AIF (Accredited Investment Fiduciary): A certified expert in the fiduciary care of investments.

Asset Allocation: The distribution of money into different asset classes, such as small-cap, midcap, and large cap funds, plus others.

Auto Enrollment: Automatic enrollment of all eligible employees; the plan participant must withdraw from the plan rather than take action to enroll.

Blackout Period: A period of time, sometimes up to 60 days, when a participant cannot make changes to his or her investment selections, usually because a plan sponsor is transitioning from one plan provider to another.

Bond Fund: An investment fund composed only of bonds; bonds are debts used by governments and private companies to raise money.

Bundled Plan: A plan offered by a single provider supplying a complete "bundle" of administration, recordkeeping, education, and investment services.

CFA (The Chartered Financial Analyst®): A person who is a CFA charterholder from the CFA Institute, which has become the most respected and recognized designation in the world.

CFP® (Certified Financial Planner): A professional who has fulfilled the certification requirements of the Certified Financial Planner Board of Standards.

Closed Architecture: A bundled plan structure limiting the sponsor to only the investments the custodian has made available.

Code: Internal Revenue Service laws regarding federal taxes.

Contributing Participant: A participant in a plan who is making financial contributions to their account.

Custodian: A bank or trust company holding the assets of a company or individual, and providing the safekeeping of the money, but not the management of the investments.

Defined Contribution Dollar Limitation: Money contributed to an investment fund that has a restricted total annual amount.

Designated Beneficiary: The named recipient of property upon the death of the owner.

Direct Rollover: Money that transfers directly from one account to another.

Diversification: Investing in several different types of asset classes to reduce risk while also increasing the opportunity for growth.

Due Diligence Plan: A plan or checklist that serves fiduciaries by ensuring they have created and maintained a 401(k) retirement plan meeting ERISA and IRS guidelines and serving the best interests of participants and their beneficiaries.

Efficient Frontier: The efficient frontier is a strategy for investing your funds based on the most growth with the least risk according to your unique circumstances.

Elective Deferral: A voluntary channeling, or deferring, of money; in this case, into a tax-deferred 401(k) plan.

Employer Discretionary Contributions: A profit sharing contribution voluntarily made by an employer to an employee retirement plan. The employer's contribution is tax deductible and employee earnings on the contributions are deferred until withdrawal.

Employer Matching Contributions: Contributions made by an employer to plan participants' accounts based on a percentage of an employee's contribution up to an identified limit (e.g., 3% of employee contributions up to 5% of salary).

ERISA: The Employee Retirement Income Security Act, a federal law approved in 1974, which sets minimum standards for employers who elect to establish and maintain pension plans.

Fidelity Bond: A bond protecting plan participants if a fiduciary mishandles or steals plan assets.

Fiduciary: An individual responsible for acting on behalf of and for the benefit of the plan participants.

Forfeiture: When an employee is not fully vested in a plan and employment is terminated, the portion of the employee's account balance composed of the employer's contributions or matching contributions is lost; an employee's salary deferrals, however, are never forfeited.

Fund: Money dedicated to an investment purpose.

Investment Manager (Investment Advisor): The person responsible for recommending the investment choices, or managing the plan's assets. (See 3(21) Fiduciary and 3(38) Fiduciary.)

Investment Policy Statement (IPS): A written statement detailing the plan's investment philosophy, objectives, responsibilities, asset classes and investment choices, evaluation of performance, and criteria for making changes to investments and service providers.

IRA: Individual Retirement Account, allowing tax-deferred savings and investment.

Large-cap Fund: An investment fund focused only on the performance of large companies, typically with over $10 billion in assets.

Mid-cap Fund: An investment fund focused only on the performance of mid-sized companies, typically with between $2 - $10 billion in assets.

Money Market Fund: A fund focused on investing in short-term debt securities; typically regarded as a safe investment, but with low return.

Non-elective: No choice; mandatory participation.

Open Architecture: An unbundled plan structure allowing the sponsor to include any investment in the plan.

Plan Administrator: The person responsible for managing the plan. The plan administrator could be the employer, a committee, the employer's appointee, or a person hired to administer the plan.

Plan Beneficiary In the event of a plan participant's death, the beneficiary receives the funds in the deceased person's account.

Plan Document: A document governing all aspects of the 401(k) plan.

Plan Fiduciary: A person who has discretionary authority of the 401(k) plan, the allocation of plan assets, or provides investment advice for compensation.

Plan Participant: An employee qualified to participate in a 401(k) retirement plan.

Plan Sponsor: The employer.

Plan Year: The 12-month period specified in the 401(k) plan document. The plan year may be a calendar year, or any 12-month period, such as a fiscal year.

Present Value: The value as of today.

Profit-sharing: Sharing the company's profits among qualified employees.

Qualified Plan: A retirement plan sponsored by an employer that meets IRS rules and regulations. Typically, contributions are tax-deductible; earnings remain untaxed until withdrawn.

Record Keeper: The record keeper's responsibility is valuing investments, keeping participants informed with statements on their accounts, and processing distribution checks.

Required Rate of Return (RRR): The minimum annual percentage an investment must earn to achieve the investment's goal for growth. The RRR is different for different investments, and for different people.

RIA (Registered Investment Advisor): A professional manager of investments registered with the Securities Exchange Commission (SEC), and thus compliant with SEC regulations.

Risk Tolerance: The amount of risk that is acceptable for your investments given your personally unique situation.

Rollover: Transferring from one retirement vehicle to another.

Roth IRA: A savings and investment vehicle funded initially with after-tax money, whose earnings then grow tax-free.

Safe Harbor 401(k) Plan: This plan is similar to a traditional 401(k), but instead of voluntary employer contributions, the employer is required to make contributions. The employer's benefit is avoiding administrative burdens regarding compliance testing with ERISA and IRS rules and regulations.

Salary Deferral: Also called employee contributions or elective deferrals, this is the dollar amount or salary percentage a participant elects to withhold from his or her paycheck for deposit into the participant's 401(k) account.

Service Provider: A company providing any service to the plan, which may include investment management, recordkeeping, plan administration, and/or employee education.

Small-cap Fund: An investment fund focused only on the performance of small companies, typically with under $2 billion in assets.

Tax-deferred Dollars: Untaxed dollars placed in a retirement plan, and taxed only upon withdrawal.

Third Party Administrator (TPA): This administrator's major responsibilities include calculating and allocating employer contributions, compliance testing, filing the annual 5500 form, tracking employee eligibility, and designing the plan that meets the employer's needs.

Trustee: The person assigned exclusive authority for managing and controlling the 401(k) plan's assets; the trustee can be subject to the direction of a named plan fiduciary.

Unbundled Plan: A plan that allows the plan sponsor to choose the TPA, record keeper, and investment advisor separately, often providing a significant decrease in cost.

Vesting: The percentage of the employer matching or profit sharing contributions owned by an employee. The company's vesting schedule is in the plan document, and is based on the number of employment years; employee contributions (salary deferrals) are always 100% vested.

Made in the USA
San Bernardino, CA
10 November 2015